NE능률 영어교과서

대한민국 고등학생 **10**명 중
4.7 명이 보는 교과서

영어 고등 교과서 점유율 1위
(7차, 2007 개정, 2009 개정, 2015 개정)

리딩튜터

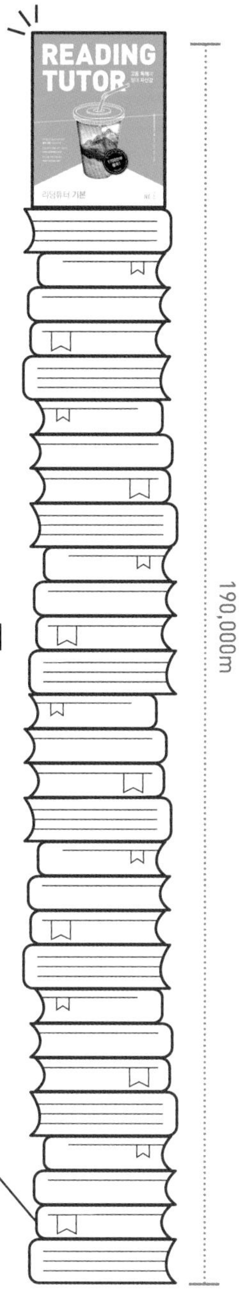

그동안 판매된
리딩튜터 1,900만 부
차곡차곡 쌓으면 19만 미터

에베레스트
21 배 높이

에베레스트 8,848m

능률보카

그동안 판매된
능률VOCA 1,100만 부

대한민국 박스오피스
천만명을 넘은 영화
단 28개

그래머존

그동안 판매된 450만 부의 그래머존을 바닥에 쭉 ~
1000km 서울-부산 왕복

KB014116

중학

천문장 LEVEL 3

지은이	NE능률 영어교육연구소
선임연구원	김지현
연구원	장경아, 가민아, 오보은
영문교열	Angela Lan, Curtis Thompson, Keeran Murphy
디자인	민유화, 안훈정, 오솔길
맥편집	한서기획
Photo Credits	www.shutterstock.com

중학

천문장

「구문이 독해로 연결되는 해석 공식」

LEVEL 3

구성과 특징

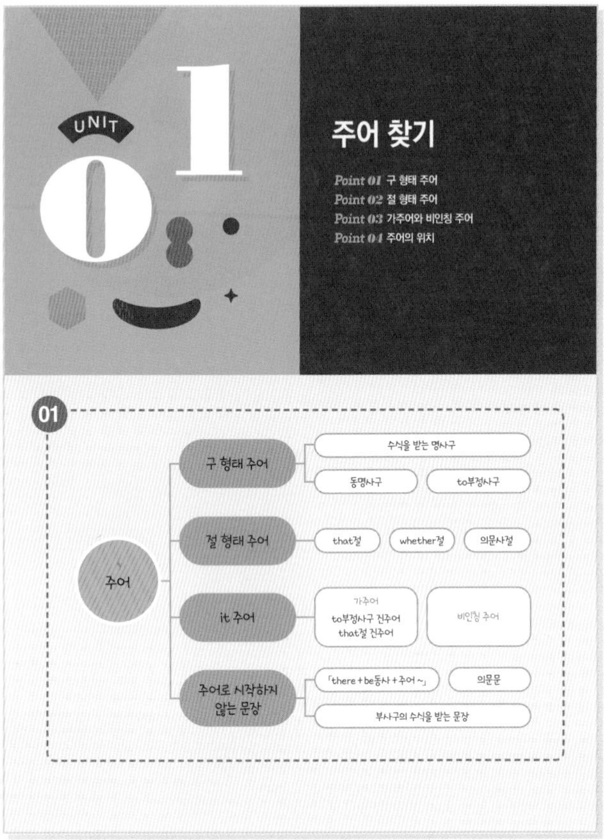

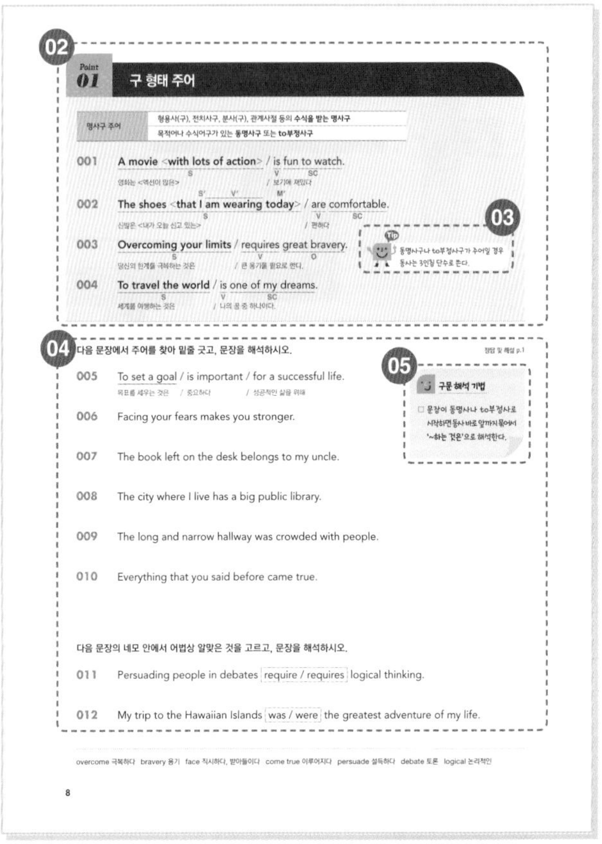

02

Point 01 구 형태 주어

명사구 주어	형용사(구), 전치사구, 분사(구), 관계사절 등의 **수식을 받는 명사구**
	목적어나 수식어구가 있는 **동명사구** 또는 **to부정사구**

001 A movie <with lots of action> / is fun to watch.
영화는 <액션이 많은> / 보기에 재밌다

002 The shoes <that I am wearing today> / are comfortable.
신발은 <내가 오늘 신고 있는> / 편하다

003 Overcoming your limits / requires great bravery.
당신의 한계를 극복하는 것은 / 큰 용기를 필요로 한다.

004 To travel the world / is one of my dreams.
세계를 여행하는 것은 / 나의 꿈 중 하나이다.

03 Tip 동명사구나 to부정사구가 주어일 경우 동사는 3인칭 단수로 쓴다.

04 다음 문장에서 주어를 찾아 밑줄 긋고, 문장을 해석하시오. 정답 및 해설 p.1

005 To set a goal / is important / for a successful life.
목표를 세우는 것은 / 중요하다 / 성공적인 삶을 위해

006 Facing your fears makes you stronger.

007 The book left on the desk belongs to my uncle.

008 The city where I live has a big public library.

009 The long and narrow hallway was crowded with people.

010 Everything that you said before came true.

다음 문장의 네모 안에서 어법상 알맞은 것을 고르고, 문장을 해석하시오.

011 Persuading people in debates [require / requires] logical thinking.

012 My trip to the Hawaiian Islands [was / were] the greatest adventure of my life.

05 구문 해석 기법
□ 문장이 동명사나 to부정사로 시작하면 동사 바로 앞까지 묶어서 '~하는 것은'으로 해석한다.

overcome 극복하다 bravery 용기 face 직시하다, 받아들이다 come true 이루어지다 persuade 설득하다 debate 토론 logical 논리적인

8

01 한눈에 들어오는 구문 도식

학습 Point를 확인하고
문장 구조를 한눈에 이해할 수 있게 구성하였습니다.

02 이해하기 쉽게 설명한 학습 Point

중학 학년별 필수 구문을 세분화한 학습 Point를
제시하고, 끊어 읽기와 직독직해를 통해 영어 문장 구조를
쉽게 이해할 수 있게 하였습니다.

03 Tip

구문을 이해하는 데 도움이 되는 문법 사항을 간략히
정리하였습니다.

04 확인 문제

학습한 Point를 바로 적용해 보는 문장별 확인 문제로
두 단계 점검이 가능하도록 구성하였습니다.

05 구문 해석 기법

학습 Point와 관련하여 독해에 유용한
해석 기법을 제공하였습니다.

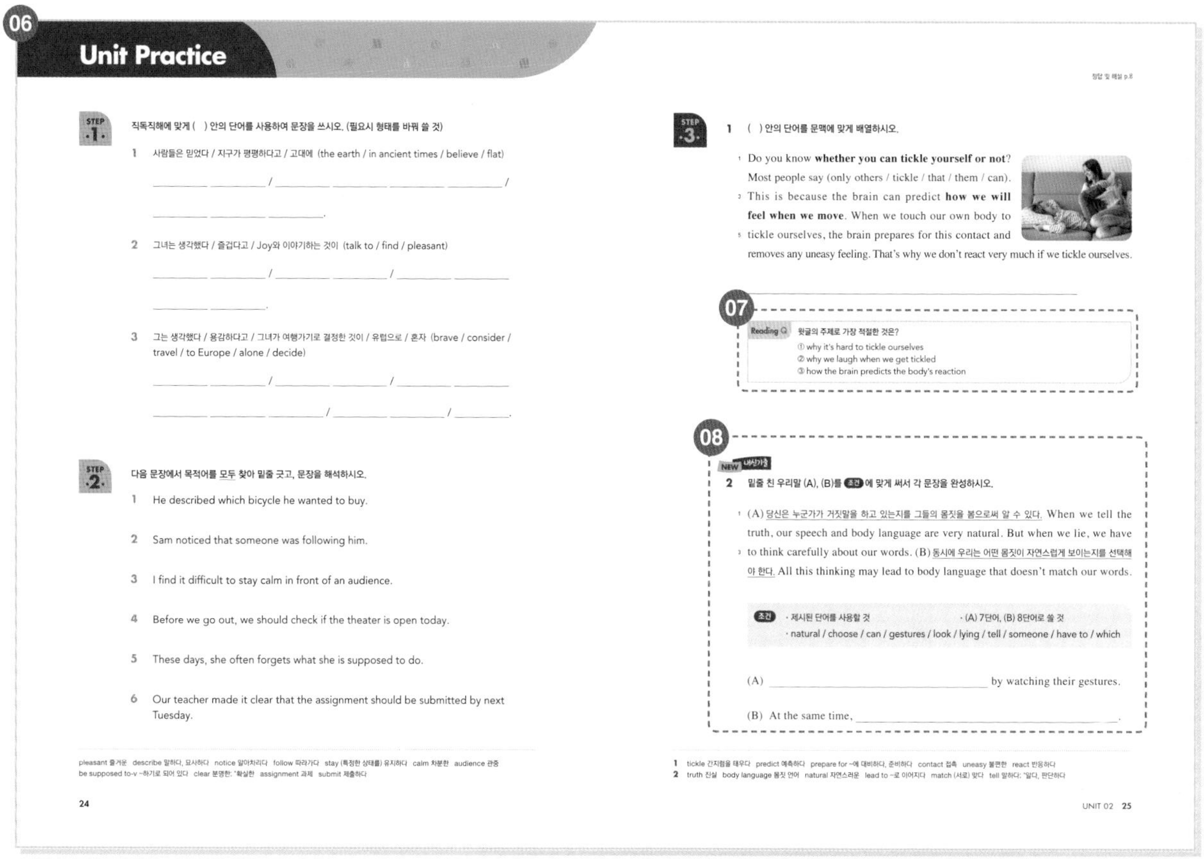
06
Unit Practice

정답 및 해설 p.8

STEP 1 직독직해에 맞게 ( ) 안의 단어를 사용하여 문장을 쓰시오. (필요시 형태를 바꿔 쓸 것)

1 사람들은 믿었다 / 지구가 평평하다고 / 고대에 (the earth / in ancient times / believe / flat)

2 그녀는 생각했다 / 즐겁다고 / Joy와 이야기하는 것이 (talk to / find / pleasant)

3 그는 생각했다 / 용감하다고 / 그녀가 여행가기로 결정한 것이 / 유럽으로 / 혼자 (brave / consider / travel / to Europe / alone / decide)

STEP 2 다음 문장에서 목적어를 모두 찾아 밑줄 긋고, 문장을 해석하시오.

1 He described which bicycle he wanted to buy.

2 Sam noticed that someone was following him.

3 I find it difficult to stay calm in front of an audience.

4 Before we go out, we should check if the theater is open today.

5 These days, she often forgets what she is supposed to do.

6 Our teacher made it clear that the assignment should be submitted by next Tuesday.

pleasant 즐거운 describe 말하다, 묘사하다 notice 알아차리다 follow 따라가다 stay (특정한 상태를) 유지하다 calm 차분한 audience 관중 be supposed to-v ~하기로 되어 있다 clear 분명한; *확실한 assignment 과제 submit 제출하다

24

STEP 3 1 ( ) 안의 단어를 문맥에 맞게 배열하시오.

Do you know **whether you can tickle yourself or not**? Most people say (only others / tickle / that / them / can). This is because the brain can predict **how we will feel when we move**. When we touch our own body to tickle ourselves, the brain prepares for this contact and removes any uneasy feeling. That's why we don't react very much if we tickle ourselves.

07
Reading Q 윗글의 주제로 가장 적절한 것은?
① why it's hard to tickle ourselves
② why we laugh when we get tickled
③ how the brain predicts the body's reaction

08
NEW 내신기출
2 밑줄 친 우리말 (A), (B)를 조건에 맞게 써서 각 문장을 완성하시오.

(A) 당신은 누군가가 거짓말을 하고 있는지를 그들의 몸짓을 봄으로써 알 수 있다. When we tell the truth, our speech and body language are very natural. But when we lie, we have to think carefully about our words. (B) 동시에 우리는 어떤 몸짓이 자연스럽게 보이는지를 선택해야 한다. All this thinking may lead to body language that doesn't match our words.

조건 · 제시된 단어를 사용할 것 · (A) 7단어, (B) 8단어로 쓸 것
· natural / choose / can / gestures / look / lying / tell / someone / have to / which

(A) ________________ by watching their gestures.

(B) At the same time, ________________.

1 tickle 간지럼을 태우다 predict 예측하다 prepare for ~에 대비하다, 준비하다 contact 접촉 uneasy 불편한 react 반응하다
2 truth 진실 body language 몸짓 언어 natural 자연스러운 lead to ~로 이어지다 match (서로) 맞다 tell 말하다; *알다, 판단하다

UNIT 02 25

06 Unit Practice

학습 Point에 대한 통합 학습 3단계로 구성하였으며, 앞에서 배운 문장을 반복함으로써 구문에 익숙해지게 하였습니다.

- STEP 1 우리말 직독직해 영작하기
- STEP 2 문장 구조를 파악하고 해석하기
- STEP 3 지문 속에서 학습 Point 적용하기

07 Reading Q

내용 확인 문제를 통해 지문 이해를 높일 수 있게 하였습니다.

08 NEW 내신기출

최신 내신 기출 유형을 반영한 서술형 문제를 통해 내신 실전 감각을 기를 수 있게 하였습니다.

09 Wrap Up

구문 도식과 주요 예문을 반복 학습으로써 학습 Point를 정리할 수 있게 하였습니다.

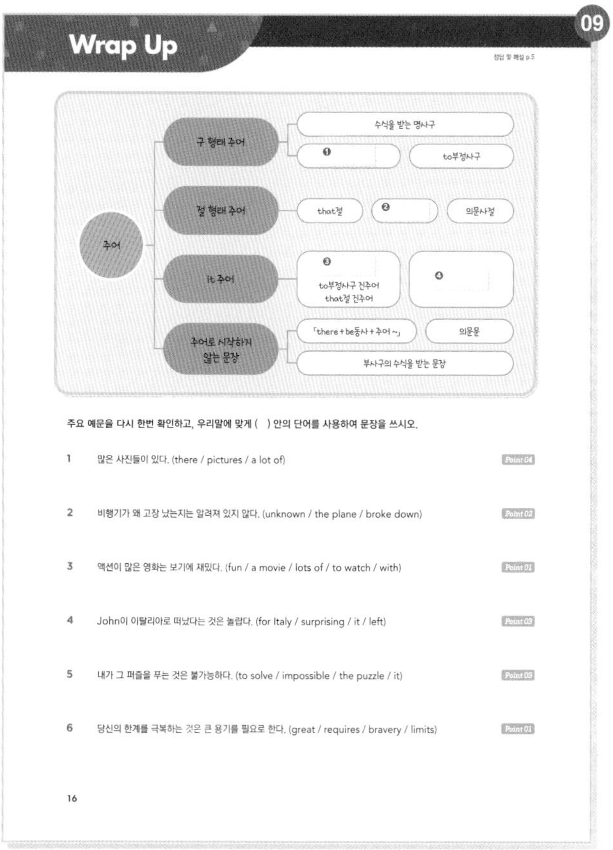
09
Wrap Up

정답 및 해설 p.5

주어
구 형태 주어
수식을 받는 명사구
❶
to부정사구
절 형태 주어
that절
❷
의문사절
it 주어
❸
to부정사구 진주어
that절 진주어
❹
주어로 시작하지 않는 문장
「there + be동사 + 주어 ~」
의문문
부사구의 수식을 받는 문장

주요 예문을 다시 한번 확인하고, 우리말에 맞게 ( ) 안의 단어를 사용하여 문장을 쓰시오.

1 많은 사진들이 있다. (there / pictures / a lot of) Point 04

2 비행기가 왜 고장 났는지는 알려져 있지 않다. (unknown / the plane / broke down) Point 02

3 액션이 많은 영화는 보기에 재밌다. (fun / a movie / lots of / to watch / with) Point 01

4 John이 이탈리아로 떠났다는 것은 놀랍다. (for Italy / surprising / it / left) Point 03

5 내가 그 퍼즐을 푸는 것은 불가능하다. (to solve / impossible / the puzzle / it) Point 03

6 당신의 한계를 극복하는 것은 큰 용기를 필요로 한다. (great / requires / bravery / limits) Point 01

16

목차

UNIT 01 주어 찾기

UNIT 02 목적어 찾기

UNIT 03 보어 찾기

이 책에 쓰인 표기법

표기법	뜻	표기법	뜻
S	주어	SC	주격보어
V	동사	OC	목적격보어
O	목적어	M	수식어(구)
IO	간접목적어	to-v	to부정사
DO	직접목적어	v-ing	동명사, 분사

표기법	뜻
S', V' 등	종속절의 주어·동사 등
( )	생략된 어구
/	끊어 읽기
//	등위절과 등위절의 구분
{[< >]}	구나 종속절의 구분

끊어 읽기는 구문 이해를 돕기 위해 의미 단위로 끊어 읽는 하나의 장치이다. 따라서 무조건 끊어 읽거나 너무 많이 끊어 읽을 필요는 없으며 자신의 독해 호흡에 따라 끊어 읽도록 한다.

UNIT 01

주어 찾기

Point 01 구 형태 주어
Point 02 절 형태 주어
Point 03 가주어와 비인칭 주어
Point 04 주어의 위치

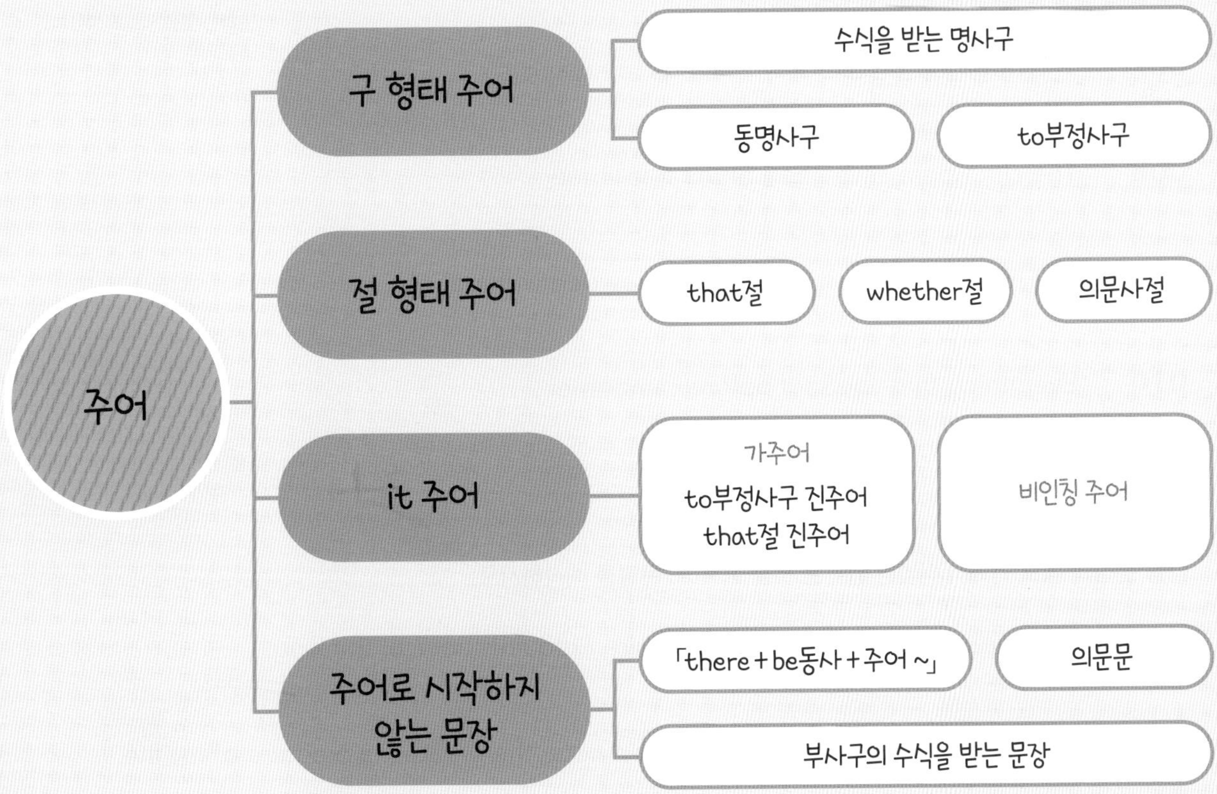

Point 01 구 형태 주어

명사구 주어	형용사(구), 전치사구, 분사(구), 관계사절 등의 **수식을 받는 명사구**
	목적어나 수식어구가 있는 **동명사구** 또는 **to부정사구**

001 **A movie <with lots of action>** / is fun to watch.
S / V / SC
영화는 <액션이 많은> / 보기에 재밌다

002 **The shoes <that I am wearing today>** / are comfortable.
(S′ V′ M′: I / am wearing / today)
S / V / SC
신발은 <내가 오늘 신고 있는> / 편하다

003 **Overcoming your limits** / requires great bravery.
S / V / O
당신의 한계를 극복하는 것은 / 큰 용기를 필요로 한다.

> Tip: 동명사구나 to부정사구가 주어일 경우 동사는 3인칭 단수로 쓴다.

004 **To travel the world** / is one of my dreams.
S / V / SC
세계를 여행하는 것은 / 나의 꿈 중 하나이다.

다음 문장에서 주어를 찾아 밑줄 긋고, 문장을 해석하시오. 정답 및 해설 p.1

> **구문 해석 기법**
> □ 문장이 동명사나 to부정사로 시작하면 동사 바로 앞까지 묶어서 '~하는 것은'으로 해석한다.

005 To set a goal / is important / for a successful life.
목표를 세우는 것은 / 중요하다 / 성공적인 삶을 위해

006 Facing your fears makes you stronger.

007 The book left on the desk belongs to my uncle.

008 The city where I live has a big public library.

009 The long and narrow hallway was crowded with people.

010 Everything that you said before came true.

다음 문장의 네모 안에서 어법상 알맞은 것을 고르고, 문장을 해석하시오.

011 Persuading people in debates [require / requires] logical thinking.

012 My trip to the Hawaiian Islands [was / were] the greatest adventure of my life.

overcome 극복하다 bravery 용기 face 직시하다, 받아들이다 come true 이루어지다 persuade 설득하다 debate 토론 logical 논리적인

Point 02 절 형태 주어

that절	That+주어+동사 ~	~하다는 것은
whether절	Whether+주어+동사 ~ (or not)	~인지 (아닌지)는
의문사절	의문사(+주어)+동사 ~	누가/무엇을/언제/어디서/어떻게/왜 ~하는지는

013 <**That she will come back / tomorrow**> / is certain.
(she: S′, will come back: V′, tomorrow: M′ / 주어절: S, is: V, certain: SC)
<그녀가 돌아올 것이라는 것은 / 내일> / 확실하다

명사절이 주어일 경우 동사는 3인칭 단수로 쓴다.

014 <**Whether I will stay or leave**> / depends on the weather.
(I: S′, will stay or leave: V′ / 주어절: S, depends on: V)
<내가 머무를지 떠날지는> / 날씨에 달려 있다.

015 <**Why the plane broke down**> / is unknown.
(the plane: S′, broke down: V′ / 주어절: S, is: V, unknown: SC)
<비행기가 왜 고장 났는지는> / 알려져 있지 않다.

다음 문장에서 주어를 찾아 밑줄 긋고, 문장을 해석하시오. 정답 및 해설 p.1

016 <That she has lied to us / once before> / is a fact.
<그녀가 우리에게 거짓말한 적이 있는 것은 / 전에 한 번> / 사실이다

017 That my friend is older than me doesn't affect our relationship.

018 Whether there is life on other planets is still a mystery.

019 When the lecture will begin is posted on the bulletin board.

020 Who the winner of the contest is will be announced tomorrow.

021 Whether he will take part in the competition is not important anymore.

다음 문장의 네모 안에서 어법상 알맞은 것을 고르고, 문장을 해석하시오.

022 Whether the projects will be successful or not [is / are] up to you.

023 How babies [learn / learns] languages [have / has] been a topic of study for many years.

affect 영향을 미치다 post 발송하다; *게시하다 bulletin board 게시판 announce 발표하다 take part in ~에 참가하다 be up to ~에 달려 있다

Unit Practice

STEP 1

직독직해에 맞게 ( ) 안의 단어를 사용하여 문장을 쓰시오. (필요시 형태를 바꿔 쓸 것)

1 너의 두려움을 직시하는 것은 / 너를 더 강하게 만든다. (strong / make / face / fears)

_______ _______ _______ / _______ _______ _______.

2 뒤뜰에 있는 나무는 / 자라고 있다 / 잘 (the tree / well / in the backyard / grow)

_______ _______ _______ _______ _______ / _______

_______ / _______.

3 우리가 이 계획을 계속할지는 / 논의될 것이다 / 추후에 (continue / later / be / plan / discuss / will)

_______ _______ _______ _______ _______ _______ /

_______ _______ _______ / _______.

STEP 2

다음 문장에서 주어를 찾아 밑줄 긋고, 문장을 해석하시오.

1 The song playing now is my father's favorite song.

2 That she was late for class was not her fault.

3 The coffee made from these beans doesn't suit my taste.

4 How carefully you brush your teeth impacts your dental health.

5 Why the dinosaurs went extinct is still a subject of scientific debate.

6 Playing a musical instrument can be a fun and creative way to express yourself.

fault 잘못 bean 콩; *원두 suit 맞다 taste 맛; *입맛 impact 영향을 주다 dental 치아의 dinosaur 공룡 extinct 멸종된 subject 주제 scientific 과학의; *과학적인 musical instrument 악기 creative 창의적인

STEP 3

1 **밑줄 친 ①~④ 중 문장의 주어가 아닌 것을 고르시오.**

① The Shakespeare and Company bookshop in Paris is a special place for writers. Famous writers such as ② Ernest Hemingway visited the shop in the past. ③ This special community provides reading material and a creative environment. ④ It also gives writers a place to stay. In exchange for working there, they can sleep there for free.

Reading Q 윗글의 주제로 가장 적절한 것은?

① a unique hotel in Paris
② a special bookstore for writers
③ Ernest Hemingway's works

NEW 내신기출

2 **다음 글을 읽고 조건 에 맞게 써서 질문에 답하시오.**

Hans Herrera is a teacher at a Chilean high school. **How he engages his students** may surprise you. He raps in his class! It began when his students learned that he once rapped for money on buses. **Whether rapping will become a popular teaching style** is uncertain. But **all his students** love his class.

*Chilean 칠레의

조건
· 관계사절의 수식을 받는 명사구를 주어로 쓸 것
· 제시된 단어만을 사용할 것 (필요시 형태를 바꿔 쓸 것)
· engage / he / by rapping / the way / students / be / his

Q. In what way does Hans Herrera engage his students?

A. ______________________________ in his class.

1 community 공동체 provide 제공하다 reading material 읽을거리 environment (주변의) 환경 in exchange for ~대신(에), ~와 교환으로
2 engage (주의·관심을) 끌다 rap (음악) 랩을 하다 once 한때 teaching style 수업 방식 uncertain 불확실한

Point **03**

가주어와 비인칭 주어

가주어 it	**to부정사구**나 **that절이 주어**일 때, **길이가 긴 주어는 뒤**로 보내고 **가주어 it을 문장 맨 앞**에 쓴다.
비인칭 주어 it	**날짜·날씨·시간·거리** 등을 나타내는 문장은 비인칭 주어 it을 쓴다.

024 **It** is necessary / **to get enough sleep.**
V: is
S(가주어) SC S(진주어)
필요하다 / 충분한 수면을 취하는 것이

025 **It** is impossible / for me / **to solve the puzzle.**
V: is
가주어 SC to부정사의 의미상 주어 S(진주어)
불가능하다 / 내가 / 그 퍼즐을 푸는 것은

026 **It** is surprising / <**that John left** / **for Italy**>.
V: is S′: John V′: left M′: for Italy
가주어 SC S(진주어)
놀랍다 / <John이 떠났다는 것은 / 이탈리아로>

027 **It** is 2 kilometers / **to Sunset Beach.**
V: is
S(비인칭 주어) SC M
2킬로미터이다 / Sunset 해변까지는

Tip
to부정사의 의미상의 주어 (행위자)
- 보통 to부정사 앞에 「for + 명사」로 쓴다.
- 사람의 성격·성질을 나타내는 형용사(kind, clever, rude, foolish 등) 뒤에는 「of + 명사」를 쓴다.

다음 문장에서 It이 가주어인지 비인칭 주어인지 쓰고, 문장을 해석하시오. 정답 및 해설 p.3

028 It will be sunny / tomorrow morning. 비인칭 주어
날씨가 화창할 것이다 / 내일 아침은

029 It is already eight o'clock. Let's go home.

030 It was lucky that I got a promotion at work.

031 It sounds exhausting to take a crowded bus every morning.

032 It is certain that our discovery will change people's lives.

033 It is important for family members to take care of each other.

다음 문장의 네모 안에서 어법상 알맞은 것을 고르고, 문장을 해석하시오.

034 It is very kind [for / of] you [helping / to help] your sick friend.

035 [It / That] takes about 2 hours to get to the stadium on foot. It may be better that you [go / to go] there by subway.

necessary 필요한 get a promotion 승진하다 sound 소리; *~인 것 같다 exhausting 진을 빼는 crowded 붐비는 discovery 발견 on foot 걸어서

Point 04 주어의 위치

주어는 보통 문장 맨 앞에 위치하지만, **「there+be동사+주어(+수식어구)」 구문, 의문문, 부사구의 수식을 받는 문장**에서는 주어의 위치가 달라질 수 있다.

036 There are / **a lot of pictures**.
V S
~이 있다 / 많은 사진들

037 What do **you** want / to eat for lunch?
S V O
넌 무엇을 원하니 / 점심으로 먹기를

038 Every morning, / **I** take a cold shower.
M S V O
아침마다, / 나는 찬물로 샤워를 한다.

039 To book a room, / **Bianca** called the hotel.
M S V O
방을 예약하기 위해, / Bianca는 그 호텔에 전화했다.

다음 문장에서 주어를 찾아 밑줄 긋고, 문장을 해석하시오. 정답 및 해설 p.3

040 Why do birds fly / in a V formation?
새들은 왜 날아가는가 / V자 대형으로

041 There will be another great opportunity.

042 At the meeting, the managers will discuss several issues.

043 To prepare for the test, Owen studied for a long time in the library.

044 Before going to bed, she always drinks a glass of warm water.

045 To overcome these obstacles and achieve our goal, what should we do?

다음 문장의 네모 안에서 어법상 알맞은 것을 고르고, 문장을 해석하시오.

046 [Do / Does] eating less help us lose weight without causing health problems?

047 According to the environmental report, there [is / are] clear signs of global warming.

formation 형성; *대형 overcome 극복하다 obstacle 장애물 achieve 성취하다 according to ~에 따르면 environmental 환경의, 환경과 관련된

Unit Practice

STEP 1

직독직해에 맞게 ( ) 안의 단어를 사용하여 문장을 쓰시오. (필요시 형태를 바꿔 쓸 것)

1 날씨가 화창할 것이다 / 내일 아침은 (tomorrow / sunny / be)

_____ _____ _____ _____ / _____ _____.

2 많은 물고기들이 있었다 / 연못에 (lots of / in the pond / be)

_____ _____ _____ _____ _____ / _____

_____ _____.

3 도움이 된다 / 많은 것들을 경험하는 것은 (be / thing / experience / helpful / many)

_____ _____ _____ / _____ _____ _____

_____.

STEP 2

다음 문장에서 주어를 모두 찾아 밑줄 긋고, 문장을 해석하시오.

1 Where are you going to go on your vacation?

2 It is exciting to watch a soccer game at the stadium.

3 There are some vegetarian dishes on the menu.

4 Back then, writing letters was a primary form of communication.

5 It is natural that everyone has different opinions and perspectives.

6 It is considerate of you to take the time to listen to my problems.

pond 연못 helpful 도움이 되는 vegetarian 채식주의(자)의 back then 예전에는 primary 주요한 form 종류, 유형; *방식 natural 자연의; *당연한 perspective 관점 considerate 사려 깊은 take the time (잠시) 시간을 내다 problem 문제; *고민

정답 및 해설 p.3

STEP 3

1 **밑줄 친 (A), (B)가 대신하는 것을 찾아 [ ]로 묶고, [ ] 부분을 해석하시오.**

(A) It is believed that drinking milk is the best way to get calcium. However, some doctors have claimed that this is not true. They agree that milk helps bones grow. Nevertheless, it has a lot of unhealthy sugar, fat, and animal protein. According to the doctors, (B) it is healthier to get calcium from beans, broccoli, and cereal.

*calcium 칼슘

(A) ____________________

(B) ____________________

Reading Q 우유의 효능에 대한 일부 의사들의 주장에 관한 윗글의 내용과 일치하지 않는 것은?

① 우유가 뼈의 성장을 돕는다는 것은 분명하다.
② 우유에는 건강에 좋은 단백질만 함유되어 있다.
③ 칼슘을 채소와 곡류에서 섭취하는 것이 건강에 더 좋다.

NEW 내신기출

2 **밑줄 친 우리말 (A), (B)에 맞게 보기 의 단어를 사용하여 각 문장을 완성하시오.**

(A) 제1차 세계 대전 중인 1914년 크리스마스 날이었다. That day, there was **a special celebration**. For several hours, **hundreds of British, German, and French soldiers** stopped fighting. (B) 상부로부터의 명령은 없었다. Everybody willingly sang Christmas carols and shared food. One British soldier even started a soccer match with the German enemies.

보기 in 1914 / orders / there / Christmas Day / no

(A) ____________________ during World War I.

(B) ____________________ from above.

1 claim 주장하다 bone 뼈 nevertheless 그럼에도 불구하고 sugar 설탕; *당분 fat 뚱뚱한; *지방 protein 단백질 bean 콩 cereal 곡류
2 celebration 기념 행사 soldier 군인 willingly 자진해서 match 성냥; *경기 enemy 적 order 순서; *명령 above 위에; *위, 상(층)부

Wrap Up

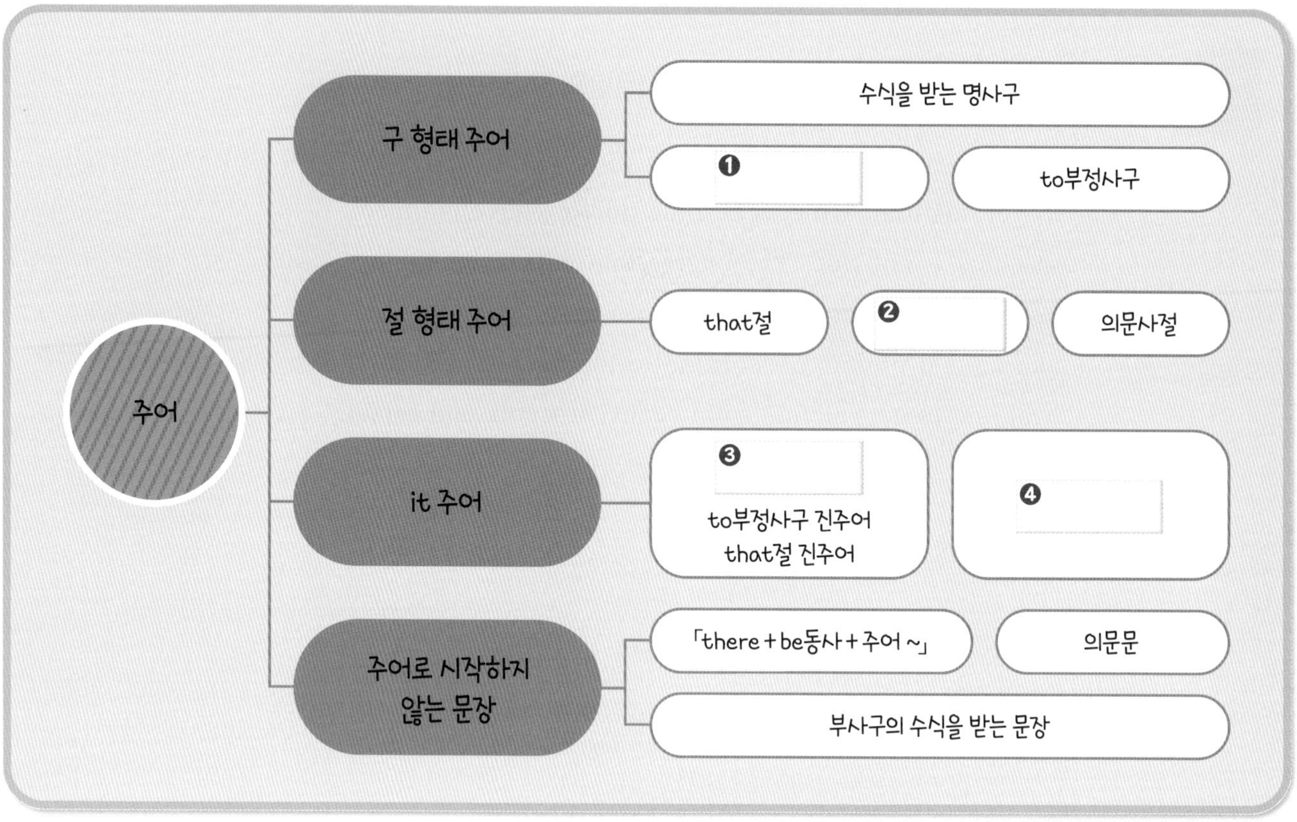

주요 예문을 다시 한번 확인하고, 우리말에 맞게 ( ) 안의 단어를 사용하여 문장을 쓰시오.

1 많은 사진들이 있다. (there / pictures / a lot of) Point 04

2 비행기가 왜 고장 났는지는 알려져 있지 않다. (unknown / the plane / broke down) Point 02

3 액션이 많은 영화는 보기에 재밌다. (fun / a movie / lots of / to watch / with) Point 01

4 John이 이탈리아로 떠났다는 것은 놀랍다. (for Italy / surprising / it / left) Point 03

5 내가 그 퍼즐을 푸는 것은 불가능하다. (to solve / impossible / the puzzle / it) Point 03

6 당신의 한계를 극복하는 것은 큰 용기를 필요로 한다. (great / requires / bravery / limits) Point 01

UNIT 02

목적어 찾기

- 목적어
  - 대명사
    - 목적격 대명사
    - 재귀대명사
  - 구 형태 목적어
    - 수식을 받는 명사구
    - 동명사구
    - to부정사구
  - 절 형태 목적어
    - that절
    - whether[if]절
    - 의문사절
  - 가목적어 it
    - to부정사구 진목적어
    - that절 진목적어

Point 01 명사와 대명사

목적어로 전치사구, 형용사(구), 분사(구), 관계사절 등의 **수식을 받는 명사구**와 **목적격 대명사**를 쓸 수 있다. 대명사 목적어의 경우, **주어와 목적어가 동일한 대상**이면 **재귀대명사**를 쓴다.

048 I wore / **the jacket** <with the red buttons>.
S V O
나는 입었다 / 재킷을 <빨간 단추가 달린>

049 Shawn played / **a song** <**which I wrote**>.
(which = O′, I = S′, wrote = V′)
S V O
Shawn은 연주했다 / 노래를 <내가 쓴>

050 Carina invited **him** / to a festival.
S V O M
Carina는 그를 초대했다 / 축제에

051 The new student introduced / **herself**.
S V O
새로 온 학생이 소개했다 / 그녀 자신을

> **Tip** 재귀대명사
> myself, yourself, himself, herself, itself, ourselves, themselves

다음 문장에서 목적어를 찾아 밑줄 긋고, 문장을 해석하시오. 정답 및 해설 p.5

052 We discussed / the city's garbage problems.
우리는 논의했다 / 그 도시의 쓰레기 문제를

053 I visited the Museum of Modern Art yesterday.

054 I told her about my vacation plan, and she loved it.

055 You should love yourself before you love others.

056 She was carrying an umbrella wet from the rain.

057 Tana saw a man playing a violin and a little girl listening to his performance.

> **구문 해석 기법**
> □ 재귀대명사는 '**주어 자신을[스스로를]**'로 해석한다.

다음 문장의 네모 안에서 어법상 알맞은 것을 고르고, 문장을 해석하시오.

058 A chameleon protects [it / itself] from danger by changing its color.

059 Some people express [them / themselves] with their clothes. They choose the styles and colors that they prefer.

button 단추 discuss 논의하다 garbage 쓰레기 modern 현대의 carry 들고 있다, 가지고 다니다 performance 공연; *연주 chameleon 카멜레온 protect 보호하다 danger 위험 express 표현하다 prefer 선호하다

Point **02**

동명사와 to부정사

동사에 따라 **동명사(구)**나 **to부정사(구)**를 목적어로 쓸 수 있고, to부정사는 **「의문사+to부정사」** 형태로도 쓰인다.

동명사를 목적어로 쓰는 동사	enjoy, avoid, mind, finish, practice, suggest, give up, imagine 등
to부정사를 목적어로 쓰는 동사	want, decide, learn, plan, ask, expect, choose, promise, hope 등

060 She enjoys / **chatting with my friends.**
S V O
그녀는 즐긴다 / 내 친구들과 수다 떠는 것을

061 Dana expects / **to pass the exam**.
S V O
Dana는 기대한다 / 시험에 통과할 것을

062 I don't know / <**what to tell him**>.
S V O
나는 모르겠다 / <그에게 무엇을 말해야 할지를>

다음 ( ) 안의 단어를 어법에 맞는 형태로 고쳐 쓰고, 문장을 해석하시오.

정답 및 해설 p.5

063 Jamie hopes / (make) new friends / soon. to make
Jamie는 바란다 / 새로운 친구들을 만들기를 / 곧

064 The taxi driver didn't know where (go).

065 I suggested (change) the date of the school festival.

066 My little brother decided (learn) how (swim).

067 Anna didn't give up (study) despite all the noise around her.

068 I sometimes imagine (be) a famous singer and (perform) on the stage.

구문 해석 기법

□ 「의문사+to-v」
who+to-v (누구를 ~해야 할지)
what+to-v (무엇을 ~해야 할지)
where+to-v (어디서 ~해야 할지)
when+to-v (언제 ~해야 할지)
how+to-v (어떻게 ~해야 할지)

다음 문장의 네모 안에서 어법상 알맞은 것을 고르고, 문장을 해석하시오.

069 I enjoy [to eat / eating] pizza, but I want [to have / having] a salad for dinner.

070 The company expects [attracting / to attract] more customers by making eco-friendly products.

suggest 제안하다 give up 포기하다 imagine 상상하다 chat 수다를 떨다 despite ~에도 불구하고 perform 공연하다 stage 단계; *무대 attract 끌어모으다 customer 고객 eco-friendly 친환경적인 product 제품

Unit Practice

STEP 1

직독직해에 맞게 ( ) 안의 단어를 사용하여 문장을 쓰시오. (필요시 형태를 바꿔 쓸 것)

1 그는 전시회를 열었다 / 그의 사진들에 대한 (an exhibition / hold / of his photos)

__________ __________ __________ __________ / __________ __________

__________.

2 우리는 결정해야 한다 / 어디에서 머물지를 (have to / stay / decide / where)

__________ __________ __________ __________ / __________ __________

__________.

3 우리는 계획하는 중이다 / 하이킹 가는 것을 / 다음 주말에 (weekend / plan / next / hiking / go)

__________ __________ __________ / __________ __________ __________ /

__________ __________.

STEP 2

다음 문장에서 목적어를 찾아 밑줄 긋고, 문장을 해석하시오.

1 Do you mind opening the window?

2 I don't know what to wear on the first date.

3 Carefully, the firefighters rescued the trapped cat.

4 He hurt himself while he was playing soccer with his friends.

5 She has lost the wireless earphones that I gave her for her birthday.

6 Dorothy and I promised to keep each other's secrets forever.

exhibition 전시회 hold 잡고 있다; *(회의·시합 등을) 열다(-held-held) mind 상관하다, 신경쓰다 rescue 구하다, 구조하다 trap (위험한 장소·궁지에) 가두다 hurt 다치게 하다(-hurt-hurt) wireless 무선의 keep a secret 비밀을 지키다 each other 서로

STEP 3

1 목적어에 유의하여 밑줄 친 문장을 해석하시오.

Today's teens use **digital devices** every day. They have been using **them** since early childhood. They amuse **themselves** by sending text messages and playing online games. In fact, they spend **most of their time** in front of computer and smartphone screens. For this reason, some people call **them** "screenagers." This is a combination of "screen" and "teenager."

*text message 문자 메시지

____

Reading Q 윗글의 제목으로 가장 적절한 것은?

① Making a Better Screen
② Why Are Teens So Busy?
③ Teens Staring at Screens

NEW 내신기출

2 다음 중 어색한 부분이 있는 문장 2개를 찾아 바르게 고쳐 쓰시오. (고친 문장 전체를 쓸 것)

These days, there are special schools for people who want becoming magicians. At these schools, future magicians learn how to perform amazing tricks. They also develop other skills needed to entertain an audience. For example, students practice to dance, act, and speak in public.

(1) ______________________________

(2) ______________________________

1 device 장치, 기구 childhood 어린 시절, 유년기 amuse 즐겁게 하다 combination 조합 stare at ~을 응시하다
2 magician 마술사 perform 공연하다 trick 마술 entertain 즐겁게 해 주다 audience 관객 act 행동하다; *연기하다 in public 대중 앞에서

Point 03 절 형태 목적어

접속사 that, whether[if]나 의문사가 이끄는 명사절은 목적어로 쓰일 수 있다.

that절	that+주어+동사 ~	~하다는 것을
whether[if]절	whether[if]+주어+동사 ~ (or not)	~인지 (아닌지)를
의문사절	의문사(+주어)+동사 ~	누가/무엇을/언제/어디서/어떻게/왜 ~하는지를

S′ V′ SC′ M′
071 I found / <**that prices are too high / in Seoul**>.
S V O
나는 알게 되었다 / <물가가 너무 높다는 것을 / 서울은>

S′ V′ SC′ M′
072 I don't know / <**whether[if] I'm allergic / to peaches**>.
S V O
나는 모른다 / <내가 알레르기가 있는지를 / 복숭아에>

S′ V′ O′
073 Luke didn't remember / <**where he put his key**>.
S V O
Luke는 기억나지 않았다 / <그가 그의 열쇠를 어디에 두었는지>

다음 문장에서 목적어를 찾아 밑줄 긋고, 문장을 해석하시오.

정답 및 해설 p.7

074 I hope / <that you do well / in the interview>.
나는 바란다 / <네가 잘하기를 / 면접에서>

075 Janice asked how the couple first met.

076 Who can explain to me why this room is so messy?

077 I wonder whether the plane will take off tomorrow.

078 People believed the earth was flat in ancient times.

079 I don't know if I'll be able to go to the amusement park with you. I'll let you know later.

다음 문장의 네모 안에서 어법상 알맞은 것을 고르고, 문장을 해석하시오.

080 Research has shown [that / which] there are some jellyfish that can live forever.

081 John wanted to buy a computer, and he asked [why / what] the most recent model was.

price 물가 allergic to ~에 대해 알레르기가 있는 interview 면접 explain 설명하다 messy 지저분한 take off 이륙하다 flat 평평한 ancient 고대의 time 시간; *시대, 시기 amusement park 놀이공원 research 연구 jellyfish 해파리 recent 최신의

Point 04 가목적어 it

to부정사구나 that절이 목적어인 경우, **길이가 긴 목적어는 뒤**로 보내고 그 자리에 **가목적어 it**을 쓴다. 특히, 형용사나 분사가 목적격보어로 사용된 5형식 구조에서 흔히 볼 수 있다.

082 She found / **it** necessary / **to get eight hours of sleep**.
S V 가목적어 OC O(진목적어)
그녀는 생각했다 / 필요하다고 / 여덟 시간 동안 자는 것이

083 Her mother's support made / **it** possible / <**that she could recover** / **quickly**>.
S V 가목적어 OC O(진목적어) S′ V′ M′
그녀의 어머니의 도움은 만들었다 / 가능하도록 / <그녀가 회복될 수 있었던 것이 / 빠르게>

다음 문장에서 진목적어를 찾아 밑줄 긋고, 문장을 해석하시오.

정답 및 해설 p.7

084 Jennifer made it clear / <that she did her best>.
Jennifer는 확실히 했다 / <그녀가 최선을 다했다는 것을>

085 Some cultures consider it embarrassing to ask another person's age.

086 Everyone thought it strange that Betty was silent on that day.

087 Good advice makes it possible to achieve better results.

088 We consider it important that kids play in a safe environment.

089 Most people think it polite to offer their seat to an elderly person.

다음 문장의 네모 안에서 어법상 알맞은 것을 고르고, 문장을 해석하시오.

090 He thought [it / that] surprising that he could buy those sneakers at that price.

091 I find it difficult [having / to have] breakfast. However, skipping breakfast makes [it harder / harder it] to have a good day.

find 찾다; *~라고 생각하다 support 지지; *도움 recover 회복되다 clear 분명한; *확실한 do one's best 최선을 다하다 consider 여기다, 생각하다 embarrassing 난처한 achieve 달성하다 offer 제안하다, 권하다 elderly 연세가 드신 sneakers 운동화 skip 거르다

Unit Practice

STEP 1 직독직해에 맞게 (   ) 안의 단어를 사용하여 문장을 쓰시오. (필요시 형태를 바꿔 쓸 것)

1 사람들은 믿었다 / 지구가 평평하다고 / 고대에 (the earth / in ancient times / believe / flat)

_______ _______ / _______ _______ _______ _______ /

_______ _______ _______.

2 그녀는 생각했다 / 즐겁다고 / Joy와 이야기하는 것이 (talk to / find / pleasant)

_______ _______ / _______ _______ / _______ _______

_______ _______.

3 그는 생각했다 / 용감하다고 / 그녀가 여행가기로 결정한 것이 / 유럽으로 / 혼자 (brave / consider / travel / to Europe / alone / decide)

_______ _______ / _______ _______ / _______ _______

_______ _______ _______ / _______ _______ / _______.

STEP 2 다음 문장에서 목적어를 모두 찾아 밑줄 긋고, 문장을 해석하시오.

1 He described which bicycle he wanted to buy.

2 Sam noticed that someone was following him.

3 I find it difficult to stay calm in front of an audience.

4 Before we go out, we should check if the theater is open today.

5 These days, she often forgets what she is supposed to do.

6 Our teacher made it clear that the assignment should be submitted by next Tuesday.

pleasant 즐거운 describe 말하다, 묘사하다 notice 알아차리다 follow 따라가다 stay (특정한 상태를) 유지하다 calm 차분한 audience 관중
be supposed to-v ~하기로 되어 있다 clear 분명한; *확실한 assignment 과제 submit 제출하다

STEP 3

1 ( ) 안의 단어를 문맥에 맞게 배열하시오.

Do you know **whether you can tickle yourself or not**? Most people say (only others / tickle / that / them / can). This is because the brain can predict **how we will feel when we move**. When we touch our own body to tickle ourselves, the brain prepares for this contact and removes any uneasy feeling. That's why we don't react very much if we tickle ourselves.

____

Reading Q 윗글의 주제로 가장 적절한 것은?

① why it's hard to tickle ourselves
② why we laugh when we get tickled
③ how the brain predicts the body's reaction

NEW 내신기출

2 밑줄 친 우리말 (A), (B)를 조건에 맞게 써서 각 문장을 완성하시오.

(A) 당신은 누군가가 거짓말을 하고 있는지를 그들의 몸짓을 봄으로써 알 수 있다. When we tell the truth, our speech and body language are very natural. But when we lie, we have to think carefully about our words. (B) 동시에 우리는 어떤 몸짓이 자연스럽게 보이는지를 선택해야 한다. All this thinking may lead to body language that doesn't match our words.

조건
· 제시된 단어를 사용할 것 · (A) 7단어, (B) 8단어로 쓸 것
· natural / choose / can / gestures / look / lying / tell / someone / have to / which

(A) ______________________________ by watching their gestures.

(B) At the same time, ______________________________.

1 tickle 간지럼을 태우다 predict 예측하다 prepare for ~에 대비하다, 준비하다 contact 접촉 uneasy 불편한 react 반응하다
2 truth 진실 body language 몸짓 언어 natural 자연스러운 lead to ~로 이어지다 match (서로) 맞다 tell 말하다; *알다, 판단하다

Wrap Up

정답 및 해설 p.9

주요 예문을 다시 한번 확인하고, 우리말에 맞게 ( ) 안의 단어를 사용하여 문장을 쓰시오.

1 Luke는 그가 그의 열쇠를 어디에 두었는지 기억나지 않았다. (remember / put / key) Point 03

2 Dana는 시험에 통과할 것을 기대한다. (the exam / expects / pass) Point 02

3 새로 온 학생이 그녀 자신을 소개했다. (the new student / introduced) Point 01

4 나는 그에게 무엇을 말해야 할지를 모르겠다. (tell / know) Point 02

5 그녀는 여덟 시간 동안 자는 것이 필요하다고 생각했다. (necessary / of sleep / found / get) Point 04

6 나는 내가 복숭아에 알레르기가 있는지 모른다. (peaches / allergic to / know / whether) Point 03

UNIT 03

보어 찾기

Point 01 주격보어_명사, 형용사, 분사
Point 02 주격보어_동명사, to부정사, 명사절
Point 03 목적격보어_명사와 형용사
Point 04 목적격보어_to부정사, 동사원형, 분사

- 보어
  - 주격보어
    - 명사(구)
    - 형용사(구)
    - 분사
    - 동명사(구)
    - to부정사(구)
    - 명사절
      - that절
      - whether절
      - 의문사절
  - 목적격보어
    - 명사(구)
    - 형용사(구)
    - to부정사(구)
    - 동사원형
    - 분사

Point 01 주격보어_명사, 형용사, 분사

명사(구), 형용사(구), 분사는 be동사, 감각을 나타내는 동사, 상태·변화를 나타내는 동사 뒤에서 주격보어로 쓰일 수 있다.

감각을 나타내는 동사	look, sound, smell, taste, feel 등
상태·변화를 나타내는 동사	keep, remain, become, get, grow, turn, go, come 등

092 This is / **one of the world's oldest museums.**
S V SC
이것은 ~이다 / 세계에서 가장 오래된 박물관들 중 하나

093 Spoiled milk / smells **terrible**.
S V SC
상한 우유는 / 지독한 냄새가 난다.

094 The way <to the store> / is **confusing**.
S V SC
길은 <그 가게로 가는> / 헷갈린다

095 He grew **tired** / because of the lecture.
S V SC M
그는 피곤해졌다 / 그 강의 때문에

다음 문장에서 주격보어를 찾아 밑줄 긋고, 문장을 해석하시오.

정답 및 해설 p.9

096 Sandra is / a cheerful teenager.
Sandra는 ~이다 / 발랄한 십 대

097 I felt depressed when my best friend moved away.

098 After adding some pepper, the soup tasted better.

099 They got excited when they heard about the free concert.

100 Edwin became the most successful businessman in the city.

101 Having a healthy diet is a good way to stay in shape.

다음 문장의 네모 안에서 어법상 알맞은 것을 고르고, 문장을 해석하시오.

102 Your idea sounds [creative / creatively], but it should be more [realistic / realistically].

103 The comedy show was [amusing / amused], so the audience was [entertaining / entertained].

spoil 상하다 cheerful 발랄한 depress 우울하게 만들다 stay in shape 건강을 유지하다 amuse 재미있게 하다 entertain 즐겁게 해주다

Point 02

주격보어_동명사, to부정사, 명사절

동명사(구), to부정사(구) 접속사 that, whether나 **의문사가 이끄는 명사절**은 **be동사** 뒤에서 주격보어로 쓰일 수 있다.

104 Our main goal is / **helping poor children**.

S V SC

우리의 주요 목표는 ~이다 / 가난한 아이들을 돕는 것

105 The only solution is / **to restart your laptop**.

S V SC

유일한 해결책은 ~이다 / 너의 노트북을 다시 시작하는 것

S′ V′ SC′

106 His best quality is / <**that he is honest**>.

S V SC

그의 최고 좋은 점은 ~이다 / <그가 정직하다는 것>

S′ V′ O′ S″ V″ O″

107 <What I want to know> / is <**whether you have vacation plans**>.

S V SC

<내가 알고 싶은 것은> / <네가 휴가 계획이 있는지>이다.

다음 문장에서 주격보어를 찾아 밑줄 긋고, 문장을 해석하시오.

정답 및 해설 p.10

108 <What Alberto really likes> is / playing soccer.

<Alberto가 정말 좋아하는 것은> ~이다 / 축구하는 것

109 The question is who will win the Nobel Prize.

110 The mystery is how he survived the accident without any injuries.

111 The most important thing for a team is to have the same goal.

112 One of my good habits is washing the dishes right after having a meal.

113 The purpose of this email is to announce a change in the schedule.

다음 문장의 네모 안에서 어법상 알맞은 것을 고르고, 문장을 해석하시오.

114 When people come [late / lately], a common excuse is [that / what] there was a traffic jam.

115 The topic of the debate was [where / whether] money brings true happiness to our lives.

restart 다시 시작하다 quality (사람의) 자질 survive 살아남다 injury 부상 purpose 목적 announce 알리다, 발표하다 common 흔한 excuse 변명

Unit Practice

STEP 1 **직독직해에 맞게 ( ) 안의 단어를 사용하여 문장을 쓰시오. (필요시 형태를 바꿔 쓸 것)**

1 약간의 후추를 넣은 뒤, / 그 수프는 더 맛있어졌다. (better / taste / add / pepper)

______ ______ ______ ______, / ______ ______

______ ______.

2 그 낡은 집은 / 언덕 위의 / 계속 잠겨 있었다 / 수년 동안 (on the hill / lock / for years / has remained / the old house)

______ ______ ______ / ______ ______ ______ /

______ ______ ______ / ______ ______.

3 문제는 ~이다 / 우리가 모으지 못했다는 것 / 충분한 돈을 / 여행을 위한 (that / save / for the trip / haven't / enough)

______ ______ ______ / ______ ______ ______

______ / ______ ______ / ______ ______ ______.

STEP 2 **다음 문장에서 주격보어를 찾아 밑줄 긋고, 문장을 해석하시오.**

1 One of my hobbies is taking pictures with my film camera.

2 I had a nightmare last night, and it was really terrifying.

3 The question is why the basketball player suddenly decided to retire.

4 The best way to comfort someone is to listen to their complaints.

5 When the storm approached, the waves grew more powerful.

6 The main question is whether the new technology will improve efficiency.

hill 언덕 remain 계속[여전히] ~이다 nightmare 악몽 terrify 무섭게 하다 retire 은퇴하다 comfort 위로하다 complaint 불평, 불만 approach 다가오다 wave 파도 grow 자라다; *~해지다 technology 기술 improve 향상시키다 efficiency 효율, 능률

STEP 3

1 밑줄 친 (A), (B)에서 주격보어를 찾아 동그라미 하고, 문장을 해석하시오.

(A) Stones are not living things. They usually don't become **larger** over time. However, stones called "Trovants" in Romania look like they grow. The rain there has minerals in it. The sand in the stones reacts chemically with the minerals. During the reaction, layers form on top of the stones. (B) Then the stones become bigger!

(A) ______________________________

(B) ______________________________

Reading Q 윗글의 제목으로 가장 적절한 것은?

① Harmful Minerals in Rain
② Romania's Growing Stones
③ Romania: A Country of Stones

NEW 내신기출

2 밑줄 친 우리말에 맞게 보기 의 단어를 사용하여 문장을 쓰시오.

When a man became **unemployed**, he decided to do something unusual. His decision was **that he would give away $10 to a poor stranger every day**. He didn't want anything in return. 그의 유일한 목표는 자신의 힘든 시기 동안 다른 사람들을 돕는 것이었다. Soon, many people knew about his kind acts. And some of them began to help the poor as well.

보기 during / to / others / his own / goal / only / times / help / difficult

____

1 over time 시간이 흐르면서 mineral 광물 react 반응하다(*n.* reaction 반응) chemically 화학적으로 layer 층, 막 form 형성하다, 형성되다 harmful 해로운
2 unemployed 실직한 unusual 특이한, 흔치 않은 decision 결심 give away 기부하다, 거저 주다 in return 답례로 as well 또한, 역시 one's own 자신의

Point 03

목적격보어_명사와 형용사

명사(구)와 **형용사(구)**는 동사의 목적어 뒤에서 목적격보어로 쓰일 수 있다.

목적격보어를 쓰는 동사	호칭·신분을 나타내는 동사	name, call, elect 등
	상태·변화를 나타내는 동사	make, keep, leave, get, turn 등
	생각·인식을 나타내는 동사	think, believe, consider, find 등

116 My classmates call / me **a comedian.**
S V O OC
나의 반 친구들은 부른다 / 나를 코미디언이라고

117 Suzy's shocking behavior left / me **speechless.**
S V O OC
Suzy의 충격적인 행동은 만들었다 / 내가 말을 못하게

118 Some people consider / the number 4 **unlucky.**
S V O OC
일부 사람들은 생각한다 / 숫자 4를 불길하다고

다음 문장에서 목적격보어를 찾아 밑줄 긋고, 문장을 해석하시오.

정답 및 해설 p.12

119 Some critics call the movie / the best film <of the year>.
몇몇 비평가들은 그 영화를 칭한다 / 최고의 영화라고 <올해의>

120 The writer named the main character of his novel Rick.

121 We found the new system fast and efficient.

122 Many people consider the *Mona Lisa* the greatest painting of all time.

123 They found the festival enjoyable and moving.

124 The members of the club elected James the next president.

구문 해석 기법

☐ 동사에 따라 '목적어를[가] 목적격보어라고[하다고/하게] 동사하다'로 해석한다.

다음 문장의 네모 안에서 어법상 알맞은 것을 고르고, 문장을 해석하시오.

125 Wearing thick boots keeps you [warm / warmly] in winter.

126 Colorful lights will make the show more [memorable / memorably].

elect (선거로) 선출하다 critic 평론가, 비평가 efficient 효율적인 moving 감동적인 president (동아리 등의) 회장 light 빛; *조명 memorable 기억에 남을 만한

Point 04 목적격보어_to부정사, 동사원형, 분사

to부정사(구), **동사원형**, **분사** 또한 목적격보어로 쓰일 수 있다.

목적격보어로	to부정사(구)가 오는 동사	want, ask, allow, order, tell, teach, advise, expect 등
	동사원형이 오는 동사	사역동사(make, have, let), 지각동사(see, hear, feel 등)
	현재분사(v-ing)가 올 때	목적어와 목적격보어가 능동 관계
	과거분사(v-ed)가 올 때	목적어와 목적격보어가 수동 관계

127 The police ordered / William **to get out of the car**.
S V O OC
경찰이 명령했다 / William이 차에서 내리도록

128 I'll let / my son **go camping** / **with his friends**.
S V O OC
나는 하게 할 것이다 / 내 아들이 캠핑을 가도록 / 그의 친구들과

129 Mark saw / his dog **running toward him**.
S V O OC
Mark는 보았다 / 그의 개가 그에게 달려오는 것을

130 I had / my computer **repaired**.
S V O OC
나는 했다 / 내 컴퓨터가 수리되도록

다음 문장에서 목적격보어를 찾아 밑줄 긋고, 문장을 해석하시오.

정답 및 해설 p.12

131 Alice wanted / me to reserve the tickets.
Alice는 원했다 / 내가 그 표를 예약하기를

132 I had all the unnecessary programs removed.

133 The prince had his servant find the owner of the shoe.

134 When the sun set, I felt the temperature drop.

135 People didn't expect the explorers to find treasure.

136 I saw him riding an electric scooter on the street.

> **구문 해석 기법**
> □ 현재분사 목적격보어
> : 목적어가 ~하고 있는
> □ 과거분사 목적격보어
> : 목적어가 ~되도록[되게]

다음 문장의 네모 안에서 어법상 알맞은 것을 고르고, 문장을 해석하시오.

137 Everyone in the room heard Christmas carols [playing / to play] on the radio.

138 Diana found herself [losing / lost] in the shopping mall.

repair 수리하다 reserve 예약하다 unnecessary 불필요한 remove 제거하다 temperature 기온, 온도 explorer 탐험가 treasure 보물

Unit Practice

STEP 1 **직독직해에 맞게 ( ) 안의 단어를 사용하여 문장을 쓰시오. (필요시 형태를 바꿔 쓸 것)**

1 George는 생각한다 / 그의 아빠가 훌륭한 음악가라고 (dad / consider / a great musician)

__________ __________ / __________ __________ __________ __________

__________.

2 그 작가는 원한다 / 그녀의 책이 베스트셀러가 되기를 (be / the writer / a bestseller / book / want)

__________ __________ __________ / __________ __________ __________

__________ __________ __________.

3 선생님께서 시키셨다 / 내가 그 시를 읽도록 / 소리내어 (out loud / let / the teacher / the poem / read)

__________ __________ __________ / __________ __________ __________

__________ / __________ __________.

STEP 2 **다음 문장에서 목적격보어를 찾아 밑줄 긋고, 문장을 해석하시오.**

1 My younger sister named her new doll Jolly.

2 You should have its battery replaced.

3 The blueberry juice turned my tongue purple when I drank it.

4 Eating spicy foods like tteokbokki makes my stomach hurt.

5 The doctor advised her to eat more fruits and vegetables.

6 I heard the dogs barking loudly from the backyard.

musician 음악가 out loud 소리내어 poem 시 battery 건전지 replace 교체하다 stomach 위, 배 hurt 아프게 하다; *아프다 advise 조언하다 bark (개가) 짖다 backyard 뒷마당

정답 및 해설 p.12

STEP 3

1 밑줄 친 (A), (B)에서 목적격보어를 찾아 동그라미 하고, 밑줄 친 부분을 해석하시오.

Houseplants look good, and (A) they also make us feel good. That's because they remove harmful chemicals from the air. People who keep houseplants in their office generally have lower blood pressure. According to research, (B) houseplants also help us to feel more creative, as they lower our stress.

(A) ______________________________

(B) ______________________________

Reading Q 윗글의 주제로 가장 적절한 것은?

① the benefits of growing houseplants
② the difficulties of caring for houseplants
③ tips for growing houseplants successfully

NEW 내신기출

2 밑줄 친 ①~④ 중 어법상 틀린 2개를 찾아 해당 번호를 쓰고 바르게 고쳐 쓰시오.

A man waves his hand and the lights turn on. What enables him ① to do this? It is a computer chip called an RFID. He had it ② place under his skin, and it can send a signal to the lights. There are many uses for RFIDs. For example, some people have them **placed in their pets**. The RFIDs help them ③ find their pets if they get lost. These special chips can make our lives more ④ conveniently in many ways!

*RFID 극소형 칩에 데이터를 저장하고 송신하는 장치

번호	적절하지 않은 단어	고쳐 쓴 단어

1 houseplant 실내 화초 harmful 해로운 chemical ((*pl.*)) 화학 물질 low 낮은(*v.* lower 낮추다) blood pressure 혈압 creative 창의적인
2 wave (손·팔을) 흔들다 turn on (TV·전기 등이) 켜지다 enable ~을 할 수 있게 하다 place 장소; *두다, 설치하다 signal 신호 get lost 길을 잃다

Wrap Up

정답 및 해설 p.13

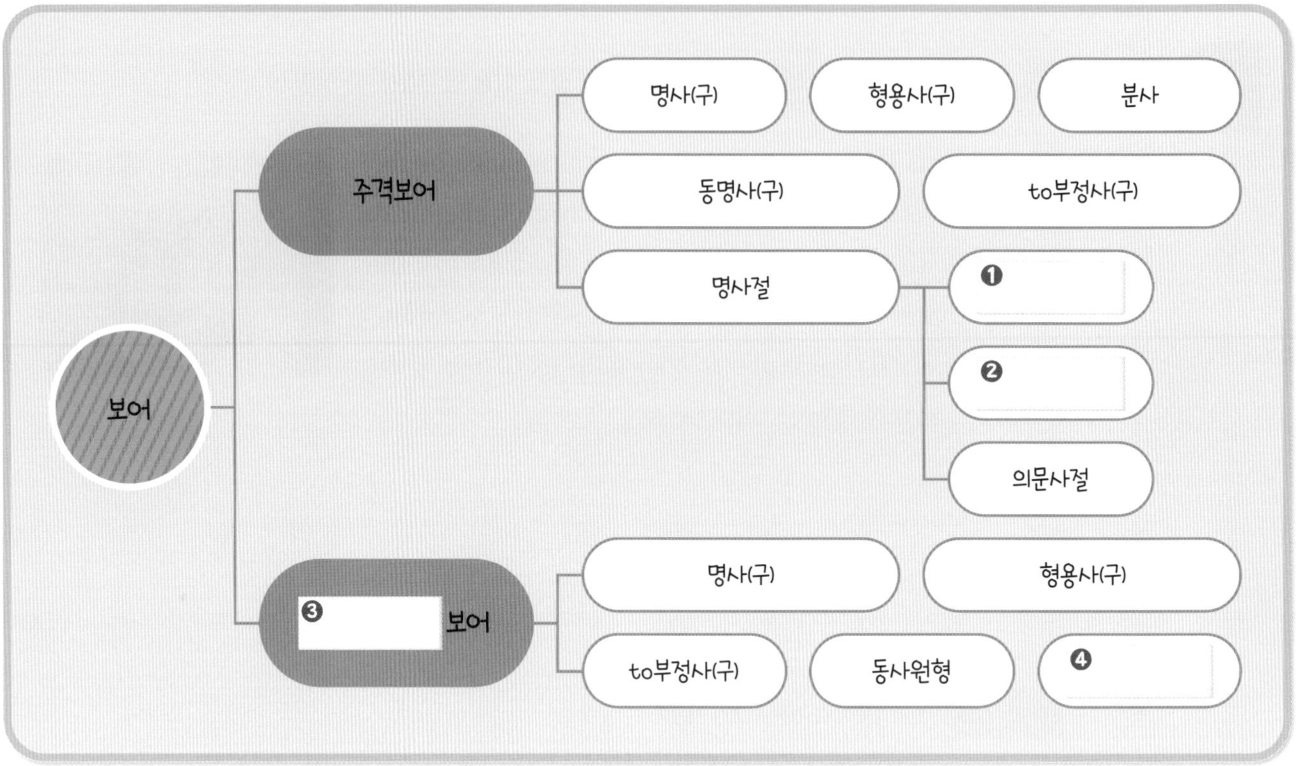

주요 예문을 다시 한번 확인하고, 우리말에 맞게 (　) 안의 단어를 사용하여 문장을 쓰시오.

1 상한 우유는 지독한 냄새가 난다. (smells / terrible / spoiled) Point 01

2 Mark는 그의 개가 그에게 달려오는 것을 보았다. (toward / saw / running) Point 04

3 그의 최고 좋은 점은 그가 정직하다는 것이다. (best / honest / quality) Point 02

4 우리의 주요 목표는 가난한 아이들을 돕는 것이다. (goal / helping / main / poor) Point 02

5 Suzy의 충격적인 행동은 내가 말을 못하게 만들었다. (speechless / shocking / left / behavior) Point 03

6 나는 내 아들이 그의 친구들과 캠핑을 가게 할 것이다. (go / with his friends / let / camping) Point 04

UNIT 04

시제와 수동태

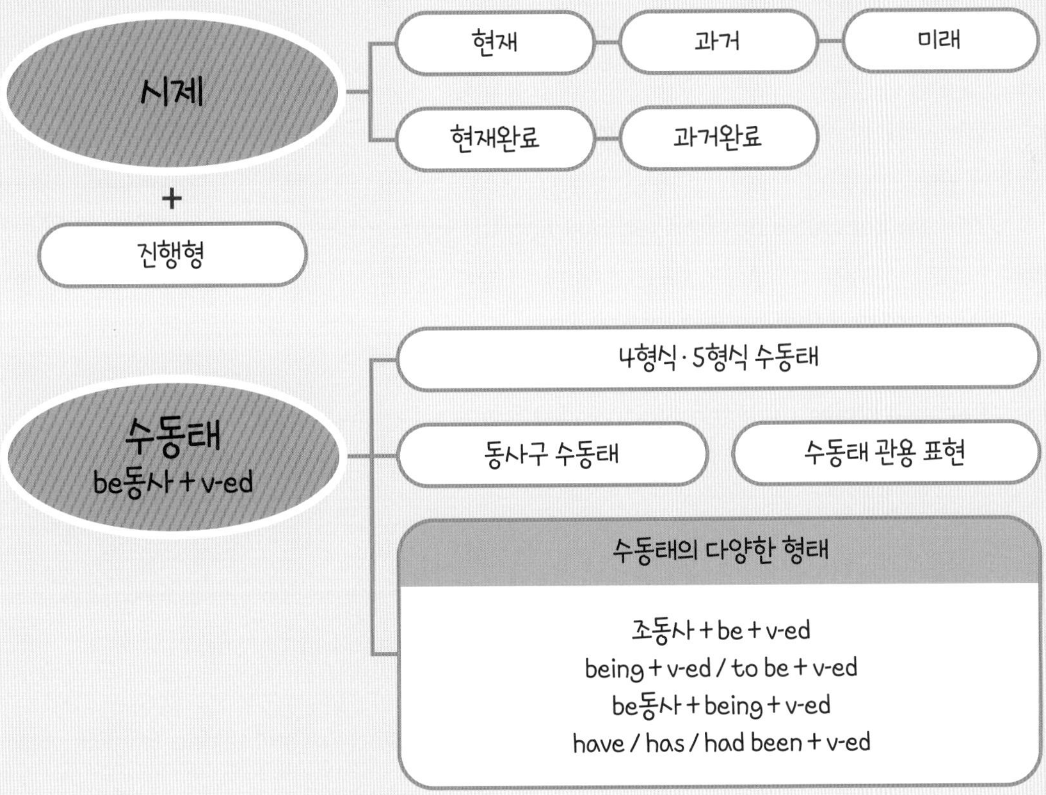

Point 01

시제와 진행형

현재·과거·미래시제는 특정 시점에 일어난 일을 나타내고, **완료시제**는 **특정 시점 이전에 일어난 일이 이후에도 영향을 미치고 있음**을 나타낸다. 또한 각 시제에 **진행형**을 써서 **동작이 일어나고 있음**을 나타낼 수 있다.

139 I **live** in Tokyo / now.
S V M1 M2
나는 도쿄에 산다 / 지금

140 I **lived** in Tokyo / <when I **was** young>.
S V M (S′ V′ SC′)
나는 도쿄에 살았다 / <내가 어렸을 때>

141 I **have lived** in Tokyo / for ten years.
S V M1 M2
나는 도쿄에 살았다 / 10년 동안 (현재도 도쿄에 살고 있음)

Tip 현재완료는 특정 과거 시점을 나타내는 표현과 함께 쓰이지 않음
ex) yesterday, last ~, ~ ago, in 2020 등

142 I **had lived** in Tokyo / <before I moved / to Osaka>.
S V M (S′ V′ M′)
나는 도쿄에 살았었다 / <내가 이사하기 전에 / 오사카로>

143 I **was living** in Tokyo / in 2013.
S V M1 M2
나는 도쿄에 살고 있었다 / 2013년에

밑줄 친 부분에 유의하여 다음 문장을 해석하시오.

정답 및 해설 p.14

144 He is fixing / his old bicycle / now.
그는 수리하고 있다 / 그의 낡은 자전거를 / 지금

145 Andrew played the drums in a band last year.

146 We were playing basketball two hours ago.

147 The workers have not finished building the gym yet.

148 Luke noticed that he had lost his key.

149 Because I have used the program for 5 years, I know it well.

구문 해석 기법

□ 현재완료는 문맥에 따라 다양하게 해석한다.
- 완료: (막/이미) ~했다
- 경험: ~한 적이 있다
- 계속: (지금까지) ~해 왔다
- 결과: ~해 버렸다

다음 문장의 네모 안에서 어법상 알맞은 것을 고르고, 문장을 해석하시오.

150 When I first met Taylor, I thought I [had / have] seen her before.

151 I [had / have] been learning English since 2022, and I'm still taking English classes.

move 움직이다; *이사하다 fix 고정시키다; *수리하다 gym 체육관 notice 알아차리다 still 아직(도) take a class 수업을 듣다, 수강하다

Point 02 주의할 시제 표현

시간·조건 부사절에서는 **현재시제로 미래를 표현**한다. 한편, 부사절이 아니더라도 **현재시제**나 **현재진행형**으로 **예정된 가까운 미래**를 나타낼 수 있다.

152 <When I **see** him / next week>, / I will hug him.
(S′ V′ O′ M′ / S V O)
<내가 그를 만날 때 / 다음 주에> / 나는 그를 안을 것이다

153 <If it **rains** tomorrow>, / I will stay home.
(S′ V′ M′ / S V M)
<내일 비가 오면> / 나는 집에 있을 것이다.

154 The bus **arrives** / at 9:00 p.m.
(S V M)
버스는 도착할 것이다 / 밤 9시에

155 I **am meeting** my friends / this weekend.
(S V O M)
나는 내 친구들을 만날 것이다 / 이번 주말에

밑줄 친 부분에 유의하여 다음 문장을 해석하시오.

정답 및 해설 p.14

156 We are going / to Berlin / next month.
우리는 갈 것이다 / 베를린에 / 다음 달에

157 Keep in mind that our plane leaves in an hour.

158 She will call you back when she gets your message.

159 You will miss the movie unless you take a taxi.

160 Daniel is coming back from China tonight.

161 He will go camping with his family after he gets his driver's license.

구문 해석 기법

□ 현재시제나 현재진행형이 가까운 미래를 나타내는 부사(구) (tomorrow, in an hour, next week 등)와 쓰였으면, 미래시제로 해석한다.

다음 문장의 네모 안에서 어법상 알맞은 것을 고르고, 문장을 해석하시오.

162 Parker will stay in the hospital until he [recovers / will recover] completely.

163 The museum [opens / opened] at 10:00 a.m. If we [arrive / will arrive] there at 9:00 a.m., we won't be able to go inside.

hug 껴안다 keep in mind 명심하다 miss 놓치다 driver's license 운전면허증 recover 회복하다 completely 완전히

Unit Practice

STEP 1

직독직해에 맞게 ( ) 안의 단어를 사용하여 문장을 쓰시오. (필요시 형태를 바꿔 쓸 것)

1 Luke는 알아차렸다 / 그가 잃어버렸다는 것을 / 그의 열쇠를 (lose / notice / key / that)

______ ______ / ______ ______ ______ ______ /

______ ______.

2 그 회사는 출시할 것이다 / 신상품을 / 내년에 (the new product / be / next year / launch)

______ ______ ______ ______ / ______ ______

______ / ______ ______.

3 우리는 길을 쓸 것이다 / 눈이 그칠 때 / 내일 (the snow / the street / when / sweep / stop)

______ ______ ______ ______ ______ ______

______ / ______ ______ ______ ______ / ______.

STEP 2

밑줄 친 부분에 유의하여 다음 문장을 해석하시오.

1 When we visited Paul, he <u>was doing</u> the dishes.

2 The science museum exhibition <u>opens</u> in a couple of days.

3 <u>I'm volunteering</u> at a local charity event next weekend.

4 If the pants I ordered <u>don't arrive</u> tomorrow, I'll just wear this skirt.

5 The pianist <u>has been playing</u> the piano for fifteen years.

6 This historic site <u>had remained</u> untouched until the explorer discovered it.

launch (상품을) 출시하다 sweep (방 등을 빗자루로) 쓸다 do the dishes 설거지를 하다 exhibition 전시회 a couple of 몇 개의 volunteer 자원봉사하다 local 지역의 charity event 자선 행사 historic site 유적지 remain 계속 ~이다 untouched 훼손되지 않은 explorer 탐험가

STEP 3

1 **(A), (B)의 각 네모 안에서 어법에 맞는 표현을 고르고, 밑줄 친 부분을 해석하시오.**

Happy Valentine's Day! Martin's Department Store **has** some special offers for you. If you (A) [visit / will visit] our store, you will see our new handmade chocolates. If you **buy** some, we will wrap them in a pretty box for free. Also, you will get free earrings if you **buy** a silver ring. These offers (B) [end / ended] on February 15th. Don't miss your chance!

(A) ____________________

(B) ____________________

Reading Q 윗글의 목적으로 가장 적절한 것은?

① 밸런타인데이를 축하하려고 ② 백화점 방문객들에게 감사를 표하려고
③ 밸런타인데이 기념 행사를 홍보하려고

NEW 내신기출

2 **밑줄 친 ①~④ 중 어법상 틀린 2개를 찾아 해당 번호를 쓰고 바르게 고쳐 쓰시오.**

Alec Greven **seems** like an ordinary kid. But he ① is the author of the best-selling book *How to Talk to Girls*. It ② has sold tens of thousands of copies around the world. In the third grade, Alec ③ has written the book during writing class and **sold** it at his school festival. Soon after, his book **became** very famous. So far, the publishing company ④ had printed his book in 17 languages.

번호	적절하지 않은 단어	고쳐 쓴 단어

1 department store 백화점 offer 제안; *할인 (행사) wrap 포장하다 for free 무료로 earring 귀걸이 end 끝나다
2 ordinary 평범한 tens of thousands of 수만의 copy (책의) 부 soon after 곧, 머지않아 so far 지금까지 print 인쇄하다; *(책 등을) 출판[발행]하다

Point 03

수동태의 개념과 형태

행위를 하는 주체가 아닌, **그 행위에 영향을 받는 대상이 주어로 올 때** 수동태를 쓴다.

형태	be동사+v-ed(+by+행위자)	시제	be동사로 시제를 표현
	부정형: be동사+not+v-ed		미래: will be v-ed

164 The gate **is locked** / every night.
S V M
그 문은 잠긴다 / 매일 밤

Tip
「by+행위자」의 생략
행위자가 일반인이거나 중요하지 않을 때 생략할 수 있음

165 The situation **was not** clearly **explained**.
S M V
그 상황은 명확하게 설명되지 않았다.

166 The car **will be washed** / by my dad.
S V by+행위자
그 차는 세차될 것이다 / 우리 아빠에 의해

밑줄 친 부분에 유의하여 다음 문장을 해석하시오.

정답 및 해설 p.16

구문 해석 기법
☐ 수동태는 '~가 (행위자에 의해) …되다/해지다'로 해석한다.

167 The wall was painted / last week.
그 벽은 페인트칠 되었다 / 지난주에

168 These pictures were drawn by a famous artist.

169 The main dish will not be served by the chef.

170 The surgery will be performed by the doctor tomorrow.

171 This book was not originally written in Korean.

172 Several paintings were moved from his house to the museum.

다음 문장의 네모 안에서 어법상 알맞은 것을 고르고, 문장을 해석하시오.

173 After the potatoes [boiled / are boiled], they are [cut / cutting] into small pieces.

174 The price of the travel package [includes / is included] your hotel bill, but breakfast is [included not / not included].

serve 차려 주다, 내어주다 perform (수)행하다 boil 삶다 cut into pieces 여러 조각으로 자르다 include 포함하다 bill 계산서; *요금

Point 04 4형식·5형식 수동태

4형식을 수동태로 쓸 때 **간접목적어와 직접목적어 둘 다 주어**로 올 수 있다. 5형식을 수동태로 쓰면 「be동사+v-ed」 뒤에 **명사(구), 형용사(구), 분사(구), to부정사(구)** 형태의 **보어**가 남는다.

175 I **was given** a gift / by him. 간접목적어 주어
S V O by+행위자
나는 선물을 받았다 / 그에게서

176 A gift **was given** / to me / by him. 직접목적어 주어
S V M by+행위자
선물이 주어졌다 / 나에게 / 그에 의해서

177 She **was made** / to wear a helmet.
S V C
그녀는 시켜졌다 / 헬멧을 쓰도록

178 He **was heard** laughing.
S V C
그가 웃고 있는 것이 들려졌다.

수동태에 유의하여 다음 문장을 해석하시오.

정답 및 해설 p.16

179 She was sent / lots of spam emails.
그녀는 받았다 / 많은 스팸 메일을

180 New sneakers were promised to her by her father.

181 They were seen singing and dancing on TV.

182 These books were bought for my son by his English teacher.

183 The old castle with the red door was believed to be haunted.

184 Visitors are not allowed to speak loudly or drink beverages here.

다음 문장의 네모 안에서 어법상 알맞은 것을 고르고, 문장을 해석하시오.

185 Since Joe was made [clean / to clean] his room, he couldn't go out.

186 I [called / was called] a "problem-solver." I was asked [solve / to solve] difficult tasks.

sneakers 운동화 haunt 귀신이 나타나다 beverage 음료 go out 외출하다 task (특히 힘든) 일, 과업

Point 05 동사구 수동태와 수동태 관용 표현

「동사+전치사」나 **「동사+부사」** 등 **두 개 이상의 단어**로 이루어진 동사구는 하나의 동사로 취급하므로, **수동태에서 한 덩어리**로 쓴다. 한편 감정이나 상태를 나타내는 수동태는 관용적으로 **by 이외의 전치사**를 쓰기도 한다.

• 수동태 관용 표현

be interested in (~에 관심이 있다)	be satisfied with (~에 만족하다)	be known as (~로 알려져 있다)
be disappointed with (~에 실망하다)	be covered with (~로 덮여있다)	be surprised at (~에 놀라다)
be filled with (~로 가득 차다)	be worried about (~에 대해 걱정하다)	

187 The baby **was looked after** / by Ann.
S V by+행위자
그 아기는 돌봐졌다 / Ann에 의해

188 The problem **was taken care of**.
S V
그 문제는 처리되었다.

189 John **was satisfied** / **with** his grade.
S V M
John은 만족했다 / 그의 성적에

밑줄 친 부분에 유의하여 다음 문장을 해석하시오. 정답 및 해설 p.16

190 His old record player is covered / with dust.
그의 오래된 레코드 플레이어는 덮여 있다 / 먼지로

191 The form was filled out by Joanna.

192 The dumplings were filled with tofu and vegetables.

193 I was surprised at the way Joel behaved yesterday.

194 Many flyers are handed out in front of the subway station.

195 Your dream is sometimes laughed at by others, but don't get discouraged.

다음 문장의 네모 안에서 어법상 알맞은 것을 고르고, 문장을 해석하시오.

196 My house [was broken by into / was broken into by] someone.

197 New York [is known / is known as] the center of fashion, and many stylish people are seen there.

take care of ~을 돌보다; *~을 처리하다 fill out 작성하다 dumpling 만두 flyer 광고지 hand out 배부하다 laugh at 비웃다, 놀리다 break into 침입하다

Point 06 수동태의 다양한 형태

수동태는 **조동사**와 쓰일 수있고, **동명사** 및 **to부정사의 수동태**도 쓰일 수 있다. 또한, **진행형**이나 **완료시제**와도 쓰일 수 있다.

조동사 수동태	조동사+be+v-ed	진행형 수동태	be동사+being+v-ed
동명사 수동태	being+v-ed	완료시제 수동태	have/has/had been+v-ed
to부정사 수동태	to be+v-ed		

198 You **may be chosen** / for the job.
S V M
네가 뽑힐지도 모른다 / 그 일자리에

199 Most people like / **being[to be] praised**.
S V O
대부분의 사람들은 좋아한다 / 칭찬받는 것을

200 The wedding **is being held** / outdoors.
S V M
그 결혼식은 열리고 있다 / 야외에서

201 Every room <for three people> / **has been booked** / already.
S V M
모든 방은 <세 명을 위한> / 예약되었다 / 이미

밑줄 친 부분에 유의하여 다음 문장을 해석하시오.

정답 및 해설 p.17

202 The plan has been canceled / again.
그 계획은 취소되었다 / 또

203 I still remember being lost at the square.

204 He wanted to be forgiven by his father for his actions.

205 Her car used to be parked next to my house.

206 My cell phone is being repaired now, so I can't answer any calls.

207 I found out that the product had been manufactured by the company years ago.

> **구문 해석 기법**
> □ 동명사 수동태는 '~되는[당하는] 것'으로 해석한다.
> □ 진행형 수동태는 '~되고 있(었)다'로, 완료형 수동태는 '~되었다/되어 왔다'로 해석한다.

다음 문장의 네모 안에서 어법상 알맞은 것을 고르고, 문장을 해석하시오.

208 Something [must is done / must be done] before the problem becomes worse.

209 I didn't know that my conversation with Ryan [was been recorded / was being recorded].

praise 칭찬하다 hold 잡고 있다; *(회의·시합 등을) 열다 book 책; *예약하다 cancel 취소하다 forgive 용서하다 manufacture 제조하다, 생산하다

Unit Practice

STEP 1

직독직해에 맞게 (   ) 안의 단어를 사용하여 문장을 쓰시오. (필요시 형태를 바꿔 쓸 것)

1 그 수술은 행해질 것이다 / 그 의사에 의해 / 내일 (perform / the surgery)

_______ _______ _______ _______ _______ / _______

_______ _______ / _______.

2 나의 호박 파이 요리법은 / 적혀 있다 / 내 일기장에 (recipe / in my diary / pumpkin pie / write down)

_______ _______ _______ _______ / _______ _______

_______ / _______ _______ _______.

3 가구를 조립하는 방법이 / 보여지고 있다 / 우리에게 / 영상으로 (the furniture / be / how / show / in the video / assemble)

_______ _______ _______ _______ _______ / _______ _______

_______ / _______ _______ / _______ _______ _______.

STEP 2

밑줄 친 부분에 유의하여 다음 문장을 해석하시오.

1 The surfer was seen riding the massive waves with ease.

2 I'm worried about the interview scheduled for tomorrow.

3 Food waste should be thrown away in plastic bags for food waste.

4 He was made to help his younger sister with her math homework by his parents.

5 Your password has not been changed for the past three months.

6 They were deeply disappointed with the lack of progress in the negotiations.

recipe 요리법 assemble 조립하다 surfer 파도타기 하는 사람, 서퍼 massive 거대한 with ease 쉽게 plastic bag 비닐봉지 food waste 음식물 쓰레기 past 과거의; *지난 deeply 깊이 lack 부족 progress 진전 negotiation 협상

STEP 3

1 (A), (B), (C)의 각 네모 안에서 어법에 맞는 표현을 고르시오.

Interestingly, piggy banks **were created** accidentally. In the 18th century, the clay that potters used (A) called / was called "pygg." Once, an English potter (B) asked / was asked to create a pygg jar. He thought the customer wanted a "pig" jar, so he (C) made / was made a jar in the shape of the animal by mistake. Years later, around the 20th century, this item became extremely popular.

*piggy bank 돼지 저금통

Reading Q 윗글의 내용과 일치하면 T, 일치하지 않으면 F를 쓰시오.

(1) 고객은 도공에게 돼지 모양의 항아리를 만들어 달라고 했다. ______

(2) 돼지 저금통은 만들어진 뒤에 바로 인기를 끌었다. ______

NEW 내신기출

2 밑줄 친 우리말 (A), (B)에 맞게 보기 의 단어를 사용하여 각 문장을 완성하시오. (필요시 형태를 바꿔 쓸 것)

According to a story, a coffee house **was opened** by Edward Lloyd in 1688. Inside, there was a container, and "To Insure Promptness" **was written** on it. Customers could put money inside it when they entered. If they did, they got fast service from the waiters. (A) 이제 이 돈은 'tip(봉사료)'이라고 불린다. (B) 오늘날에는 고객들이 서비스를 제공받은 뒤에 종업원들에게 봉사료가 주어진다.

보기 a "tip" / this / tips / to waiters / give / serve / call / money

(A) Now, ______ ______ ______ ______ ______ ______.

(B) Today, ______ ______ ______ ______ ______ after customers ______ ______ ______.

1 accidentally 우연히 clay 점토 potter 도공 jar 단지, 항아리 customer 고객 by mistake 실수로 item 물품 extremely 극도로, 매우

2 according to ~에 따르면 container 그릇, 용기 insure 보험에 들다; *보장하다 promptness 재빠름, 신속 serve 제공하다

Wrap Up

정답 및 해설 p.19

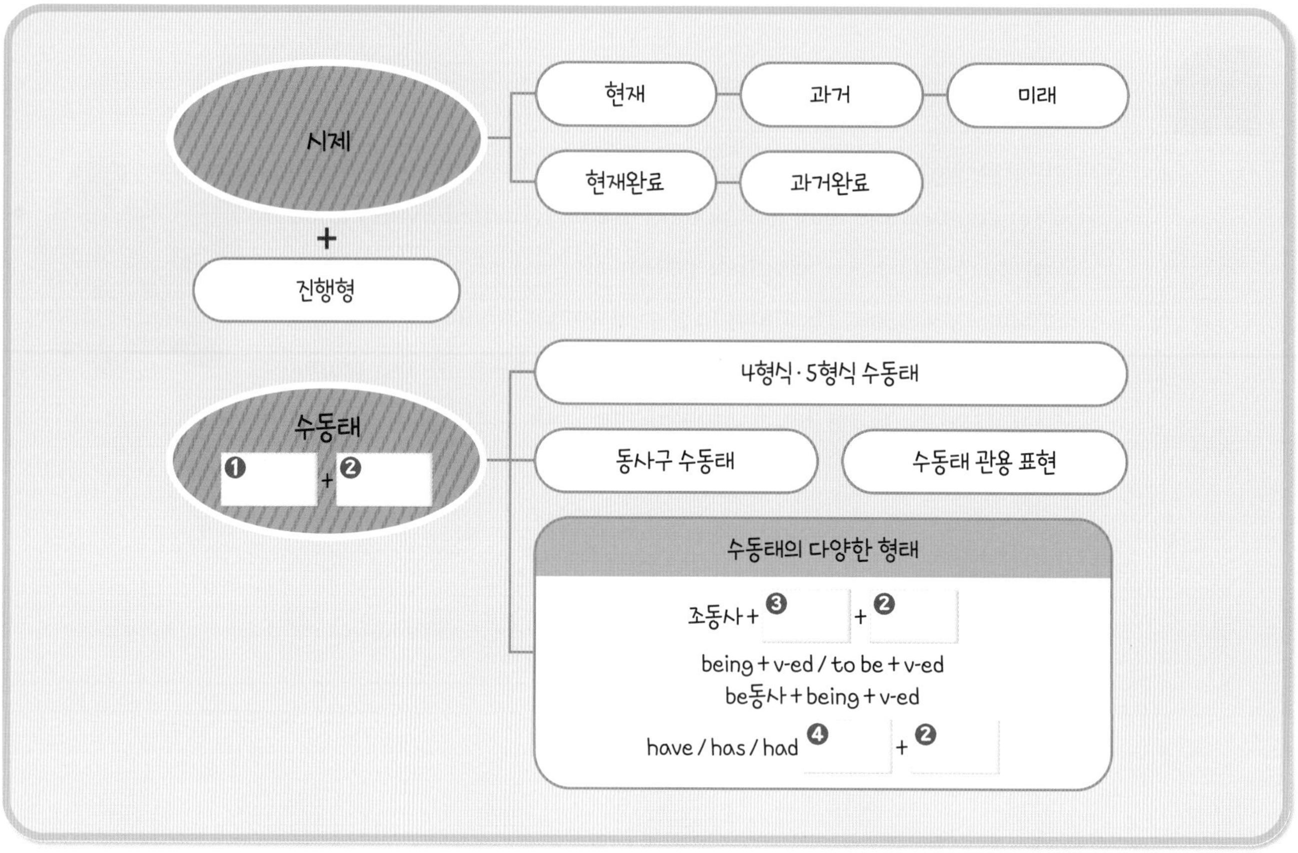

주요 예문을 다시 한번 확인하고, 우리말에 맞게 ( ) 안의 단어를 사용하여 문장을 쓰시오.

1 나는 이번 주말에 내 친구들을 만날 것이다. (this / friends / weekend / meeting) Point 02

2 그에 의해서 나에게 선물이 주어졌다. (a gift / to me / given) Point 04

3 그 차는 우리 아빠에 의해 세차될 것이다. (dad / washed / the car) Point 03

4 John은 그의 성적에 만족했다. (satisfied / with his grade) Point 05

5 그 결혼식은 야외에서 열리고 있다. (outdoors / the wedding / held) Point 06

6 나는 오사카로 이사하기 전에 도쿄에 살았었다. (in Tokyo / before / lived / to Osaka / moved) Point 01

UNIT 05

조동사와 가정법

조동사

- 미래·예정·의지
  will
- 능력·가능·허가·추측
  can / may / must
- 의무·충고·금지
  must / have to / should / had better
- 과거 일에 대한 추측·후회
  cannot / must / may / should + have v-ed
- 다양한 표현
  used to
  would rather
  would
  would like to

가정법

- 가정법 과거
- 가정법 과거완료
- 혼합 가정법
  If+주어+had v-ed, 주어+조동사 과거형+동사원형
- I wish 가정법
  I wish+주어+동사의 과거형 (가정법 과거)
  I wish+주어+had v-ed (가정법 과거완료)
- as if 가정법
  as if+주어+동사의 과거형 (가정법 과거)
  as if+주어+had v-ed (가정법 과거완료)

Point 01

조동사의 의미 I

미래·예정·의지	will	~할 것이다
능력·가능	can	~할 수 있다(= be able to), ~할 가능성이 있다
허가	can, may	~해도 된다
추측 / 강한 확신	may(= might) / must, cannot	~일지도 모른다 / ~임이 틀림없다, ~일 리가 없다

210 We **will** go on a picnic / this spring.
S V M_1 M_2
우리는 소풍을 갈 것이다 / 이번 봄에

211 We **can** see / a full moon / on Chuseok.
S V O M
우리는 볼 수 있다 / 보름달을 / 추석에

212 They **must** be home / now.
S V M_1 M_2
그들은 집에 있는 것이 틀림없다 / 지금

밑줄 친 부분에 유의하여 다음 문장을 해석하시오.

정답 및 해설 p.19

213 Nelly is able to fix / your computer.
Nelly는 고칠 수 있다 / 네 컴퓨터를

214 He must be very thirsty after finishing a race.

215 You can stay here if you promise to be quiet.

216 Clara will take care of my cat while I'm on vacation.

217 You may look around the museum, but you may not take pictures.

218 My little brothers are still afraid of heights. They will not ride this rollercoaster.

구문 해석 기법

- ☐ might는 may보다 더 불확실한 추측을 나타낸다.
- ☐ must나 cannot[can't] 뒤에 be가 오면 추측의 의미인 경우가 많다.

다음 문장의 네모 안에서 문맥상 알맞은 것을 고르고, 문장을 해석하시오.

219 She's avoiding eye contact, and her voice is shaking. She [might / would] be lying.

220 Those people claim that they have seen a dragon in the sky, but it [can / cannot] be true.

full moon 보름달 promise 약속하다 take care of ~을 돌보다 look around (주변을) 둘러보다 height 높이; *높은 곳 avoid 피하다 shake 떨다, 흔들다 claim 주장하다 dragon 용

Point 02

조동사의 의미 II

의무	must, have to, should	~해야 한다
충고	should, had better	~하는 것이 좋겠다[낫다]
금지	must not	~해서는 안 된다

221 Everyone **must** wear / a swimming cap / in the pool.
S V O M
모든 사람들은 써야 한다 / 수영모를 / 수영장에서

222 You **had better** take / some cold medicine.
S V O
너는 먹는 것이 좋겠다 / 약간의 감기약을

223 You **must not** throw trash / on the street.
S V O M
너는 쓰레기를 버려서는 안 된다 / 거리에

Tip
must[have to]의 시제 표현
• had to: ~해야 했다 (과거)
• will have to: ~해야 할 것이다 (미래)

밑줄 친 부분에 유의하여 다음 문장을 해석하시오.

정답 및 해설 p.19

224 You should take / a bigger suitcase.
너는 가져가는 것이 좋겠다 / 더 큰 여행 가방을

225 You will have to come to my office before nine o'clock.

226 People must not park their cars in this area.

227 You had better go to bed early on the night before the exam.

228 You should not bully or make fun of others.

229 As he always breaks his promises, you had better not trust him.

구문 해석 기법
☐ must not, should not
: ~해서는 안 된다 (금지)
☐ don't / doesn't have to
: ~할 필요가 없다 (불필요)

다음 문장의 네모 안에서 문맥상 또는 어법상 알맞은 것을 고르고, 문장을 해석하시오.

230 Before you go abroad, you [must / must not] visit City Hall and [get / to get] a passport.

231 You [don't have to / had better] pay the entrance fee if you have a membership card.

swimming cap 수영모 suitcase 여행 가방 park 주차하다 bully 괴롭히다 make fun of ~을 놀리다 break 깨다; *(법·약속 등을) 어기다 trust 믿다 abroad 해외로 City Hall 시청 passport 여권 entrance 입구; *입장 fee 요금

Point 03 조동사+have v-ed

「조동사+have v-ed」는 **과거의 일에 대한 추측·후회·유감**을 나타낸다.

cannot[can't] have v-ed	~했을 리가 없다	may[might] have v-ed	~했을지도 모른다
must have v-ed	~했음이 틀림없다	should have v-ed	~했어야 했다

232 She **cannot have said** / that.
S V O
그녀가 말했을 리가 없다 / 그것을

233 He **may have left** / his cell phone / in the classroom.
S V O M
그는 두고 왔을지도 모른다 / 그의 휴대 전화를 / 교실에

234 I **should have taken** / her advice.
S V O
나는 받아들였어야 했다 / 그녀의 충고를

밑줄 친 부분에 유의하여 다음 문장을 해석하시오.

정답 및 해설 p.20

235 She may have told / my secret / to someone.
그녀가 말했을지도 모른다 / 나의 비밀을 / 누군가에게

236 Joey cannot have heard our conversation.

237 You should not have driven so fast on the highway.

238 The tennis player must have trained hard for the match.

239 They cannot have cleaned their rooms. They're still a mess.

240 Felix should have apologized to her when he had the chance.

구문 해석 기법

□ should have v-ed는 '~했어야 했는데 실제로 하지 못했다'는 의미를 담고 있다.

다음 문장의 네모 안에서 어법상 알맞은 것을 고르고, 문장을 해석하시오.

241 He thought that he might [has / have] given his friends the wrong information.

242 You may have been tired, but you [must / should] have gone to work. Your colleagues must have [be / been] angry.

highway 고속도로 train 훈련하다 match 성냥; *경기, 시합 mess 지저분한 상태 apologize 사과하다 chance 가능성; *기회 colleague 동료

Point 04 다양한 조동사 표현

조동사를 사용해 다양한 의미를 표현할 수 있으며, **조동사 뒤**에는 항상 **동사원형**이 온다.

used to	~하곤 했다 (과거의 습관) ~이었다 (과거의 상태)	would	~하곤 했다 (과거의 습관)
would rather ~ (than ...)	(…하느니) 차라리 ~하겠다	would like to	~하고 싶다

243 He **used to** play soccer / <when he was young>.
S V O / S′ V′ SC′
그는 축구를 하곤 했다 / <그가 어렸을 때>

244 She **would** drink coffee / every morning.
S V O M
그녀는 커피를 마시곤 했다 / 아침마다

245 We **would like to** take / a yoga class.
S V O
우리는 듣고 싶다 / 요가 수업을

밑줄 친 부분에 유의하여 다음 문장을 해석하시오.

정답 및 해설 p.20

246 I would like to read / more books / this year.
나는 읽고 싶다 / 더 많은 책을 / 올해에

247 Alberto and I would go skiing every winter.

248 I would like to talk about my worries.

249 I would rather drive than go by train.

250 Jimmy used to eat a lot of junk food on weekends.

251 I would rather have one true friend than a million fake ones.

구문 해석 기법

☐ 조동사 used to는 '(과거에) ~하곤 했으나 지금은 그렇지 않다'는 의미를 담고 있다.

다음 문장의 네모 안에서 어법상 알맞은 것을 고르고, 문장을 해석하시오.

252 I would like [to ask / asking] someone to help me because I cannot do it by myself.

253 Sophia [used to / would] have long hair, but she cut it short yesterday.

worry 고민, 걱정 junk food 정크푸드(패스트푸드) true 사실인; *진정한 a million 수많은 fake 거짓된 by oneself 홀로, 혼자서

Unit Practice

STEP 1

직독직해에 맞게 ( ) 안의 단어를 사용하여 문장을 쓰시오. (필요시 형태를 바꿔 쓸 것)

1 그는 틀림없다 / 매우 목이 마른 것이 / 경주를 끝낸 뒤에 (very / after / a race / finishing / thirsty)

__________ __________ __________ / __________ __________ / __________

__________ __________ __________.

2 나는 숨을 참을 수 없다 / 물속에서 / 30초 동안 (seconds / my breath / for / hold / underwater)

__________ __________ __________ __________ __________ / __________ /

__________ __________ __________.

3 너는 확인했어야 했다 / 네 답을 / 답안지를 제출하기 전에 (submitting / answers / check / have / the answer sheet)

__________ __________ __________ __________ / __________ __________ /

__________ __________ __________ __________ __________.

STEP 2

밑줄 친 부분에 유의하여 다음 문장을 해석하시오.

1 I <u>would like to order</u> a large pizza with extra cheese.

2 You <u>had better turn down</u> the music or the neighbors will complain.

3 Victor <u>used to have</u> a fear of water, but he has overcome it.

4 The package <u>might have been delivered</u> to the wrong address.

5 She <u>would</u> always <u>read</u> a bedtime story to her children when they were young.

6 We <u>cannot have missed</u> the bus because we were there earlier than the planned schedule.

---

hold one's breath 숨을 참다 underwater 물속에서 submit 제출하다 answer sheet 답안지 extra 추가의 turn down (소리·온도 등을) 낮추다 complain 불평[항의]하다 overcome 극복하다(-overcame-overcome) package 소포 bedtime story 잠자기 전 동화

STEP 3

1 (A), (B)의 각 네모 안에서 문맥상 알맞은 조동사를 고르시오.

When you feel depressed, you **should** get out and meet other people. If you stay home, you **might** end up feeling worse. Exercise also helps. You (A) [have to / will] feel better if you're physically active. These activities (B) [might not / should not] chase away your depression completely, but they **will** help.

Reading Q 윗글의 요지로 가장 적절한 것은?

① 우울할 때는 활동적으로 행동하라.
② 새로운 사람들에게 먼저 다가가라.
③ 긍정적인 태도가 우울함을 예방한다.

NEW 내신기출

2 밑줄 친 우리말에 맞게 보기 의 단어를 사용하여 문장을 완성하시오. (필요시 형태를 바꿔 쓸 것)

According to a survey, people care a lot about their weight. <u>절반 이상의 사람들은 그들이 9킬로그램을 찌우느니 차라리 1,000달러를 잃겠다고 응답했다.</u> This surprising result **might** be related to society's opinion of overweight individuals. They are often considered to be lazy and less attractive.

보기 1,000 dollars / gain / nine kilograms / lose

More than half the people responded that ______________________________

______________________________.

1 depressed 우울한(*n.* depression 우울함) end up 결국 ~하게 되다 physically 신체적으로 chase away ~을 쫓아내다 completely 완전히
2 survey (설문) 조사 care about ~에 신경 쓰다 related to ~와 관련된 overweight 비만의 individual 개인; *(특정한 유형의) 사람 attractive 매력적인

Point 05

가정법 과거/과거완료, 혼합 가정법

가정법 과거는 **현재 사실과 반대되는 일**을, 가정법 과거완료는 **과거 사실과 반대되는 일을 가정·상상**하여 말할 때 사용한다. 혼합 가정법은 **과거 사실과 반대되는 가정·상상이 현재 상황에 영향을 미칠 때** 쓴다.

가정법 과거	If+주어+동사의 과거형/were ~, 주어+조동사 과거형+동사원형 …	(만약) ~하면 …할 텐데
가정법 과거완료	If+주어+had v-ed ~, 주어+조동사 과거형+have v-ed …	(만약) ~했더라면 …했을 텐데
혼합 가정법	If+주어+had v-ed ~, 주어+조동사 과거형+동사원형 …	(만약) ~했더라면 …할 텐데

254 <If I(S′) **had**(V′) / a lot of money(O′)>, / I(S) **could buy**(V) / a fancy car(O).
<내가 가지고 있다면 / 많은 돈을>, / 나는 살 수 있을 텐데 / 비싼 차를

255 <If Ethan(S′) **had studied**(V′) / harder(M′)>, / he(S) **might have passed**(V) / the exam(O).
<Ethan이 공부했더라면 / 더 열심히>, / 그는 통과했을지도 모를 텐데 / 시험을

256 <If I(S′) **had not seen**(V′) / the movie(O′)>, / I(S) **would watch**(V) it(O) / with you(M).
<내가 보지 않았더라면 / 그 영화를>, / 나는 그것을 볼 텐데 / 너와 함께

가정법에 유의하여 다음 문장을 해석하시오. 정답 및 해설 p.22

257 <If I were born / again>, / I would become / a pilot.
<내가 태어난다면 / 다시>, / 나는 될 텐데 / 조종사가

258 If he had worn a helmet, he might not have injured his head.

259 If we took a different route, we might avoid the traffic jam.

260 If he had not sat on the chair, it would not be broken now.

261 If she had gotten the award, she would have been proud of herself.

262 If I had known that he was in the hospital, I would have visited him.

다음 문장의 네모 안에서 어법상 알맞은 것을 고르고, 문장을 해석하시오.

263 If we [have not played / had not played] computer games all night, we would not feel sleepy now.

264 If I had lived in Paris in the 1920s, I could [meet / have met] many famous artists.

fancy 값비싼 pilot 조종사, 비행사 injure 부상을 입다 route 길 avoid 방지하다; *피하다 traffic jam 교통 체증 proud of ~이 자랑스러운

Point 06 I wish/as if 가정법

I wish +	주어+동사의 과거형/were ~	~하면 좋을 텐데 (가정법 과거)
	주어+had v-ed ~	~했더라면 좋았을 텐데 (가정법 과거완료)
as if +	주어+동사의 과거형/were ~	마치 ~인 것처럼 (가정법 과거)
	주어+had v-ed ~	마치 ~였던 것처럼 (가정법 과거완료)

265 **I wish** / <I **had exercised** / this morning>.
S V / S′ V′ M′
좋았을 텐데 / <내가 운동을 했더라면 / 오늘 아침에>

266 Ron talks / <**as if** he **knew** / everything>.
S V / S′ V′ O′
Ron은 말한다 / <마치 그가 아는 것처럼 / 모든 것을>

267 She screamed / <**as if** she **had seen** / a ghost>.
S V / S′ V′ O′
그녀는 비명을 질렀다 / <마치 그녀가 봤던 것처럼 / 귀신을>

가정법에 유의하여 다음 문장을 해석하시오.

정답 및 해설 p.22

268 I wish / <I had my own room>.
좋을 텐데 / <내가 나만의 방을 가지면>

269 I wish Bob had come to London with me.

270 Daniel acted as if we had not had a fight.

271 The car looks as if it had been in an accident.

272 I wish today were Saturday so I could take a nap.

273 She treats me as if I were her private secretary.

다음 문장의 네모 안에서 어법상 알맞은 것을 고르고, 문장을 해석하시오.

274 I wish I [said / had said] goodbye to all of my friends before I left.

275 Kamila always talks to me as if she [were / had been] older than me.

scream 비명을 지르다 act 행동하다 take a nap 낮잠을 자다 treat 대하다, 다루다 private 개인 소유의, 사적인 secretary 비서

Unit Practice

STEP 1 직독직해에 맞게 ( ) 안의 단어를 사용하여 문장을 쓰시오. (필요시 형태를 바꿔 쓸 것)

1 그가 앉지 않았더라면 / 그 의자에, / 그것은 부서져 있지 않을 텐데 / 지금 (break / on / sit)

________ ________ ________ ________ ________ / ________ ________

________, / ________ ________ ________ ________ ________ / ________.

2 좋을 텐데 / 내가 귀여운 반려동물을 가지고 있다면 / 집에 (a cute pet / wish / at home / have)

________ ________ / ________ ________ ________ ________

________ / ________ ________.

3 그는 그 치킨을 먹었다 / 마치 그가 아무것도 안 먹었던 것처럼 / 며칠간 (anything / in days / the chicken / eat)

________ ________ ________ ________ / ________ ________ ________

________ ________ ________ ________ / ________ ________.

STEP 2 가정법에 유의하여 다음 문장을 해석하시오.

1 I wish he had let me know that he needed some help.

2 Jason and Ellen talked as if they had known each other for years.

3 If you had listened to the instructions, you wouldn't be in trouble now.

4 If the sun did not exist, we would not be here today.

5 If we had read the reviews, we could have avoided going to the restaurant.

6 When Lily is in the water, she swims as if she were a mermaid.

break 부서지다(-broke-broken) pet 반려동물 instruction 설명 in trouble 난처하여 review 검토; *비평 avoid 막다; *피하다 mermaid 인어

STEP 3

1 네모 안에서 어법상 알맞은 것을 고르고, 밑줄 친 문장을 해석하시오.

If you **went** to the moon, you **would see** mountain ranges and bowl-shaped holes called craters. They were formed when rocks from space crashed into the moon. They pushed up some parts of its surface and made holes in others. **If** you [traveled / had traveled] to the moon, you **would** also **see** huge plains. Many of these plains were made by lava after it cooled and hardened in craters.

*crater 분화구 **lava 용암

____

Reading Q 윗글의 주제로 가장 적절한 것은?

① 달 지형의 형성 과정 ② 달이 지구에 미치는 영향
③ 달의 온도와 표면 모양의 관계

NEW 내신기출

2 밑줄 친 우리말 (A), (B)를 조건에 맞게 써서 각 문장을 완성하시오.

One day, a young reindeer saw himself in a lake. He said, "My horns are beautiful. (A) 하지만 내가 이 못생긴 다리들을 가지고 있지 않다면 좋을 텐데. (B) 내가 아름다운 다리들을 가지고 태어났다면 내 인생은 더 행복할 텐데!" Just then, he heard a hunter's gun. As he tried to run away, his horns became caught in some branches. But his legs helped him escape. "Phew!" he said. "**If I didn't have** these strong legs, I **would be** dead now!"

조건
- 가정법으로 쓸 것
- 제시된 단어를 사용할 것
- happier / ugly / have / these / life
- (A) 6단어, (B) 5단어로 쓸 것

(A) But I wish ______________________________.

(B) If I had been born with beautiful legs, ______________________!

1 mountain range 산맥 crash into ~와 충돌하다 push up 밀어 올리다 surface 표면 travel 여행하다; *가다 plain 평원, 평지 cool 식다 harden 굳다
2 reindeer 순록 lake 호수 horn 뿔 hunter 사냥꾼 run away 도망가다 branch (나뭇)가지 escape 달아나다, 탈출하다

Wrap Up

정답 및 해설 p.24

조동사

- 미래·예정·의지: will
- 능력·가능·허가·추측: can / may / must
- ❶ ______: must / have to / should / had better
- 과거 일에 대한 ❷ ______: cannot / must / may / should + have v-ed
- 다양한 표현: used to / would rather / would / would like to

가정법

- 가정법 과거
- 가정법 과거완료
- 혼합 가정법: If + 주어 + had v-ed, 주어 + 조동사 과거형 + ❸ ______
- I wish 가정법: I wish + 주어 + 동사의 과거형 (가정법 ❹ ______) / I wish + 주어 + had v-ed (가정법 과거완료)
- as if 가정법: as if + 주어 + 동사의 과거형 (가정법 과거) / as if + 주어 + had v-ed (가정법 ❺ ______)

주요 예문을 다시 한번 확인하고, 우리말에 맞게 ( ) 안의 단어를 사용하여 문장을 쓰시오.

1 너는 거리에 쓰레기를 버려서는 안 된다. (trash / on the street / throw) Point 02

2 그녀는 마치 귀신을 봤던 것처럼 비명을 질렀다. (screamed / a ghost / seen) Point 06

3 우리는 추석에 보름달을 볼 수 있다. (on Chuseok / see / a full moon) Point 01

4 그녀는 아침마다 커피를 마시곤 했다. (every morning / coffee / drink) Point 04

5 내가 많은 돈을 가지고 있다면 비싼 차를 살 수 있을 텐데. (a lot of / a fancy car/ buy) Point 05

6 그는 교실에 그의 휴대 전화를 두고 왔을지도 모른다. (left / in the classroom / cell phone) Point 03

UNIT 06

수식어구의 쓰임

Point 01 형용사적 수식어구_형용사와 전치사구
Point 02 형용사적 수식어구_분사와 to부정사
Point 03 부사적 수식어구_부사와 전치사구
Point 04 부사적 수식어구_to부정사

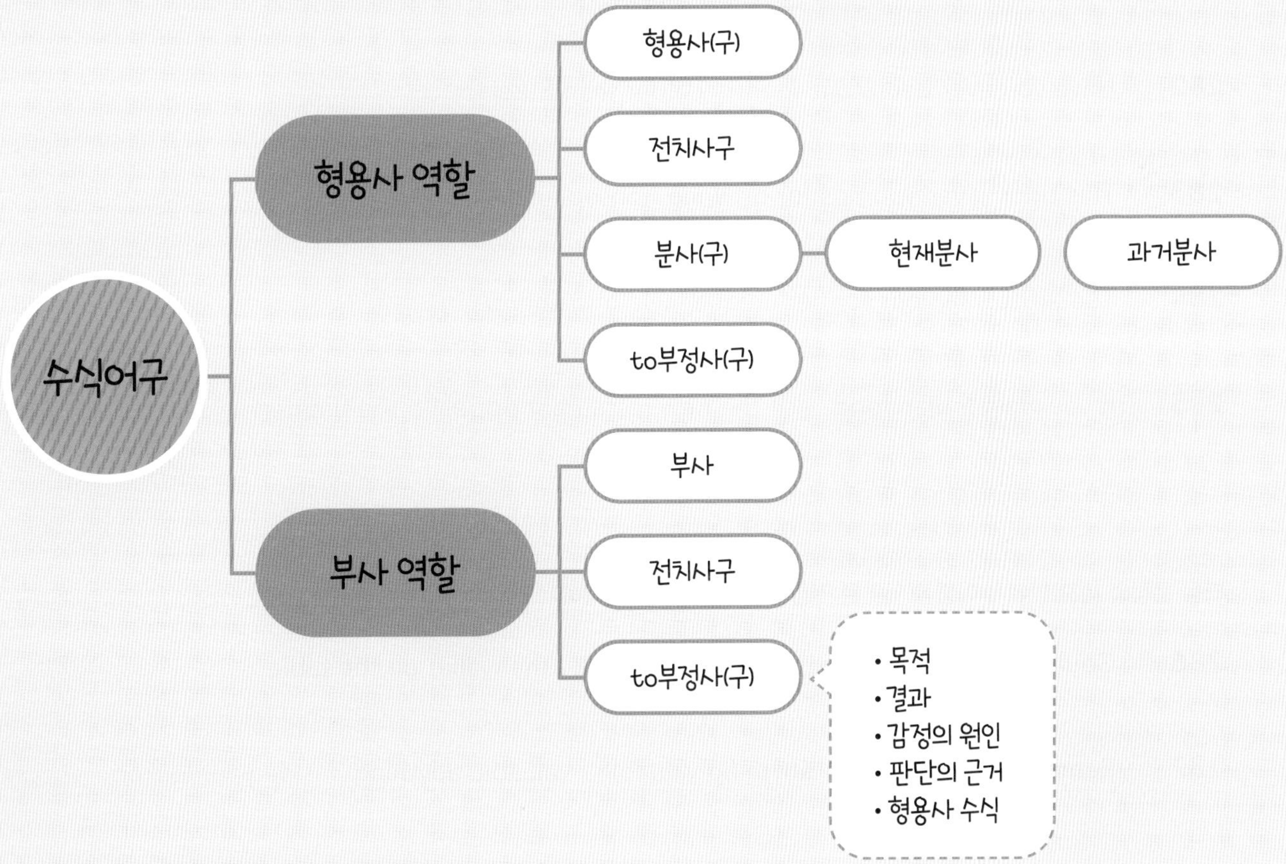

Point 01

형용사적 수식어구_형용사와 전치사구

형용사(구)는 명사 앞 또는 뒤에서, **-thing, -body, -one으로 끝나는 대명사 뒤**에서 수식한다. **전치사구는 명사 뒤**에서 수식한다.

276 George gave / an **impressive** speech.
S V O
George는 했다 / 인상적인 연설을

277 Suji learned / skills <**useful for her job**>.
S V O
Suji는 배웠다 / 기술들을 <그녀의 직업에 유용한>

278 I need / something <**delicious to eat** / **for dinner**>.
S V O
나는 필요하다 / 무언가가 <먹을 맛있는 / 저녁 식사로>

279 The elementary school <**near my home**> / will be closed.
S V
그 초등학교가 <우리 집 근처에 있는> / 폐교될 것이다

다음 문장에서 밑줄 친 부분을 수식하는 수식어(구)를 모두 찾아 < >로 묶고, 문장을 해석하시오. 정답 및 해설 p.24

280 My mom likes to collect / <bright and colorful> vases.
우리 엄마는 모으는 것을 좋아하신다 / <선명하고 형형색색인> 꽃병을

281 The government introduced a law against spitting on the street.

282 Have you ever been to a country colder than Russia?

283 This book gives you tips for growing houseplants.

284 The artist is famous for her unique style of painting.

285 If you want Indian food, visit the new restaurant opposite the theater.

다음 문장의 네모 안에서 어법상 알맞은 것을 고르고, 문장을 해석하시오.

286 Could you bring me [on the table the wallet / the wallet on the table]?

287 Remember not to keep [anything valuable / valuable anything] inside your locker.

impressive 인상적인 vase 꽃병 government 정부 introduce 소개하다; *내놓다[도입하다] spit 침을 뱉다 houseplant 실내 화초 valuable 귀중한

Point 02 형용사적 수식어구_분사와 to부정사

단독으로 쓰인 분사는 명사 앞에서, 다른 어구와 함께 쓰인 분사나 to부정사(구)는 명사 뒤에서 수식한다.

288 I am afraid of / **barking** dogs.
S V O
나는 무섭다 / 짖고 있는 개가

Tip
현재분사(v-ing): 능동 · 진행(~하는, ~하고 있는)
과거분사(v-ed): 수동 · 완료(~된, ~한)

289 The girl <**smiling brightly**> / must be Luna.
S V SC
그 소녀가 <환하게 웃고 있는> / Luna임이 틀림없다

290 The poem <**written by the poet**> / is moving.
S V SC
그 시는 <그 시인에 의해 쓰인> / 감동적이다

291 I have / a question <**to ask you**>.
S V O
나는 있다 / 질문이 <너에게 물어볼>

다음 문장에서 밑줄 친 부분을 수식하는 수식어(구)를 모두 찾아 < >로 묶고, 문장을 해석하시오. 정답 및 해설 p.24

292 The company is hiring / <new> employees <to work in our department>.
그 회사는 채용 중이다 / <새로운> 직원들을 <우리 부서에서 일할>

293 The police officer found the stolen car last night.

294 When I was young, I had nothing to worry about.

295 I ate the waffle covered with strawberries and syrup.

296 A boy singing on the stage waved his hand at me.

297 Tara heard the people riding on the roller coaster scream.

다음 문장의 네모 안에서 어법상 알맞은 것을 고르고, 문장을 해석하시오.

298 Because the doctor had many [patients to take care of / to take care of patients], she couldn't rest.

299 The shopping mall sets up a Christmas tree [decorating / decorated] with lights and ribbons every December.

bark (개가) 짖다 brightly 환하게 poem 시 poet 시인 moving 감동시키는 hire 고용하다 scream 비명을 지르다 set up 설치하다 decorate 장식하다

Unit Practice

STEP 1

직독직해에 맞게 (   ) 안의 단어를 사용하여 문장을 쓰시오. (필요시 형태를 바꿔 쓸 것)

1 항공권의 가격은 / 꽤 비싸다 / 요즘 (of an airline ticket / these days / fairly / the price / high)

________ ________ ________ ________ ________ ________ /

________ ________ ________ / ________ ________.

2 Tara는 들었다 / 사람들이 / 롤러코스터를 타고 있는 / 비명을 지르는 것을 (the people / scream / hear / on the roller coaster / ride)

________ ________ / ________ ________ / ________ ________

________ ________ ________ / ________.

3 그는 찾고 있었다 / 냉장고 안에서 / 우유를 / 그의 시리얼에 넣을 (on his cereal / look / put / in the refrigerator / for milk)

________ ________ ________ / ________ ________ ________ / ________

________ / ________ ________ ________ ________ ________.

STEP 2

다음 문장에서 명사를 수식하는 수식어(구)를 찾아 밑줄 긋고, 문장을 해석하시오.

1 I love looking up at the sky full of stars on a clear night.

2 The fallen leaves covered the ground like a soft blanket.

3 Having friends to rely on makes life more pleasant.

4 My mom often tries to change clothes of no use into unique items.

5 Ivan doesn't like math because it's the most challenging subject for him.

6 I saw someone strange leave a note on my desk.

airline ticket 항공권 fairly 상당히, 꽤 look up ~을 올려다보다 clear 분명한; *(날씨가) 맑은 blanket 담요 rely on ~에 의지하다 pleasant 즐거운
of no use 쓸모없는 unique 독특한 item 항목; *물품 challenging 도전적인 subject 주제; *과목

STEP 3

1 (A), (B)의 단어를 어법에 맞는 형태로 고쳐 쓰시오.

Dancing Lessons for the Advanced in Age is a novel (A) (write) by **Czech** author Bohumil Hrabal. In the story, there is an **elderly** man (B) (describe) his life. Unlike **other** books, Hrabal's book has **only one** sentence! However, the book is 128 pages. Hrabal's writing method is a **unique** style **great for grabbing attention**.

*Czech 체코의

(A) ____________________ (B) ____________________

Reading Q Hrabal의 소설에 관한 윗글의 내용과 일치하지 않는 것은?

① 한 노인이 자기 인생에 대해 이야기한다.
② 128개의 문장으로 이루어져 있다.
③ 독자의 관심을 끌 수 있는 독특한 형식으로 쓰였다.

NEW 내신기출

2 밑줄 친 우리말을 조건에 맞게 써서 문장을 완성하시오.

In the United States, the foods **eaten on New Year's Day** are different in **each** area. <u>예를 들어 남부에 사는 사람들은 완두콩으로 만들어진 걸쭉한 수프인 Hoppin' John을 먹는다.</u> They also eat **green** vegetables, such as cabbage. These vegetables symbolize money. People hope to earn **a lot of** money by eating them.

조건 · 분사를 쓸 것 · 제시된 단어만을 사용할 것 (필요시 형태를 바꿔 쓸 것)
· make / Hoppin' John / people / eat / with peas / in the South / live

For example, ____,

a thick soup ____________________________.

1 novel 소설 author 작가 elderly 연세가 드신 describe 서술하다 unlike ~와는 달리 method 방법 grab attention 관심을 끌다
2 cabbage 양배추 symbolize 상징하다 earn (일을 하여 돈을) 벌다 pea 완두콩 thick 두꺼운; *걸쭉한

Point 03 부사적 수식어구_부사와 전치사구

부사와 전치사구는 **동사, 형용사, 부사, 문장 전체를 수식**한다.

300 She **probably** likes / your present. 동사 수식
S M V O
그녀는 아마도 좋아할 것이다 / 네 선물을

301 Stretching is good / **for your body**. 형용사 수식
S V SC M
스트레칭 하는 것은 좋다 / 너의 몸에

302 The cake was baked **very** well. 부사 수식
S V M_1 M_2
그 케이크는 아주 잘 구워졌다.

303 **In a hurry**, / we ran across the road. 문장 전체 수식
M_1 S V M_2
서둘러서, / 우리는 길을 가로질러 달렸다.

다음 문장에서 밑줄 친 부분을 수식하는 부분을 찾아 < >로 묶고, 문장을 해석하시오. 정답 및 해설 p.26

304 Cats are known to be / <highly> sensitive animals.
고양이는 알려져있다 / 매우 예민한 동물로

305 For a long time, shells were used as money.

306 The musical instruments in this store are quite expensive.

307 She is worried about her upcoming job interview.

308 Since we have met fairly often, we know each other well.

309 Unfortunately, the game was canceled due to bad weather.

다음 문장의 네모 안에서 어법상 알맞은 것을 고르고, 문장을 해석하시오.

310 She [careful / carefully] read the instructions before starting the experiment.

311 Nancy was [terrible at cooking / at cooking terrible], but now she is pretty good at it.

highly 매우 sensitive 세심한; *예민한 shell 조개껍데기 upcoming 곧 있을 fairly 꽤 cancel 취소하다 read 읽다(-read-read)

Point 04 부사적 수식어구_to부정사

의미	목적	~하기 위해 (= in order to[so as to])	감정의 원인	~해서, ~하게 되어서
	결과	~해서 결국 …하다	판단의 근거	~하는 것을 보면, ~하다니
	형용사 수식	~하기에		

312 We turned on the TV / **to watch the news.** 목적
S V O M
우리는 TV를 켰다 / 뉴스를 보기 위해

313 Jimmy grew up / **to become a professor.** 결과
S V M
Jimmy는 자라서 / 교수가 되었다.

314 We're glad / **to see you graduate.** 감정의 원인
S V SC M
우리는 기쁘다 / 네가 졸업하는 것을 보게 되어

315 He must be foolish / **to believe her words.** 판단의 근거
S V SC M
그는 어리석음이 틀림없다 / 그녀의 말을 믿다니

다음 문장에서 밑줄 친 to부정사구가 어떤 의미로 쓰였는지 쓰고, 문장을 해석하시오. 정답 및 해설 p.27

316 Natalie is brave / to travel around the world alone. 판단의 근거
Natalie는 용감하다 / 혼자 세계를 여행하다니

317 Everyone was shocked to hear the price of the tickets.

318 My great-grandfather lived to be ninety-five.

319 She joined the school choir to develop her singing skills.

320 My mother was disappointed to hear that I failed the test.

321 After it snows, the slope freezes and becomes dangerous to walk on.

다음 문장의 네모 안에서 어법상 알맞은 것을 고르고, 문장을 해석하시오.

322 He went to the store [to buy / buying] groceries, but it was already [closed / closing].

323 Many paintings in the museum [is / are] hard [understanding / to understand].

grow up 성장하다 choir 합창단, 성가대 disappointed 실망한 slope 경사지, 비탈 freeze 얼다 dangerous 위험한 grocery 식료품

Unit Practice

STEP 1 직독직해에 맞게 (   ) 안의 단어를 사용하여 문장을 쓰시오. (필요시 형태를 바꿔 쓸 것)

1 그녀는 걱정한다 / 그녀의 곧 있을 취업 면접에 대해 (upcoming / worried / job interview)

__________ __________ __________ / __________ __________ __________

__________ __________.

2 Eric은 인터넷을 검색했다 / 가사를 찾기 위해 / 그 노래의 (of the song / search / find / the lyrics / on the internet)

__________ __________ __________ __________ __________ / __________

__________ __________ __________ / __________ __________ __________.

3 나는 항상 너무 졸리다 / 월요일 아침마다 (sleepy / feel / on Monday mornings / too / always)

__________ __________ __________ __________ __________ / __________

__________ __________.

STEP 2 다음 문장에서 [ ] 표시된 부분을 수식하는 수식어(구)를 찾아 밑줄 긋고, 문장을 해석하시오.

1 My rival runs really [fast], so I must practice running as best as I can.

2 It seemed that she was [embarrassed] to forget her lines during the school play.

3 A nice hotel room is [expensive] to book during the holiday season.

4 In the morning, Matthew [woke up] to find himself late for school.

5 With his creativity and talent, Steve Jobs absolutely [deserved] to win the Nobel Prize.

6 The movie [must be amazing] to have been seen by so many people.

search 찾아보다, 검색하다 lyric 서정시; *((pl.)) 가사 rival 경쟁 상대 embarrassed 당황스러운 line 선; *대사 play 놀이; *연극 holiday season 휴가철 creativity 창의력 talent 재능 absolutely 틀림없이 deserve ~을 받을 만하다

정답 및 해설 p.27

STEP 3

1 수식어구에 유의하여 밑줄 친 문장을 해석하시오.

Tigerfish are found **in Africa**. As you can guess **from their name**, they have large teeth. Tigerfish can grow **to be 1.5 meters long**, and they can weigh **over 70 kilograms**. Some hungry tigerfish grab flying birds **out of the air**! This was **even** caught **on film**. People are **often** surprised **to see them jump to catch their prey**.

Reading Q 타이거피시에 관한 윗글의 내용과 일치하지 않는 것은?

① 아프리카에서 볼 수 있다.
② 호랑이보다 큰 이빨을 가지고 있다.
③ 먹이를 잡기 위해 수면 위로 뛰어오르기도 한다.

NEW 내신기출

2 밑줄 친 ①~④ 중 어법상 틀린 2개를 찾아 해당 번호를 쓰고 바르게 고쳐 쓰시오.

People **often** eat ① to relieve stress. The problem is that they **generally** choose junk food. **Over time**, this behavior is likely ② causing weight gain and high cholesterol. Therefore, think ③ careful when you're stressed. When you need to relax, why not go **for a walk** instead of ④ eating french fries?

번호	적절하지 않은 단어	고쳐 쓴 단어

1 guess 추측하다, 짐작하다 weigh 무게가 ~이다 grab (단단히) 붙잡다 catch 잡다; *(장면을) 포착하다 prey 먹이
2 relieve 없애주다, 완화하다 generally 일반적으로, 대개 junk food 정크푸드 over time 시간이 흐르면서 likely ~할 것 같은 weight gain 체중 증가

정답 및 해설 p.28

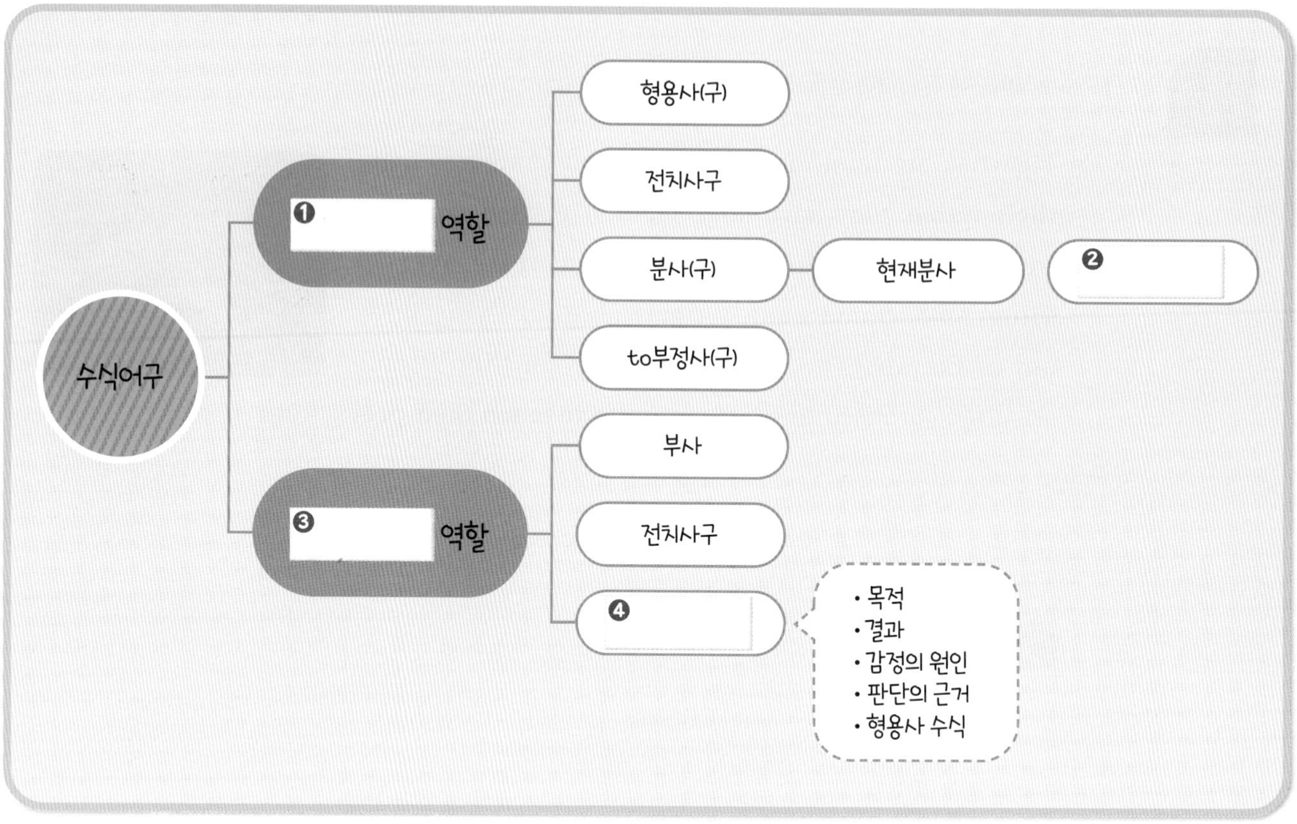

주요 예문을 다시 한번 확인하고, 우리말에 맞게 ( ) 안의 단어를 사용하여 문장을 쓰시오.

1 우리는 네가 졸업하는 것을 보게 되어 기쁘다. (glad / graduate / see) Point 04

2 Jimmy는 자라서 교수가 되었다. (become / grew up / a professor) Point 04

3 그녀는 아마도 네 선물을 좋아할 것이다. (likes / present / probably) Point 03

4 서둘러서 우리는 길을 가로질러 달렸다. (ran / in a hurry / across the road) Point 03

5 우리 집 근처에 있는 그 초등학교가 폐교될 것이다. (near my home / closed / the elementary school) Point 01

6 환하게 웃고 있는 그 소녀가 Luna임이 틀림없다. (brightly / the girl / smiling) Point 02

UNIT 07

관계사절

Point 01 관계대명사와 관계부사
Point 02 관계사의 계속적 용법과 생략
Point 03 관계대명사 what
Point 04 복합관계사

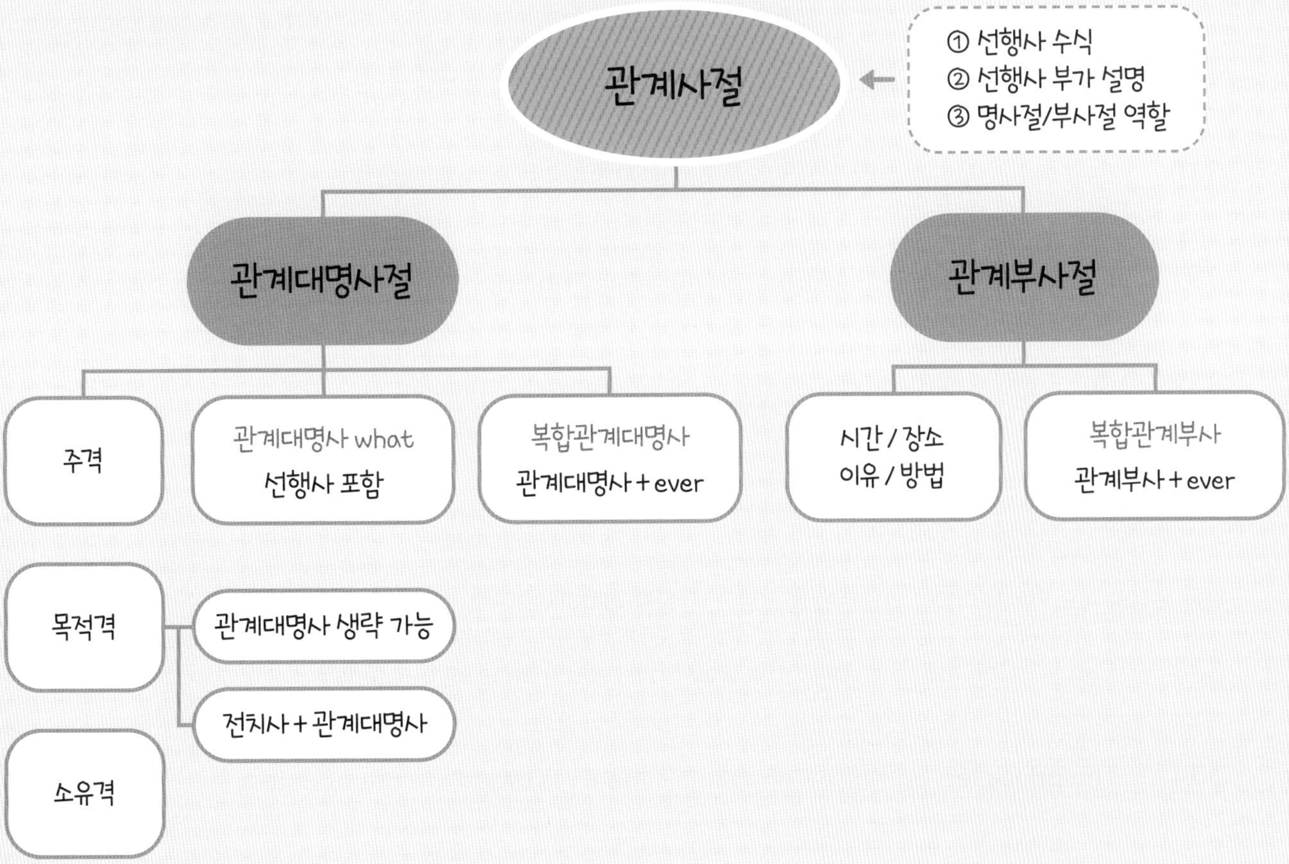

Point 01 관계대명사와 관계부사

관계대명사(who, which, that, whom, whose)와 관계부사(when, where, why, how)는 두 개의 절을 연결하는 **접속사**인 동시에 각각 **대명사**와 **부사 역할**을 하며, 이들이 이끄는 절은 **선행사인 명사를 수식**한다.

• 관계부사 how와 선행사 the way는 함께 쓰지 않고 둘 중 하나만 사용한다.

S′ V′ O′

324 Linda is / *the neighbor* <**who has two children**>.

S V SC

Linda는 ~이다 / 이웃 <두 명의 아이가 있는>

M′ S′ V′

325 Brooks is / *my friend* <**with whom I exercise**>.

S V SC

Brooks는 ~이다 / 내 친구 <내가 함께 운동하는>

Tip 전치사+관계대명사
- 선행사가 전치사의 목적어일 때 전치사는 앞으로 이동 가능
- 관계대명사가 that인 경우는 이동 불가

S′ V′ M′

326 Tell me / *the reason* <**why you are here**>.

V IO DO

내게 말해줘 / 이유를 <네가 여기에 있는>

다음 문장에서 관계사절을 찾아 밑줄 긋고, 문장을 해석하시오.

정답 및 해설 p.29

구문 해석 기법

□「전치사+관계대명사절」은「전치사+선행사」를 관계대명사절 뒤에 놓고 의미를 파악한다.

327 I found / *the key* <that you were looking for> / on the shelf.

나는 발견했다 / 열쇠를 <네가 찾던> / 선반 위에서

328 The man who saved the child from drowning is a hero.

329 Do you know the reason why they changed their minds?

330 Last Saturday was the day when my best friend got married.

331 I need a big bag into which I can put all my books.

332 Be careful when you drive on a road where traffic is heavy.

다음 문장의 네모 안에서 어법상 알맞은 것을 고르고, 문장을 해석하시오.

333 Can you tell me [the way / the way how] you manage your time?

334 The principles [on which / on that] his theory is based are out of date.

---

drown 물에 빠지다 heavy 무거운; *심한 principle 원리 theory 이론 base ~의 기초를 쌓다; *~의 근거로 하다 out of date 구식이 된

Point **02**

관계사의 계속적 용법과 생략

역할	선행사에 대한 부가적인 설명
형태	선행사와 관계사 사이에 콤마(,)를 씀 (~인데[이나], 그것/그 사람은[을] …)
특징	관계대명사 that은 계속적 용법으로 쓰이지 않음 계속적 용법으로 쓰인 관계대명사 which는 앞 절의 일부나 전체를 선행사로 할 수 있음

335 I went to *Paris*, / [**which is the capital** <**of France**>]. 선행사 부가 설명
(S: I, V: went, M: to Paris / S′: which, V′: is, SC′: the capital)
나는 파리에 갔는데, / [그곳은 수도이다 <프랑스의>]

336 *He won the lottery*, / <**which surprised everyone**>. 선행사 부가 설명
(S: He, V: won, O: the lottery / S′: which, V′: surprised, O′: everyone)
그는 복권에 당첨되었는데, / <이는 모두를 놀라게 했다>.

337 This is / *the game* <(**which**) **we used to play**>.
(S: This, V: is, SC: the game / O′: (which), S′: we, V′: used to play)
이것은 ~이다 / 게임 <우리가 하곤 했던>

Tip 목적격 관계대명사(who, whom, which, that)는 생략 가능

다음 문장에서 관계사절을 찾아 밑줄 긋고, 문장을 해석하시오. 정답 및 해설 p.29

338 This is *my new ring*, / <which I got for my birthday>.
이것은 나의 새 반지인데, / <그것은 내가 생일에 받은 것이다>.

339 James is going out with Clara, who is his classmate.

340 Rudolph was a reindeer others laughed at.

341 Ally met a man, who was a firefighter, on the train.

342 Who is the person you traveled to Vietnam with?

343 Benjamin said he lived in Toronto, which turned out to be false.

다음 문장의 네모 안에서 어법상 알맞은 것을 고르고, 문장을 해석하시오.

344 Louis spent the summer with his aunt, [taught / who taught] him to speak English.

345 Mechanical problems were found with the cars, [which / that] led to lower sales.

win the lottery 복권에 당첨되다 go out with ~와 사귀다 reindeer 순록 mechanical 기계와 관련된, 기계상의 lead to ~로 이어지다 sale ((*pl.*)) 판매량

Unit Practice

STEP 1 **직독직해에 맞게 ( ) 안의 단어를 사용하여 문장을 쓰시오. (필요시 형태를 바꿔 쓸 것)**

1 그는 소파를 구매했다 / 네 사람이 앉을 수 있는 (four / a sofa / sit on / people / buy / that)

__________ __________ __________ __________ / __________ __________

__________ __________ __________ __________.

2 나의 가장 친한 친구는 Katlin인데, / 그녀는 정직하고 성실하다. (diligent / honest / close / and)

__________ __________ __________ __________ __________, / __________

__________ __________ __________ __________.

3 너는 이유를 아니 / 그들이 그들의 마음을 바꾼 (the reason / minds / do / changed / know)

__________ __________ __________ __________ __________ / __________

__________ __________ __________ __________?

STEP 2 **다음 문장에서 관계사절을 찾아 밑줄 긋고, 문장을 해석하시오.**

1 The fireworks exploded, which made the sky look colorful.

2 The high school gives a scholarship to students whose grades are excellent.

3 Fabian does volunteer work at the hospital where he was born.

4 He was excited to interview the woman he had read about in a magazine article.

5 I saw a bird building a nest, which was common in my area.

6 She returned the product to the clerk from whom she had made the purchase.

close (시간·공간상) 가까운; *친밀한(-closer-closest) firework 폭죽 explode 터지다 scholarship 장학금 grade 품질; *성적 article 기사 nest 둥지 common 흔한 return 돌아오다; *반납하다 clerk (가게의) 점원 purchase 구입, 구매

STEP 3

1 밑줄 친 (A), (B)의 각 네모 안에서 어법에 맞는 표현을 고르고, 관계대명사절을 찾아 < >로 묶으시오.

Plants are caring. (A) <u>They look after the ecosystems in [that / which] they grow.</u> For example, plants pay attention to the needs of the soil around them. If the soil lacks a nutrient, they start to produce that particular nutrient. What's more, healthy plants help nearby injured plants too. (B) <u>They send nutrients [who / which] injured plants need through their root networks.</u>

Reading Q 윗글의 주제로 가장 적절한 것은?

① why plants need healthy soil
② how to communicate with plants
③ how plants help their communities

NEW 내신기출

2 밑줄 친 우리말 (A), (B)를 조건에 맞게 써서 각 문장을 완성하시오.

Scientists are interested in female sea turtles, (A) <u>그들은 알을 낳기 위해 물에서 나온다</u>. They have found that these turtles return to the same beach (B) <u>그들이 태어났던</u>. They dig a hole in the sand and lay their eggs. Then they bury the eggs to hide them from animals **that eat them**. Finally, they go back into the sea.

*sea turtle 바다거북

조건
· 관계대명사와 to부정사를 쓸 것
· 제시된 단어를 사용할 것
· eggs / born / lay / leave / the water / on
· (A) 7단어, (B) 5단어로 쓸 것

(A) ______________________________

(B) ______________________________

1 caring 배려하는, 보살피는 ecosystem 생태계 nutrient 영양소 particular 특정한 injured 다친 community 공동체
2 female 암컷, 여성 dig 파다 hole 구멍, 구덩이 lay 놓다, 두다; *(알을) 낳다 bury (땅 속에) 묻다 hide 숨기다

Point 03

관계대명사 what

what은 **선행사를 포함하는 관계대명사**로 **the thing which[that](~하는 것)**의 의미이다. 관계대명사 what이 이끄는 절은 명사절로, 문장에서 **주어, 목적어, 보어의 역할**을 할 수 있다.

O′ S′ V′
346 <**What I heard**> / was an unbelievable story. 주어
S V SC
<내가 들은 것은> / 믿기 어려운 이야기였다.

O′ S′ V′
347 I showed him / <**what I bought**>. 목적어
S V IO DO
나는 그에게 보여 주었다 / <내가 산 것을>

O′ S′ V′
348 This is not / <**what I expected**>. 보어
S V SC
이것은 ~이 아니다 / <내가 예상했던 것>

다음 문장에서 관계대명사절을 찾아 밑줄 긋고, 문장을 해석하시오. 정답 및 해설 p.31

349 This app is / <what I use / to book hotel rooms>.
이 앱은 ~이다 / <내가 사용하는 것 / 호텔 방을 예약하기 위해>

350 People couldn't believe what they were seeing.

351 Students should bring what they need for class.

352 What you experienced at the camp sounds very interesting.

353 What happened to Eric can happen to anyone.

354 I went shopping, but I couldn't find what I wanted to buy.

다음 문장의 네모 안에서 어법상 알맞은 것을 고르고, 문장을 해석하시오.

355 [That / What] you did for us today was very brave, and I'm proud of you.

356 Volunteering at an orphanage is what [has she / she has] done for over ten years.

unbelievable 믿기 어려운 experience 경험하다 brave 용감한 be proud of ~을 자랑스러워하다 orphanage 보육원

Point 04 복합관계사

복합관계대명사	명사절 또는 부사절을 이끎	**whoever**(~하는 사람은 누구든지), **whichever**(~하는 것은 어느 것이나), **whatever**(무엇을 ~하더라도)
복합관계부사	부사절을 이끎	**whenever**(~할 때마다), **wherever**(어디에 ~하더라도), **however**(아무리 ~하더라도, 어떻게 ~할지라도)

S′ V′ O′

357 <**Whoever violates the law**> / will be punished. 복합관계대명사 (명사절)

V

<법을 위반하는 사람은 누구든지> / 처벌받을 것이다.

O′ S′ V′

358 <**Whatever they say**>, / I don't care. 복합관계대명사 (양보 부사절)

S V

<그들이 무슨 말을 하더라도>, / 나는 상관하지 않는다.

M′ S′ V′ O′

359 <**Whenever he visits me**>, / he brings cookies. 복합관계부사 (시간 부사절)

S V O

<그가 나를 방문할 때마다>, / 그는 쿠키를 가져온다.

M′ SC′ S′ V′

360 Money can't buy happiness / <**however rich you are**>. 복합관계부사 (양보 부사절)

S V O

돈은 행복을 살 수 없다 / <네가 아무리 부자라 하더라도>

다음 문장에서 복합관계사절을 찾아 밑줄 긋고, 문장을 해석하시오. 정답 및 해설 p.31

361 I will read / <whichever book you recommend>.

나는 읽을 것이다 / <네가 추천하는 어떤 책이든지>

362 Wherever I go, I always bring my smartphone.

363 Whenever I feel sad, my little puppy comforts me.

364 He doesn't wear a scarf however cold it is outside.

365 Whatever you do to persuade me, I won't change my mind.

366 Whoever leaves the classroom last should turn off the lights.

다음 문장의 네모 안에서 어법상 알맞은 것을 고르고, 문장을 해석하시오.

367 [However / Whichever] busy you are, you should help with the group project.

368 If you feel hungry, you can have [whatever / wherever] is in the refrigerator.

violate 위반하다 punish 처벌하다 care 상관하다 recommend 추천하다 comfort 위로하다 persuade 설득하다 refrigerator 냉장고

Unit Practice

STEP 1

직독직해에 맞게 (   ) 안의 단어를 사용하여 문장을 쓰시오. (필요시 형태를 바꿔 쓸 것)

1 이것이 내가 준비한 것이다 / 아빠 생신을 위해 (prepare / this / for my father's birthday)

_______ _______ _______ _______ _______ / _______

_______ _______ _______.

2 내가 필요로 하는 것은 / 요즘 / 약간의 평온함과 고요함이다 (need / quiet / these days / peace / some)

_______ _______ _______ / _______ _______ / _______

_______ _______ _______ _______.

3 네가 아무리 바쁘더라도, / 너는 그룹 과제를 도와야 한다. (should / busy / with the group project / help)

_______ _______ _______ _______, / _______ _______

_______ _______ _______ _______ _______.

STEP 2

다음 문장에서 관계사절을 찾아 밑줄 긋고, 문장을 해석하시오.

1 Honestly, I don't understand what you're trying to say.

2 Whichever route you take during rush hour, there will be a traffic jam.

3 Whenever Charlotte eats delicious food, she likes to take pictures of it.

4 What you've learned in today's class will be tested in our quiz next week.

5 Wherever we looked, there were singing birds and blossoming flowers.

6 Whoever wants to join the club needs to fill out this application.

quiet 조용한; *고요(함) these days 요즘 route 길 rush hour 혼잡 시간대 blossom 꽃이 피다 join 연결하다; *가입하다 club 동아리, 동호회 fill out ~을 작성하다 application 지원서

STEP 3

1 (A), (B)의 ( ) 안의 단어를 문맥에 맞게 배열하고, 밑줄 친 부분을 해석하시오.

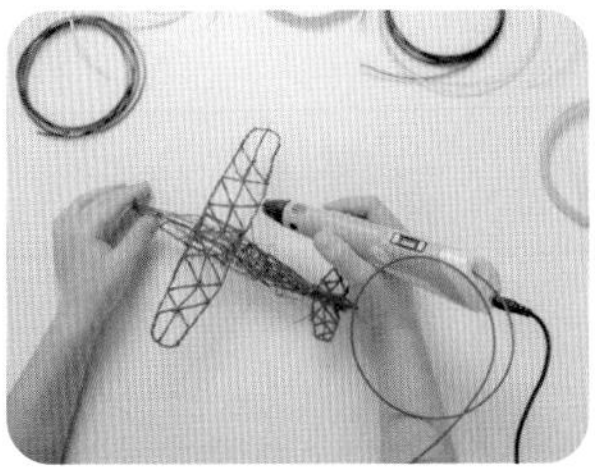

Drawing is great! But drawings made with a normal pen are only two-dimensional. That's why you need a 3D pen! You can draw (A) (want / whatever / you) in three dimensions. Just put some plastic into the pen and plug it in. Heated plastic will come out (B) (the pen / wherever / move / you), even in the air. The plastic quickly cools and becomes solid. How fun!

(A) ______________________________

(B) ______________________________

Reading Q 3D 펜에 관한 윗글의 내용과 일치하면 T, 일치하지 않으면 F를 쓰시오.

(1) 펜 안에 플라스틱을 넣어서 3차원 조형물을 만들 수 있다. ______

(2) 펜에서 나온 플라스틱은 굳는 데 시간이 오래 걸린다. ______

NEW 내신기출

2 밑줄 친 ①~④ 중 어법상 틀린 2개를 찾아 해당 번호를 쓰고 바르게 고쳐 쓰시오.

At concerts, you clap ① whenever the music stops. But it is tough ② to know when to clap at a classical music concert. Classical songs have many parts that have their own endings. Thus, it is hard to recognize the ending for ③ that you should clap. If you're unsure, just wait until others clap. ④ However starts first probably knows best.

번호	적절하지 않은 단어	고쳐 쓴 단어

1 dimensional ~차원의(*n.* dimension 차원) plug in 전원을 연결하다 cool 시원한; *식다[차가워지다] solid 고체의; *단단한

2 clap 박수를 치다 tough 어려운, 힘든 classical 고전적인; *클래식의 recognize 알아보다, 알다 unsure 확실치 않은 probably 아마(도)

Wrap Up

정답 및 해설 p.33

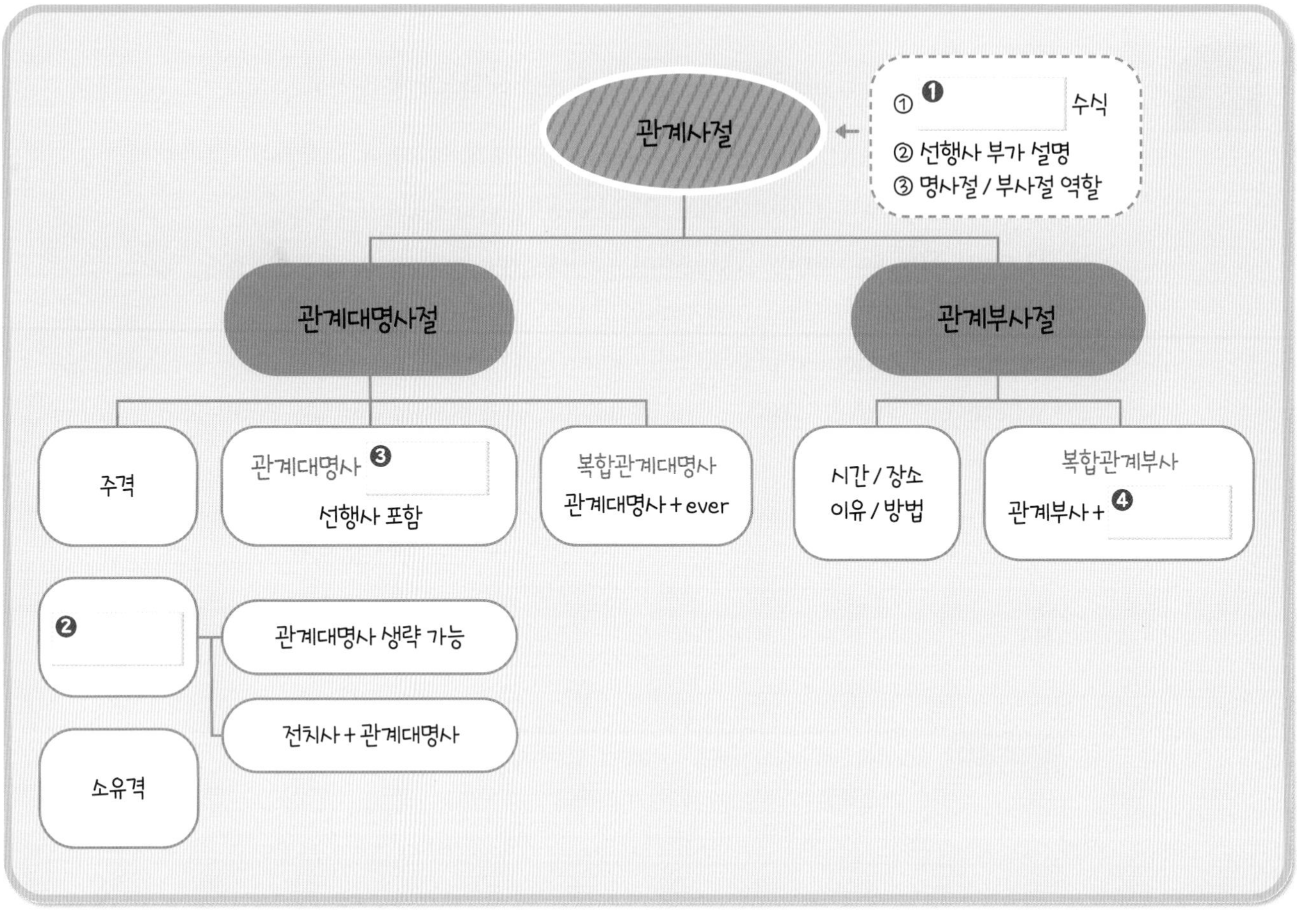

주요 예문을 다시 한번 확인하고, 우리말에 맞게 ( ) 안의 단어를 사용하여 문장을 쓰시오.

1 법을 위반하는 사람은 누구든지 처벌받을 것이다. (violates / punished / the law / will) *Point 04*

2 이것은 우리가 하곤 했던 게임이다. (play / used to / the game) *Point 02*

3 그는 나를 방문할 때마다 쿠키를 가져온다. (cookies / visits / brings) *Point 04*

4 Brooks는 내가 운동을 함께 하는 내 친구이다. (exercise / friend / with) *Point 01*

5 나는 그에게 내가 산 것을 보여 주었다. (bought / showed / what) *Point 03*

6 그는 복권에 당첨되었는데, 이는 모두를 놀라게 했다. (everyone / the lottery / won / surprised) *Point 02*

UNIT 08

부사절과 분사구문

Point 01 시간·이유 부사절
Point 02 조건·양보 부사절
Point 03 분사구문의 의미
Point 04 분사구문의 다양한 형태

부사절
접속사 + 주어 + 동사

- 시간
  when, before, after, as, while, until[till], since, as soon as
- 이유
  because[since, as]
- 조건
  if, unless, as long as
- 양보
  though[although, even though], even if

분사구문
v-ing ~

분사가 이끄는 수식어구

- 동시동작
- 시간
- 이유
- 조건

완료형 분사구문
수동형 분사구문
접속사 + 분사구문
주어 + 분사구문
분사구문 관용 표현

Point 01

시간·이유 부사절

부사절은 「접속사+주어+동사 ~」의 형태로, **주절에 의미를 더하는 부사 역할**을 한다. 접속사에 따라 부사절은 **시간**이나 **이유**를 나타낼 수 있다.

시간	when(~할 때), before(~하기 전에), after(~한 뒤에), as(~할 때, ~하면서), while(~하는 동안), until[till](~할 때까지), since(~한 이래로), as soon as(~하자마자) 등 시간 부사절에서는 현재시제로 미래를 나타낸다.
이유	because[since, as] (~ 때문에, ~해서)

369 <**When** I come home>, / my dog welcomes me.
(S′ V′ M′ / S V O)
<내가 집에 올 때>, / 내 개가 나를 반겨준다.

370 She washes bottles / <**before** she recycles them>.
(S V O / S′ V′ O′)
그녀는 병들을 씻는다 / <그녀가 그것들을 재활용하기 전에>

371 <**Since** this shirt is big / for me>, / I'll get / it tailored.
(S′ V′ SC′ M′ / S V O OC)
<이 셔츠는 크기 때문에 / 내게>, / 나는 할 것이다 / 그것이 딱 맞게 수선되도록

다음 문장에서 부사절을 찾아 밑줄 긋고, 문장을 해석하시오. 정답 및 해설 p.33

372 <After I repair / the printer>, / I will give you a call.
<내가 수리한 뒤에 / 프린터를>, / 나는 너에게 전화를 줄 것이다

373 You can rest on the sofa until your clients arrive.

374 Sam didn't bring his laptop because it was not working.

375 Five years have passed since Monica went abroad to study.

376 As she was allergic to seafood, she couldn't eat the shrimp dish.

377 As soon as my younger sister looked at my picture, she laughed aloud.

다음 문장의 네모 안에서 어법상 알맞은 것을 고르고, 문장을 해석하시오.

378 You should not answer your phone [before / while] you're inside the theater.

379 As [is he / he is] busy these days, he won't be able to come to the wedding.

recycle 재활용하다 tailored 잘[딱] 맞도록 만든 client 고객 go abroad 해외에 가다 allergic to ~에 알레르기가 있는 aloud 소리 내어; *크게

Point 02 조건·양보 부사절

접속사에 따라 부사절은 **조건**이나 **양보**를 나타낼 수 있다.

조건	if(만약 ~라면), unless(만약 ~하지 않으면), as long as(~하는 한) 등 조건 부사절에서는 현재시제로 미래를 나타낸다.
양보	though[although, even though](비록 ~하지만), even if(만약 ~할지라도)

S' V' O'

380 <**If you have any questions**>, / please ask me.

V O

<질문이 있으시면>, / 제게 물어봐주세요.

S' V' SC'

381 <**Although he was tired**>, / he went to the library.

S V M

<그는 비록 피곤했지만>, / 그는 도서관에 갔다.

S' V' SC'

382 We won't give up / <**even if the situation is bad**>.

S V

우리는 포기하지 않을 것이다 / <만약 상황이 나쁠지라도>

다음 문장에서 부사절을 찾아 밑줄 긋고, 문장을 해석하시오. 정답 및 해설 p.34

383 <Though it is raining>, / the match will continue.

<비가 내리고 있지만>, / 경기는 계속될 것이다.

384 I won't see him again unless he says sorry to me.

385 If you want to make good friends, be kind to others first.

386 Even though Finn took some medicine, his symptoms didn't get better.

387 Although she was holding back her tears, everyone knew that she felt sad.

388 Even if I work hard, it may be difficult to earn enough money to buy a house.

다음 문장의 네모 안에서 어법상 알맞은 것을 고르고, 문장을 해석하시오.

389 The dog won't attack you [if / unless] you move suddenly or scare him.

390 As long as you [follow / will follow] the rules, you can use the school library.

take medicine 약을 먹다 symptom 증상 get better (병·상황 따위가) 좋아지다, 호전되다 hold back one's tears 눈물을 참다 earn (돈을) 벌다

Unit Practice

STEP 1

직독직해에 맞게 (　) 안의 단어를 사용하여 문장을 쓰시오. (필요시 형태를 바꿔 쓸 것)

1 비록 그것은 꽤 비쌌지만, / 그것은 근사한 저녁 식사였다. (quite / a nice dinner / expensive)

_______ _______ _______ _______ _______ _______, /

_______ _______ _______ _______ _______.

2 그 선생님이 쓰시는 동안 / 칠판에, / 그 학생들은 필기를 했다 (take notes / on the blackboard)

_______ _______ _______ _______ / _______ _______

_______, / _______ _______ _______ _______.

3 네가 만들기를 원한다면 / 좋은 친구들을, / 다른 사람들에게 친절해라 / 먼저 (first / make / want / good / to others / kind)

_______ _______ _______ _______ _______ / _______

_______, / _______ _______ _______ _______ /_______.

STEP 2

다음 문장에서 부사절을 찾아 밑줄 긋고, 문장을 해석하시오.

1 I didn't see the sign because I was too busy looking at my cell phone.

2 It is bad for your health to go to sleep as soon as you finish your meal.

3 When he tasted the soup, he realized that he had put too much salt in it.

4 My parents allow me to stay out late as long as I let them know where I am.

5 After we baked some cookies, we shared them with our neighbors.

6 Unless you hurry, you won't be able to buy the concert tickets.

quite 꽤　expensive 비싼　take notes 필기를 하다　sign 징후; *간판, 표지판　meal 식사　taste 맛이 ~하다; *맛보다　realize 깨닫다　put 넣다(-put-put)
stay out 집에 안 들어오다　share 공유하다; *나누다　hurry 서두르다

정답 및 해설 p.34

STEP 3

1 빈칸 (A), (B), (C)에 들어갈 접속사를 바르게 짝지은 것을 고르시오.

____(A)____ you need to cook something quickly, a microwave oven is very helpful. But how does it work? ____(B)____ you press the start button, the oven sends microwaves through your food. The energy in the microwaves affects the water molecules in the food. They begin to move quickly back and forth. ____(C)____ this movement produces heat, the microwave oven can cook the food.

*microwave 마이크로파 (주파수가 매우 높은 전자파)
**molecule 분자 (물체의 성질을 가진 최소 단위)

	(A)		(B)		(C)
①	When	……	Before	……	If
②	When	……	If	……	Since
③	Unless	……	If	……	After
④	Unless	……	When	……	Since

Reading Q 윗글의 제목으로 가장 적절한 것은?
① Quick and Easy Recipes to Cook in a Microwave Oven
② The Principle of Heating Food in a Microwave Oven
③ Various Uses of a Microwave Oven in Our Daily Lives

NEW 내신기출

2 밑줄 친 단어를 문맥에 맞게 배열하시오. (접속사를 쓸 것)

Beans have many health benefits. For example, they help prevent heart disease and cancer. And **although they are high in calories**, they are also high in fiber. Fiber makes you feel full quickly, so you can avoid eating too much. Moreover, <u>good / taste / beans / with many other foods</u>, it's easy to add them to your diet.

____

1 microwave oven 전자레인지 affect 영향을 미치다 back and forth 앞뒤로 movement 움직임 produce 만들어 내다 principle 원리
2 bean 콩 benefit 이점 prevent 예방하다 heart disease 심장 질환 cancer 암 high in ~의 함유량이 높은 fiber 섬유질 avoid 피하다

Point **03**

분사구문의 의미

부사절의 주어가 주절의 주어와 같을 때 부사절에서 「**접속사+주어**」를 **생략**하고 **동사를 분사(v-ing)**로 바꾼 형태이다.

의미	동시동작	~하면서(as)	이유	~ 때문에, ~해서(because, since, as)
	시간	~할 때(when), ~하는 동안(while), ~후에(after)	조건	(만약) ~라면, ~한다면(if)

391 <**Cooking dinner**>, / she burned her hand. 동시동작
S V O
<저녁을 요리하면서>, / 그녀는 그녀의 손을 데었다.

392 <**Walking out of the room**>, / Amy turned off / the light. 시간
S V O
<방에서 나올 때>, / Amy는 껐다 / 전등을

393 <**Taking this train**>, / you will arrive / at the town / by 2:00 p.m. 조건
S V M_1 M_2
<이 기차를 타면>, / 너는 도착할 것이다 / 그 마을에 / 오후 2시까지

밑줄 친 분사구문과 주어진 부사절의 의미가 같도록 네모 안에서 문맥상 알맞은 것을 고르시오. 정답 및 해설 p.36

394 <Getting off the bus>, / Jason slipped / and fell.
<버스에서 내리면서>, / Jason은 미끄러졌다 / 그리고 넘어졌다
= < As / Because he got off the bus>

395 Turning right, you will find a bank.
= If / Because you turn right

396 Having no money, Issac couldn't pay for dinner.
= After / Because he had no money

397 Looking out the window, I saw a stranger wandering.
= Since / When I looked out the window

398 Taking a shower, he sang a song from his favorite movie.
= As / Since he took a shower

399 Driving down the road in heavy rain, David witnessed an accident.
= While / Since he drove down the road in heavy rain

400 Listening to loud music through earphones, you'll damage your hearing.
= If / Before you listen to loud music through earphones

burn (불이) 타오르다; *데다 slip 미끄러지다 stranger 낯선 사람 wander 돌아다니다 witness 목격하다 damage 손상을 주다 hearing 청력, 청각

Point 04 분사구문의 다양한 형태

부사절의 주어가 주절의 주어와 다를 때 부사절의 **주어를 생략하지** 않고 분사 앞에 남기기도 하고, 분사구문의 의미를 분명히 하기 위해 **접속사를 남기기도** 한다. 분사구문은 시제와 태에 따라 **완료형**과 **수동형**으로 쓸 수 있다.

완료형 분사구문	Having v-ed	분사구문의 시제가 주절의 시제보다 앞설 때
수동형 분사구문	(Being / Having been) v-ed	Being과 Having been은 생략 가능

분사구문 관용 표현	frankly speaking(솔직히 말하면), considering (that)(~을 고려하면), generally speaking(일반적으로 말하면), judging from(~로 판단하건대)

401 <**The weather being good**>, / we went to the beach.
(S: we / V: went / M: to the beach)
<날씨가 좋아서>, / 우리는 해변에 갔다.

402 <**Having quit his job**>, / he started a new business.
(S: he / V: started / O: a new business)
<직장을 그만둔 뒤>, / 그는 새로운 사업을 시작했다.

밑줄 친 부분에 유의하여 다음 문장을 해석하시오. 정답 및 해설 p.36

403 <Judging from his accent>, / he must be / from Busan.
<그의 말투로 판단하건대>, / 그는 틀림없다 / 부산에서 온 것이

404 When buying something online, you should compare prices.

405 The test being difficult, many of the students failed.

406 Considering it's his first job, he is doing pretty well.

407 Frankly speaking, I don't think that our plan is a good idea.

408 Surrounded by the police, the criminal came out of the house.

다음 문장의 네모 안에서 어법상 알맞은 것을 고르고, 문장을 해석하시오.

409 [Having hidden / Hidden] by a big tree, this "no smoking" sign is easy to miss.

410 [Being / Having] already read the book several times, she knew the whole story.

quit 그만두다 accent 말씨, 말투 compare 비교하다 surround 둘러싸다 criminal 범인 hide 숨기다, 가리다(-hid-hidden) whole 전체의

Unit Practice

STEP 1

직독직해에 맞게 ( ) 안의 단어를 사용하여 문장을 쓰시오. (필요시 형태를 바꿔 쓸 것)

1 그 시험이 어려워서, / 많은 학생들이 / 낙제했다. (difficult / of the students / fail / the test / many)

_______ _______ _______ _______, / _______ _______

_______ _______ / _______.

2 그녀의 집을 청소하면서, / Emma는 몇몇 오래된 사진들을 발견했다. (some / find / clean / photos / old / house)

_______ _______ _______, / _______ _______ _______

_______ _______.

3 응원을 받았기 때문에 / 군중에게, / 그 운동선수는 용기를 얻었다 (by the crowd / encourage / the athlete / cheer / feel)

_______ _______ / _______ _______ _______, / _______

_______ _______ _______.

STEP 2

다음 문장에서 분사구문을 찾아 밑줄 긋고, 문장을 해석하시오.

1 Taking a taxi, we will be able to save time and avoid walking in the rain.

2 While talking on the phone, I looked at the calendar to check my schedule.

3 Generally speaking, taking breaks from studying improves your concentration.

4 Not remembering the password, Samuel couldn't log into his account.

5 Warned about the storm, they decided to cancel their outdoor activities.

6 Having seen the accident, he called an ambulance at once.

crowd 군중 encourage 격려하다, 용기를 북돋우다 cheer 환호하다; *응원하다 save (죽음 등에서) 구하다; *절약하다 take breaks 휴식을 취하다 improve 개선하다, 향상시키다 concentration 집중; *집중력 log into ~에 접속하다 account 계좌; *계정 cancel 취소하다 outdoor 야외의

STEP ·3·

1 분사구문에 유의하여 밑줄 친 문장을 해석하시오.

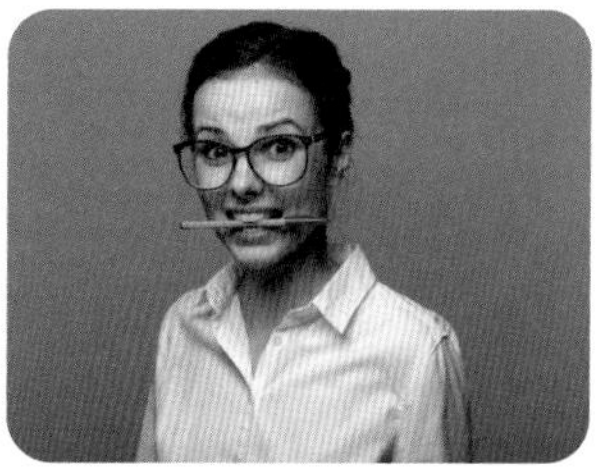

We can judge if a smile is real by __________ it. In a study, people guessed whether a smile was real **while holding a pencil in their mouth**. This stopped them from smiling. When they were holding the pencil in their mouth, they had a hard time deciding. But they found it easier without the pencil. This is because they could smile the same way and understand the emotions of the smiler.

____

Reading Q 빈칸에 들어갈 말로 가장 적절한 것은?

① hiding ② imitating ③ imagining

NEW 내신기출

2 밑줄 친 우리말에 맞게 보기 의 단어를 사용하여 문장을 쓰시오. (필요시 형태를 바꿔 쓸 것)

Oymyakon is a Russian town with a population of about 500 people. **Considered the coldest populated place on the planet**, it is nicknamed the "Pole of Cold." 날씨가 끔찍하기 때문에, Oymyakon에서 사는 것은 매우 어렵다. Batteries die quickly, and metal sticks to skin. Some residents even keep their car engine running from fall till spring to prevent it from freezing.

보기 difficult / in Oymyakon / be / very / terrible / live / the weather

________ ________ ________ ________, ________ ________

________ ________ ________ ________.

1 judge 판단하다 study 공부하다; *연구 guess 추측하다 hold 잡고 있다 emotion 감정 imitate 흉내 내다
2 populated 거주하는 planet 행성; *지구 nickname 별명; *별명을 붙이다 pole 극지 die 죽다; *(기계가) 멎다 stick to ~에 달라붙다 resident 주민

Wrap Up

정답 및 해설 p.38

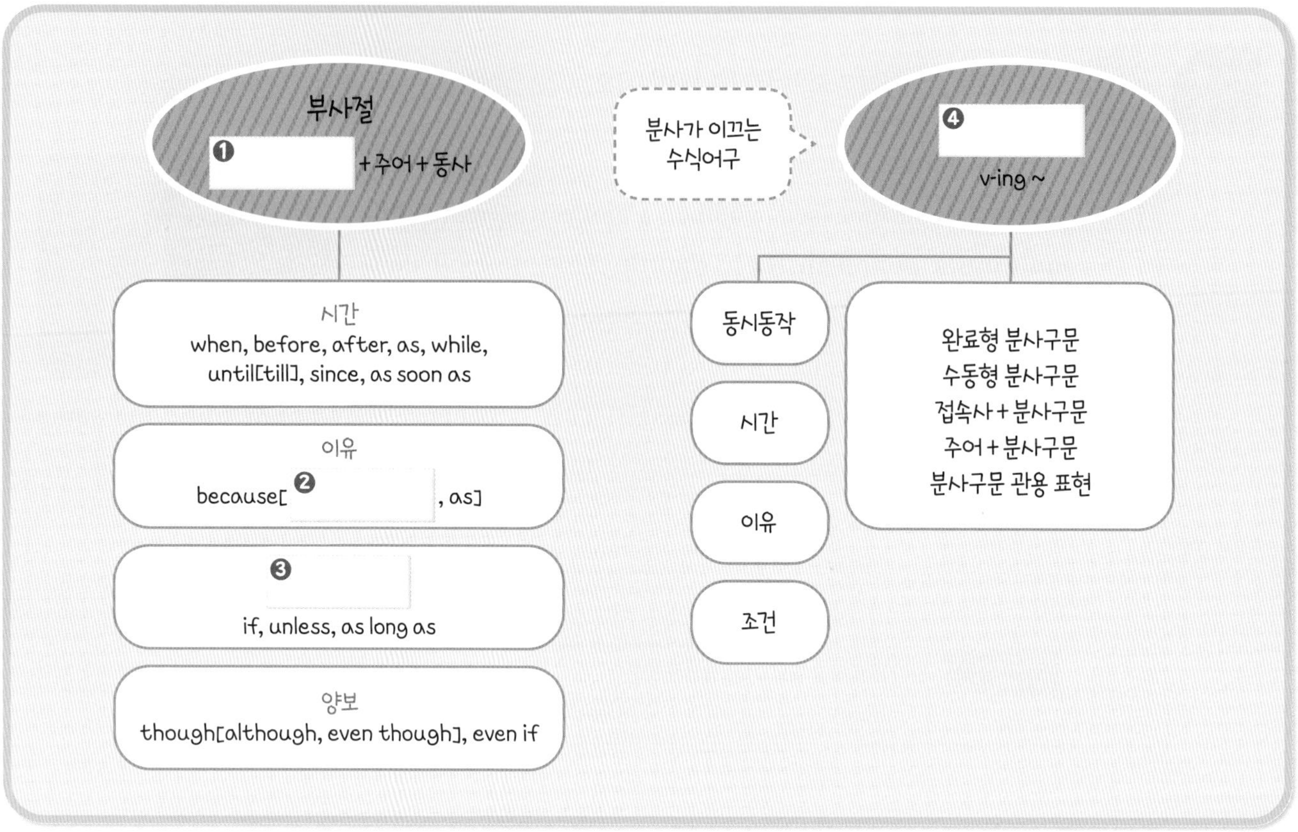

주요 예문을 다시 한번 확인하고, 우리말에 맞게 ( ) 안의 단어를 사용하여 문장을 쓰시오.

1 그는 비록 피곤했지만 도서관에 갔다. (the library / tired / although) Point 02

2 이 셔츠는 내게 크기 때문에 나는 그것을 딱 맞게 수선할 것이다. (since / for me / big / tailored / get) Point 01

3 직장을 그만둔 뒤 그는 새로운 사업을 시작했다. (his job / quit / a new business / started / having) Point 04

4 방에서 나올 때 Amy는 전등을 껐다. (out of the room / the light / turned off / walking) Point 03

5 날씨가 좋아서 우리는 해변에 갔다. (the weather / the beach / good / being) Point 04

6 저녁을 요리하면서 그녀는 그녀의 손을 데었다. (dinner / hand / cooking / burned) Point 03

UNIT 09

특수구문

- *Point 01* 짝을 이루는 접속사
- *Point 02* 강조와 생략
- *Point 03* 부정 표현
- *Point 04* 도치

특수구문

- 짝을 이루는 접속사
  - both A and B
  - either A or B
  - neither A nor B
  - not only A but (also) B
  - not A but B
- 강조
  - it is / was ~ that ...
  - 조동사 do
- 생략
  - 반복되는 어구
  - 부사절의 「주어 + be동사」
- 부정 표현
  - 전체부정
  - 부분부정
  - 부정부사
- 도치
  - 부정어
  - 장소 · 방향의 부사 / 전치사구
  - so / neither[nor]
  - \+ 동사 + 주어

Point 01 짝을 이루는 접속사

두 개 이상의 단어가 짝을 이루는 접속사를 상관접속사라고 한다. 상관접속사가 연결하는 A, B는 **문법적인 성격이 같아야** 한다.

both A and B	A와 B 둘 다	not only A but (also) B	A 뿐만 아니라 B도 (= B as well as A)
either A or B	A 또는 B (둘 중 하나)	not A but B	A가 아니라 B
neither A nor B	A도 B도 아닌		

411 **Both** *my sister* **and** *I* / caught a cold.
S / V / O
여동생과 나 둘 다 / 감기에 걸렸다.

412 You can choose / to **either** *walk* **or** *take* the bus.
S / V / O_1 / O_2
너는 선택할 수 있다 / 걷거나 그 버스를 타는 것 둘 중 하나를

413 This coat is / **not only** *light* / **but also** *warm*.
S / V / SC_1 / SC_2
이 코트는 ~이다 / 가벼울 뿐만 아니라 / 따뜻한

다음 문장에서 밑줄 친 상관접속사로 연결된 말을 찾아 동그라미 하고, 문장을 해석하시오. 정답 및 해설 p.38

414 Neither he nor I / expected this kind of problem.
그도 나도 / 이런 종류의 문제를 예상하지 못했다.

415 You may send it either by email or by fax.

416 I like both watching sports and playing them.

417 Lily will go to Japan not for travel, but for work.

418 When I speak in front of a lot of people, I feel both excited and nervous.

419 Ken donates money to charity not because he is rich, but because he wants to help others.

다음 문장의 네모 안에서 어법상 알맞은 것을 고르고, 문장을 해석하시오.

420 Yoga helps you relieve stress as well as [strengthen / to strengthen] your body.

421 I go to work by bike not only to help the environment but also [to stay / staying] healthy.

light (빛이) 밝은; *가벼운 expect 예상하다 donate 기부[기증]하다 charity 자선 단체 relieve 없애 주다; *완화하다 strengthen 강화하다, 더 튼튼하게 하다

Point 02 강조와 생략

강조	it is/was ~ that ...	it is/was와 that 사이에 강조할 어구 삽입 (…한 것은 바로 ~이다/이었다)
	조동사 do	「do/does/did+동사원형」 형태로 동사 강조 (정말 ~하다/했다)
생략	반복되는 어구	없어도 내용을 파악할 수 있을 때 반복되는 어구 생략
	부사절의 「주어+be동사」	부사절의 주어가 주절의 주어와 같을 때 부사절의 「주어+be동사」 생략

422 **It is** Bob / <**that[who]** works / at the post office>.
S V SC (V′, M′)
바로 Bob이다 / <일하는 사람은 / 우체국에서>

강조하는 어구가 사람이면 that 대신 who를 쓸 수 있다.

423 I **do like** horror movies.
S V O
나는 공포 영화를 정말 좋아한다.

424 <While (**I was**) in the hospital>, / I kept a diary.
(S′ V′ M′) S V O
<병원에 있는 동안>, / 나는 일기를 썼다.

밑줄 친 부분에 유의하여 다음 문장을 해석하시오.

정답 및 해설 p.39

425 We do agree / <that we need a change>.
우리는 정말 동의한다 / <우리는 변화가 필요하다는 것에>

426 Kali's son is as old as Owen's.

427 Although tired, we waited until the game was over.

428 My family was worried about my injury more than I was.

429 It was in Paris that he got his first job as a model.

430 It was at the mall that I found the perfect birthday gift for my friend.

다음 문장의 네모 안에서 어법상 알맞은 것을 고르고, 문장을 해석하시오.

431 When [asking / asked] about the accident, Patrick didn't say anything.

432 I do [believe / believed] it was Kelly [that / what] sent me the invitation.

horror movie 공포 영화 keep a diary 일기를 쓰다 over 끝이 난 injury 부상 get a job 일자리를 구하다 invitation 초대; *초대장

Unit Practice

STEP 1

직독직해에 맞게 (   ) 안의 단어를 사용하여 문장을 쓰시오. (필요시 형태를 바꿔 쓸 것)

1 바로 나의 담임 선생님이었다 / 내가 만난 사람은 / 길에서 (meet / on the street / homeroom teacher)

______ ______ ______ ______ ______ / ______

______ ______ / ______ ______ ______.

2 너는 그 책을 살 수 있거나 / 온라인으로 / 또는 그것을 빌릴 수 있다 / 도서관에서 (the book / borrow / from the library / buy / online / can)

______ ______ ______ ______ ______ ______ / ______ /

______ ______ ______ / ______ ______ ______.

3 나의 가족은 스키 타러 가는 것을 즐긴다 / 겨울뿐만 아니라 / 여름에도 (go / family / in summer / skiing / enjoy / in winter)

______ ______ ______ ______ ______ / ______ ______

______ ______ / ______ ______ ______ ______.

STEP 2

밑줄 친 부분에 유의하여 다음 문장을 해석하시오.

1 While walking in the forest, we saw some ducks swimming in a pond.

2 Though some people may not remember, I did win an award for painting in school.

3 Blake was asked to try bungee jumping, but he didn't want to.

4 It was the book that I couldn't put down until the end.

5 Suffering from colds, neither Carter nor Sofia could go on the field trip.

6 The concert hall has standing areas that are close to the stage as well as seating options.

homeroom teacher 담임 선생님 pond 연못 award 상 ask 묻다; *요청하다 put ~ down ~을 내려놓다 suffer from ~로 고생하다[고통받다]
field trip 현장 학습 option 선택할 수 있는 것

정답 및 해설 p.39

STEP 3

1 ( ) 안의 단어를 문맥에 맞게 배열하고 해석하시오.

In the past, toys were mostly made of clay or wood. **It was** in the 1700s **that** people first began to make toys with other materials. They realized they could use (as / clay and wood / well / leather and paper / as). And later, after the invention of machines, metals were used. Today, of course, most toys are made of plastic.

____

Reading Q 윗글의 내용을 한 문장으로 요약하고자 한다. 빈칸 (A)와 (B)에 들어갈 말로 가장 적절한 것은?

Toys were made of clay and wood until people ___(A)___ making them out of leather, paper, and metals, but now, plastic is the ___(B)___ material for most toys.

	(A)		(B)
①	quit	……	major
②	began	……	minor
③	started	……	primary

NEW 내신기출

2 빈칸 (A), (B)에 알맞은 말을 조건에 맞게 써서 요약문을 완성하시오.

Do you text **while walking**? Then you should stop. One study has shown that it is more dangerous than texting **while driving**. You might think walking is simple, but researchers say it isn't. To walk safely, you must focus on your surroundings. However, **when texting**, you mostly focus on the screen. This can cause a dangerous accident.

조건
· 제시된 단어를 사용할 것 (필요시 형태를 바꿔 쓸 것)　· (A) 3단어, (B) 7단어로 쓸 것
· from / walk / prevents / texting / while / focus / on your surroundings

(A) ______________________ is very dangerous because texting
(B) ______________________.

1 mostly 주로　clay 점토　material 재료　realize 깨닫다　leather 가죽　invention 발명　machine 기계　metal 금속　major 주요한　minor 사소한
2 text 글; *문자 메시지를 보내다　safely 안전하게　focus on ~에 집중하다　surrounding ((*pl.*)) (주변) 환경　prevent A from B　A가 B하는 것을 막다

Point 03 부정 표현

부정문은 not을 써서 표현하는 것이 기본이지만 not 외에도 여러 표현을 사용할 수 있다. 또한, 전체가 아닌 부분을 부정하는 표현을 쓰기도 한다.

전체부정	no, none, never, neither[not ~ either], nobody	어떤 누구도[결코, 둘 다, 아무도] ~않다
부분부정	not + every / all / always / necessarily / both	모두가[항상, 반드시, 둘 다] ~한 것은 아니다
부정부사	hardly, rarely, seldom	거의[좀처럼] ~하지 않다

433 Luckily, / **none** of the passengers were hurt.
M S V
운 좋게도, / 어떤 승객도 다치지 않았다.

434 **Not every** girl likes flowers.
S V O
모든 여자아이들이 꽃을 좋아하는 것은 아니다.

435 I can **hardly** understand / his words.
S M V O
나는 거의 이해할 수가 없다 / 그의 말을

밑줄 친 부분에 유의하여 다음 문장을 해석하시오.

정답 및 해설 p.41

436 The bus never arrives / on time / in the morning.
버스는 결코 도착하지 않는다 / 제시간에 / 아침에는

437 Ariana seldom expresses her thoughts.

438 Nobody knows how lonely I am now.

439 Asking forgiveness is not always easy, but it is important.

440 Neither of us had the patience to wait in a long line at a restaurant.

441 Even though Jason rarely exercises, he has never been overweight.

다음 문장의 네모 안에서 어법상 알맞은 것을 고르고, 문장을 해석하시오.

442 That doesn't [necessary / necessarily] mean you have to pay the charge at once.

443 [No / Not] all people achieve their dreams, but [no / not] one succeeds without dreaming.

necessarily 반드시 on time 제시간에 forgiveness 용서 patience 참을성; *인내심 overweight 과체중의 charge 요금 at once 즉시, 당장

Point 04

도치

강조하고자 하는 어구가 문장의 맨 앞에 나와 **주어와 동사의 순서가 바뀌는 것**을 **도치**라 한다.

부정어(no, not, never, little, hardly 등)	부정어+be동사+주어 ~ 부정어+조동사[do/does/did]+주어+동사원형 ~
장소·방향의 부사(here, there 등) / 전치사구	부사/전치사구+동사+주어 ~
so / neither[nor]	so/neither[nor]+(조)동사+주어 ~

444 **Never** *will I* lose / my wallet / again.
조동사 S V O M
나는 절대로 잃어버리지 않을 것이다 / 내 지갑을 / 다시는

445 **Under the ocean** / *live various kinds of fish*.
M V S
바다 아래에 / 다양한 종류의 물고기가 산다.

446 I worked hard // and **so** *did Jack*.
S_1 V_1 M V_2 S_2
나는 열심히 일했다 // 그리고 Jack도 그랬다

주어와 동사의 순서에 유의하여 다음 문장을 해석하시오.

정답 및 해설 p.41

447 Here comes the train / five minutes late.
여기 기차가 온다 / 5분 늦게

448 Not only is he intelligent, but he is also kind.

449 Out of the trash can came a terrible smell.

450 In New York Harbor stands the Statue of Liberty.

451 Hardly can we imagine a world without the Internet.

452 My friend does not like broccoli, and neither do I.

구문 해석 기법

□ so나 neither[nor] 다음에 주어와 동사가 도치된 문장은 '~도 그렇다[마찬가지이다]'로 해석한다.

다음 문장의 네모 안에서 어법상 알맞은 것을 고르고, 문장을 해석하시오.

453 Little [I did / did I] imagine that our team would actually win the match.

454 These sculptures were created by the ancient Greeks, and so [these paintings were / were these paintings].

various 다양한 terrible 끔찍한; *지독한 harbor 항구 the Statue of Liberty 자유의 여신상 sculpture 조각품 ancient 고대의 Greek 그리스인

Unit Practice

STEP 1

직독직해에 맞게 ( ) 안의 단어를 사용하여 문장을 쓰시오. (필요시 형태를 바꿔 쓸 것)

1 아무도 알지 못한다 / 내가 얼마나 외로운지 / 지금 (lonely / now / know / how / nobody)

_________ _________ / _________ _________ _________ _________ / _________.

2 Becky는 전혀 생각하지 않았다 / 그녀가 그 복권에 당첨될 것이라고 (win / think / would / that / the lottery / never)

_________ _________ _________ _________ / _________ _________

_________ _________ _________ _________.

3 저기에 강이 흐른다 / 중심을 관통하여 / 도시의 (of the city / flow / through the heart / a river)

_________ _________ _________ _________ / _________ _________

_________ / _________ _________ _________.

STEP 2

밑줄 친 부분에 유의하여 다음 문장을 해석하시오.

1 In the night sky shines the bright full moon.

2 You can't drop things in space because there is no gravity.

3 Nathan doesn't believe in any superstitions, and nor do I.

4 After a long day, little was she expecting the surprise party waiting at home.

5 Not every city has a convenient public transportation system like Seoul.

6 Even though it is winter, it rarely snows these days due to the warm weather.

lottery 복권 flow 흐르다 heart 심장; *중심 bright (빛이) 밝은 full moon 보름달 drop 떨어뜨리다 gravity 중력 superstition 미신 expect 예상하다 convenient 편리한 public transportation 대중교통

STEP 3

1 ( ) 안의 단어를 문맥에 맞게 배열하고 해석하시오.

Meteora is one of the largest groups of monasteries in Greece. It is located on top of sandstone peaks. **Nobody** can easily climb them, but monks managed to build monasteries on them in the early 11th century. There were originally 24 buildings, but (them / all / remain / not / of) — only six are left today.

*monastery 수도원 **sandstone 사암(沙巖)

____

Reading Q Meteora에 관한 윗글의 내용과 일치하지 않는 것은?

① 사람들이 쉽게 접근할 수 없는 곳에 있다. ② 11세기 초에 수도승들이 지었다.
③ 24개의 건물 중에서 6개가 손실되었다.

NEW 내신기출

2 밑줄 친 ①~④ 중 어법상 틀린 2개를 찾아 해당 번호를 쓰고 바르게 고쳐 쓰시오.

A small ocean wave sees the waves in front of him ① crashing into the seashore. "I'm doomed!" he screams. ② Along another wave comes and asks, "What's the matter?" "Look!" the little wave cries. "Those waves will crash and disappear forever, and ③ so we will! I'm afraid of disappearing!" The second wave says, "Don't be frightened. Crashing ④ never means disappearing. We are not just waves but part of the ocean."

번호	적절하지 않은 어구	고쳐 쓴 어구

1 peak 봉우리 monk 수도승 manage 간신히[용케] 해내다 century 세기(백년) originally 원래 remain 남다
2 ocean 바다 crash into ~와 충돌하다 seashore 해변 doomed 운이 다한 scream 소리치다 disappear 사라지다 frightened 무서워하는

Wrap Up

정답 및 해설 p.43

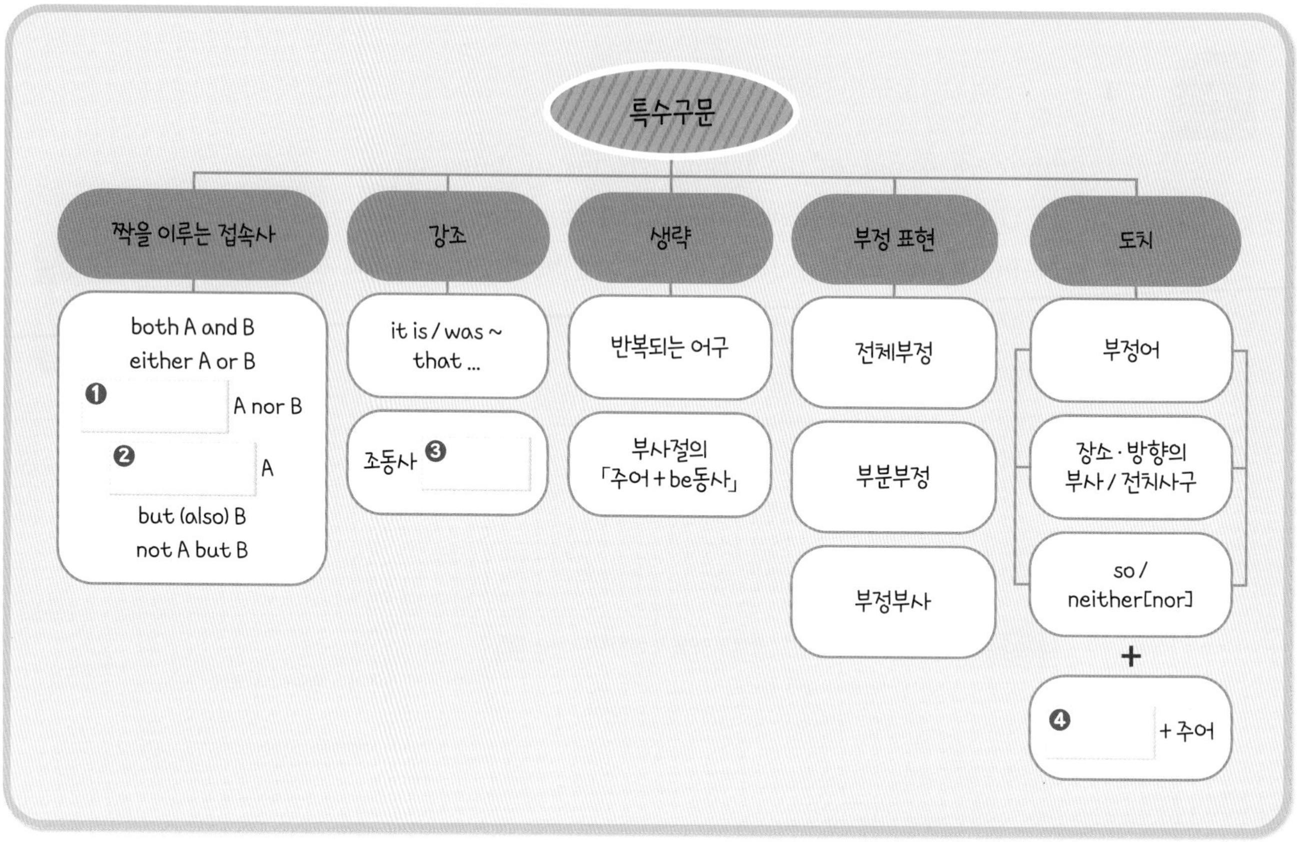

주요 예문을 다시 한번 확인하고, 우리말에 맞게 ( ) 안의 단어를 사용하여 문장을 쓰시오.

1 나는 열심히 일했고 Jack도 그랬다. (so / hard / worked) Point 04

2 우체국에서 일하는 사람은 바로 Bob이다. (at the post office / works) Point 02

3 너는 걷거나 그 버스를 타는 것 둘 중 하나를 선택할 수 있다. (either / take / to / walk / choose) Point 01

4 운 좋게도, 어떤 승객도 다치지 않았다. (of the passengers / luckily / hurt / none) Point 03

5 모든 여자아이들이 꽃을 좋아하는 것은 아니다. (likes / not / flowers / girl / every) Point 03

6 병원에 있는 동안 나는 일기를 썼다. (a diary / in the hospital / kept) Point 02

MEMO

MEMO

MEMO

지은이

NE능률 영어교육연구소

NE능률 영어교육연구소는 혁신적이며 효율적인 영어 교재를 개발하고
영어 학습의 질을 한 단계 높이고자 노력하는 NE능률의 연구조직입니다.

중학 천문장 〈LEVEL 3〉

펴 낸 이	주민홍
펴 낸 곳	서울특별시 마포구 월드컵북로 396(상암동) 누리꿈스퀘어 비즈니스타워 10층 (주)NE능률 (우편번호 03925)
펴 낸 날	2024년 1월 5일 개정판 제1쇄 발행 2024년 2월 15일 제2쇄
전 화	02 2014 7114
팩 스	02 3142 0356
홈페이지	www.neungyule.com
등록번호	제 1-68호
I S B N	979-11-253-4295-3
정 가	13,000원

고객센터

교재 내용 문의 : contact.nebooks.co.kr (별도의 가입 절차 없이 작성 가능)
제품 구매, 교환, 불량, 반품 문의 : 02-2014-7114
☎ 전화문의는 본사 업무시간 중에만 가능합니다.

중학

천문장

LEVEL 3

「구문이 독해로 연결되는 해석 공식」

정답 및 해설

NE 능률

UNIT 01

주어 찾기

Point 01 구 형태 주어 p.8

006 Facing your fears / makes you stronger.
너의 두려움을 직시하는 것은 / 너를 더 강하게 만든다.

007 The book <left on the desk> / belongs to my uncle.
그 책은 <책상 위에 놓인> / 우리 삼촌의 것이다
책상 위에 놓인 그 책은 우리 삼촌 것이다.

008 The city <where I live> / has a big public library.
도시는 <내가 사는> / 큰 공립 도서관을 가지고 있다
내가 사는 도시에는 큰 공립 도서관이 있다.

009 The long and narrow hallway / was crowded / with people.
그 길고 좁은 복도는 / 붐볐다 / 사람들로
그 길고 좁은 복도는 사람들로 붐볐다.

010 Everything <that you said / before> / came true.
모든 것이 <네가 말했던 / 전에> / 이루어졌다
네가 전에 말했던 모든 것이 이루어졌다.

011 Persuading people <in debates> / requires logical thinking.
사람들을 설득하는 것은 <토론에서> / 논리적인 사고를 필요로 한다
토론에서 사람들을 설득하는 것은 논리적인 사고를 필요로 한다.

012 My trip <to the Hawaiian Islands> / was the greatest adventure <of my life>.
나의 여행은 <하와이 섬들로의> / 가장 큰 모험이었다 <내 인생의>
나의 하와이 섬들로의 여행은 내 인생의 가장 큰 모험이었다.

Point 02 절 형태 주어 p.9

017 <That my friend is older / than me> / doesn't affect / our relationship.
<내 친구가 나이가 더 많은 것은 / 나보다> / 영향을 미치지 않는다 / 우리의 관계에
내 친구가 나보다 나이가 더 많은 것은 우리의 관계에 영향을 미치지 않는다.

018 <Whether there is life / on other planets> / is still a mystery.
<생명체가 있는지는 / 다른 행성들에> / 여전히 수수께끼이다
다른 행성들에 생명체가 있는지는 여전히 수수께끼이다.

019 <When the lecture will begin> / is posted / on the bulletin board.
<그 강의가 언제 시작할지는> / 게시되어 있다 / 게시판에
그 강의가 언제 시작할지는 게시판에 게시되어 있다.

020 [Who the winner <of the contest> is] / will be announced / tomorrow.
[우승자가 <그 대회의> 누구인지는] / 발표될 것이다 / 내일
그 대회의 우승자가 누구인지는 내일 발표될 것이다.

021 <Whether he will take part / in the competition> / is not important / anymore.
<그가 참가할지는 / 그 대회에> / 중요하지 않다 / 더 이상
그가 그 대회에 참가할지는 더 이상 중요하지 않다.

022 <Whether the projects will be successful or not> / is up to you.
<그 프로젝트들이 성공적일지 아닐지는> / 너에게 달려 있다.

023 <How babies learn languages> / has been a topic <of study> / for many years.
<아기들이 어떻게 언어를 배우는지는> / 주제가 되어 왔다 <연구의>/ 여러 해 동안
아기들이 어떻게 언어를 배우는지는 여러 해 동안 연구 주제가 되어 왔다.

Unit Practice pp.10~11

STEP 1

1 Facing your fears / makes you stronger.
풀이 동명사구 Facing your fears가 문장의 주어이며, 동사 makes, 목적어 you, 목적격보어 stronger인 5형식 문장이다.
구문 ▶ makes+목적어+목적격보어(형용사): 목적어가 ~하게 만들다
▶ 형용사-er: 더 ~한 (비교급)

2 The tree in the backyard / is growing / well.
풀이 명사구 The tree ~ backyard가 문장의 주어이다. 전치사구 in the backyard는 명사 The tree를 수식한다. 또한 '~하고 있다'로 해석되므로 동사는 현재진행형으로 쓴다.
구문 am/are/is+v-ing: ~하고 있다 (현재진행)

3 Whether we will continue this plan / will be discussed / later.

풀이 접속사 Whether가 이끄는 명사절 주어는 「접속사(Whether)+주어(we)+동사(will continue) ~」의 순서로 배열한다. 또한 '~될 것이다'로 해석되므로 동사는 미래시제 수동태로 쓴다.

구문 will be+v-ed: ~될 것이다 (미래시제 수동태)

STEP 2

1 The song playing now is my father's favorite song.

지금 재생 중인 노래는 우리 아버지가 가장 좋아하시는 노래이다.

풀이 명사구 The song ~ now가 문장의 주어이다. 현재분사구 playing now는 명사 The song을 수식한다.

2 That she was late for class was not her fault.

그녀가 수업에 늦은 것은 그녀의 잘못이 아니었다.

풀이 접속사 that이 이끄는 명사절 That ~ class가 문장의 주어이고 that절 주어는 '~하다는 것은'으로 해석한다. 명사절이 주어이므로 3인칭 단수 동사 was를 썼다.

구문 late for: ~에 늦은[지각한]

3 The coffee made from these beans doesn't suit my taste.

이 원두로 만든 커피는 내 입맛에 맞지 않는다.

풀이 명사구 The coffee ~ beans가 문장의 주어이다. made from these beans는 명사 The coffee를 수식하는 과거분사구이므로, beans에 수를 일치시켜 복수 동사를 쓰지 않도록 유의한다.

구문 made from: ~로 만든

4 How carefully you brush your teeth impacts your dental health.

치아를 얼마나 세심하게 닦는지가 너의 치아 건강에 영향을 준다.

풀이 의문사 how가 이끄는 명사절 How ~ teeth가 문장의 주어이고 How절 주어는 '어떻게 ~하는지가'로 해석한다. 명사절이 주어이므로 3인칭 단수 동사 impacts를 썼다. 동사 앞에 있는 복수 명사 teeth를 주어로 혼동하여 복수 동사를 쓰지 않도록 유의한다.

5 Why the dinosaurs went extinct is still a subject of scientific debate.

공룡이 왜 멸종했는지는 여전히 과학적 논쟁의 주제이다.

풀이 의문사 why가 이끄는 명사절 Why ~ extinct가 문장의 주어, is가 동사이다. Why절 주어는 '왜 ~하는지는'으로 해석한다.

6 Playing a musical instrument can be a fun and creative way to express yourself.

악기를 연주하는 것은 너 자신을 표현하는 재미있고 창의적인 방법이 될 수 있다.

풀이 동명사구 Playing ~ instrument가 문장의 주어이고, 명사구 a musical instrument는 동명사 Playing의 목적어이다. 동명사구 주어는 '~하는 것은'으로 해석한다.

구문 ▶ to express yourself: 명사 way를 수식하는 형용사 역할의 to부정사구

▶ yourself: to부정사 to express의 목적어 (재귀대명사)

STEP 3

1 ②
Q ②

해석 파리에 있는 The Shakespeare and Company 서점은 작가들에게 특별한 장소이다. 어니스트 헤밍웨이와 같은 유명한 작가들이 과거에 그 서점을 방문했다. 이 특별한 공동체는 읽을거리와 창의적인 환경을 제공한다. 그곳은 또한 작가들에게 머무를 장소를 제공한다. 그곳에서 일하는 대신, 그들은 그곳에서 무료로 숙박할 수 있다.

구문해설

2행 Famous writers **such as** Ernest Hemingway visited the shop *in the past*.

▶ such as: ~와 같은

▶ in the past: 과거에

4행 It also **gives writers a place** ***to stay.***

▶ give+간접목적어+직접목적어: ~에게 …을 주다

▶ to stay: 명사 a place를 수식하는 형용사 역할의 to부정사

문제해설

1 ② Ernest Hemingway는 전치사구 such as의 목적어이며, 문장의 주어는 Famous writers ~ Hemingway이다.

Q 작가들에게 읽을거리와 창의적인 환경, 머무를 곳을 제공하는 the Shakespeare and Company 서점에 관한 내용이므로, 글의 주제로는 ② '작가들을 위한 특별한 서점'이 가장 적절하다.

① 파리에 있는 독특한 호텔

③ 어니스트 헤밍웨이의 작품들

2 The way he engages his students is by rapping

해석 Hans Herrera는 칠레의 한 고등학교 교사이다. 그가 어떻게 학생들의 관심을 끄는지는 여러분을 놀라게 할지도 모른다. 그는 수업에서 랩을 한다! 그것은 학생들이 그가 한때 돈을 위해 버스에서 랩을 했다는 것을 알게 되었을 때 시작되었다. 랩을 하는 것이 인기 있는 수업 방식이 될 것인지는 불확실하다. 하지만 그의 모든 학생들은 그의 수업을 매우 좋아한다.

구문해설

2행 It began **when** his students learned *that* he once rapped for money on buses.

▶ when: ~할 때

▶ that: 동사 learned의 명사절 목적어를 이끄는 접속사 (생략 가능)

4행 But **all his students love** his class.

▶ all+복수 명사+복수 동사: 모든 ~가 …하다

문제해설

2
Q. Hans Herrera는 어떤 방법으로 그의 학생들의 관심을 끄는가?
A. 그가 학생들의 관심을 끄는 방법은 수업 시간에 랩을 하는 것이다.

관계사절의 수식을 받는 명사구를 주어로 써야 하므로, 관계부사 how 대신 선행사 the way를 써서 「the way+주어+동사 ~」의 순서로 배열한다. 주어가 단수이므로 동사는 3인칭 단수 동사 is를 쓴다. 「by+v-ing」는 '~함으로써'의 의미로 동명사구 rapping in his class는 전치사 by의 목적어로 쓰였다.

Point 03 가주어와 비인칭 주어 p.12

029 It is already eight o'clock. Let's go home.
비인칭 주어
벌써 8시다. 집에 가자.

030 It was lucky / <that I got a promotion / at work>. 가주어
행운이었다 / <내가 승진한 것은 / 직장에서>
내가 직장에서 승진한 것은 행운이었다.

031 It sounds exhausting / to take a crowded bus / every morning. 가주어
지칠 것 같다 / 붐비는 버스를 타는 것은 / 아침마다
아침마다 붐비는 버스를 타는 것은 지칠 것 같다.

032 It is certain / <that our discovery will change / people's lives>. 가주어
확실하다 / <우리의 발견이 바꿀 것이라는 것은 / 사람들의 삶을>
우리의 발견이 사람들의 삶을 바꿀 것이라는 것은 확실하다.

033 It is important / for family members / to take care of each other. 가주어
중요하다 / 가족 구성원들이 / 서로를 돌보는 것은
가족 구성원들이 서로를 돌보는 것은 중요하다.

034 It is very kind / of you / to help your sick friend.
매우 친절하다 / 네가 / 아픈 친구를 도와주다니
아픈 친구를 도와주는 것을 보니 너는 매우 친절하구나.

035 It takes about 2 hours / to get to the stadium / on foot. It may be better / <that you go there / by subway>.
약 2시간이 걸린다 / 경기장까지 가는 것은 / 걸어서. 더 나을 것이다 / <네가 그곳에 가는 것이 / 지하철을 타고>
경기장까지 가는 것은 걸어서 약 2시간이 걸린다. 그곳에 지하철을 타고 가는 것이 더 나을 것이다.

Point 04 주어의 위치 p.13

041 There will be / another great opportunity.
~이 있을 것이다 / 또 다른 멋진 기회가
또 다른 멋진 기회가 있을 것이다.

042 At the meeting, / the managers will discuss / several issues.
회의에서, / 관리자들은 토론할 것이다 / 몇 가지 안건들을
회의에서 관리자들은 몇 가지 안건들을 토론할 것이다.

043 To prepare for the test, / Owen studied / for a long time / in the library.
시험을 준비하기 위해, / Owen은 공부했다 / 오랫동안 / 도서관에서
시험을 준비하기 위해 Owen은 오랫동안 도서관에서 공부했다.

044 Before going to bed, / she always drinks / a glass of warm water.
잠자리에 들기 전에, / 그녀는 항상 마신다 / 따뜻한 물 한 잔을
잠자리에 들기 전에 그녀는 항상 따뜻한 물 한 잔을 마신다.

045 To overcome these obstacles / and achieve our goal, / what should we do?
이 장애물들을 극복하기 위해 / 그리고 우리의 목표를 달성하기 위해, / 우리는 무엇을 해야 할까
이 장애물들을 극복하고 우리의 목표를 달성하기 위해 우리는 무엇을 해야 할까?

046 Does eating less help / us lose weight / without causing health problems?
덜 먹는 것은 도와주는가 / 우리가 살을 빼도록 / 건강 문제를 야기하는 것 없이
덜 먹는 것은 건강 문제를 야기하는 것 없이 우리가 살을 빼도록 도와주는가?

047 According to the environmental report, / there are / clear signs <of global warming>.
환경 보고서에 따르면, / ~이 있다 / 확실한 징후들 <지구 온난화의>
환경 보고서에 따르면 지구 온난화의 확실한 징후들이 있다.

Unit Practice pp.14~15

STEP 1

1 It will be sunny / tomorrow morning.
풀이 날씨를 나타내는 비인칭 주어 it을 문장의 주어로 쓴다.

2 There were lots of fish / in the pond.

풀이 「there+be동사+주어+수식어구」 구문으로, 주어가 복수이므로 be동사 were를 쓰고, 그 뒤에 주어 lots of fish가 오도록 배열한다.

3 It is helpful / to experience many things.

풀이 가주어 it을 문장 앞에 쓰고 진주어를 뒤로 보낸 형태이다. 진주어 자리의 빈칸 개수로 보아 that절이 아닌 to부정사구 주어를 써야 하므로, 진주어 to experience many things를 뒤로 보내고 문장 맨 앞에 가주어 it을 쓴다.

STEP 2

1 Where are you going to go on your vacation?

너는 휴가에 어디를 갈 거니?

풀이 의문사 Where가 사용된 의문문으로, 동사 are 뒤에 나온 you가 문장의 주어이다.

구문 be going to+동사원형: ~할 것이다

2 It is exciting to watch a soccer game at the stadium.

경기장에서 축구 경기를 보는 것은 신난다.

풀이 가주어 it을 문장 맨 앞에 두고 진주어 to부정사구 to watch ~ stadium을 뒤로 보낸 형태이다. 가주어 it 자리에 진주어인 to부정사구의 내용을 넣어 해석한다.

3 There are some vegetarian dishes on the menu.

메뉴에 몇 가지의 채식주의 요리가 있다.

풀이 「there+be동사+주어+수식어구」 구문은 '~가 있다'로 해석한다. be동사 다음에 나온 명사구 some vegetarian dishes가 문장의 주어이며, 주어가 복수이므로 are를 썼다.

4 Back then, writing letters was a primary form of communication.

예전에는 편지를 쓰는 것이 주된 의사소통 방식이었다.

풀이 문장 전체를 수식하는 부사구 Back then이 문장 맨 앞에 오고, 그 뒤에 문장의 주어인 동명사구 writing letters가 쓰였다.

5 It is natural that everyone has different opinions and perspectives.

모든 사람이 다른 의견과 관점을 가지고 있는 것은 당연하다.

풀이 가주어 It, 진주어 that절 구문이다. 가주어 It 자리에 진주어 that절의 내용을 넣어 해석한다.

6 It is considerate of you to take the time to listen to my problems.

네가 나의 고민을 들어주려고 시간을 내다니 사려깊구나.

풀이 가주어 it, 진주어 to부정사구 구문이다. 가주어 it 자리에 진주어 to부정사구의 내용을 넣어 해석한다.

구문 of+명사: 사람의 성격 · 성질을 나타내는 형용사 considerate 뒤에 to부정사의 의미상 주어는 「of+명사」를 씀

STEP 3

1 (A) that drinking milk is the best way to get calcium
(B) to get calcium from beans, broccoli, and cereal
문장 해석은 아래 해석 참조

Q ②

해석 (A) 우유를 마시는 것이 칼슘을 얻는 최고의 방법이라고 생각된다. 하지만 일부 의사들은 이것이 사실이 아니라고 주장해 왔다. 그들은 우유가 뼈가 자라도록 돕는다는 것에는 동의한다. 그럼에도 불구하고 그것은 건강에 좋지 않은 당분과 지방, 그리고 동물성 단백질을 많이 함유하고 있다. 그 의사들에 따르면, (B) 콩, 브로콜리, 그리고 곡류에서 칼슘을 얻는 것이 건강에 더 좋다.

구문해설

1행 ~ **drinking milk** is the best way *to get calcium*.

▶ drinking milk: 동명사구 주어

▶ to get calcium: 명사구 the best way를 수식하는 형용사 역할의 to부정사구

2행 However, some doctors **have claimed** *that* this is not true.

▶ have/has+v-ed: ~해 왔다 (현재완료)

▶ that: 동사 have claimed의 명사절 목적어를 이끄는 접속사

3행 They agree **that** milk *helps bones grow*.

▶ that: 동사 agree의 명사절 목적어를 이끄는 접속사

▶ help+목적어+목적격보어(동사원형): 목적어가 ~하도록 돕다

문제해설

1 (A) It은 가주어이며, 진주어는 명사절 that drinking ~ calcium이다.
(B) it은 가주어이며, 진주어는 to부정사구 to get ~ cereal이다.

Q 우유에는 건강에 좋지 않은 동물성 단백질이 많다고 했으므로, 글의 내용과 일치하지 않는 것은 ②이다.

2 (A) It was Christmas Day in 1914
(B) There were no orders

해석 (A) 제1차 세계 대전 중인 1914년 크리스마스 날이었다. 그날 특별한 축하 행사가 있었다. 몇 시간 동안 수백 명의 영국, 독일, 프랑스 병사들이 전투를 중단했다. (B) 상부로부터의 명령은 없었다. 모두가 자진해서 크리스마스 캐럴을 부르고 음식을 나누었다. 한 영국 병사는 심지어 독일 적군들과 축구 경기를 시작하기도 했다.

구문해설

1행 **That day**, *there was* a special celebration.

▶ That day: Christmas Day in 1914를 가리키는 명사구

▶ there was+단수 명사: ~이 있었다

2행 **For** several hours, *hundreds of* British, German, and French soldiers **stopped fighting**.

▶ for+시간: ~ 동안

▶ hundreds of: 수백의 ~

▶ stop+v-ing: ~하는 것을 멈추다

3행 **There were no** orders *from above*.

▶ there were no+복수 명사: ~이 없었다

▶ from above: 명사 orders를 수식하는 전치사구

문제해설

2 (A) 날짜를 나타내는 비인칭 주어 It, be동사 과거형 was, 주격보어 Christmas Day, 수식어구 in 1914의 순서로 배열한다.
(B) '~이 있었다'는 「there+be동사(was/were)+주어」로 나타낸다. no orders from above가 주어이므로 be동사는 were로 쓴다.

Wrap Up p.16

❶ 동명사구 ❷ whether절 ❸ 가주어 ❹ 비인칭 주어

1 There are a lot of pictures.
2 Why the plane broke down is unknown.
3 A movie with lots of action is fun to watch.
4 It is surprising that John left for Italy.
5 It is impossible for me to solve the puzzle.
6 Overcoming[To overcome] your limits requires great bravery.

UNIT 02 목적어 찾기

Point 01 명사와 대명사 p.18

053 I visited / the Museum <of Modern Art> / yesterday.
나는 방문했다 / 박물관을 <현대 미술> / 어제
나는 어제 현대 미술 박물관을 방문했다.

054 I told her / about my vacation plan, // and she loved it.
나는 그녀에게 말했다 / 나의 휴가 계획에 대해, // 그리고 그녀는 그것을 매우 좋아했다
나는 그녀에게 나의 휴가 계획에 대해 말했고 그녀는 그것을 매우 좋아했다.

055 You should love yourself / <before you love others>.
너는 너 자신을 사랑해야 한다 / <다른 사람들을 사랑하기 전에>
너는 다른 사람들을 사랑하기 전에 너 자신을 사랑해야 한다.

056 She was carrying / an umbrella <wet from the rain>.
그녀는 들고 있었다 / 우산을 <비에 젖은>
그녀는 비에 젖은 우산을 들고 있었다.

057 Tana saw / a man <playing a violin> / and a little girl <listening to his performance>.
Tana는 보았다 / 한 남자를 <바이올린을 연주하는> / 그리고 한 어린 소녀를 <그의 연주를 듣고 있는>
Tana는 바이올린을 연주하는 한 남자와 그의 연주를 듣고 있는 한 어린 소녀를 보았다.

058 A chameleon protects itself / from danger / by changing its color.
카멜레온은 스스로를 보호한다 / 위험으로부터 / 자신의 색을 바꿈으로써
카멜레온은 자신의 색을 바꿈으로써 위험으로부터 스스로를 보호한다.

059 Some people express themselves / with their clothes. They choose / the styles and colors <that they prefer>.
어떤 사람들은 그들 자신을 표현한다 / 옷으로. 그들은 선택한다 / 스타일과 색상을 <그들이 선호하는>
어떤 사람들은 옷으로 그들 자신을 표현한다. 그들은 그들이 선호하는 스타일과 색상을 선택한다.

Point 02 동명사와 to부정사 p.19

064 The taxi driver didn't know / where to go.
그 택시 기사는 몰랐다 / 어디로 가야 할지를
그 택시 기사는 어디로 가야 할지를 몰랐다.

065 I suggested changing / the date <of the school festival>.
나는 변경할 것을 제안했다 / 날짜를 <학교 축제의>
나는 학교 축제 날짜를 변경할 것을 제안했다.

066 My little brother decided to learn / how to swim.
내 남동생은 배우기로 결심했다 / 수영하는 법을
내 남동생은 수영하는 법을 배우기로 결심했다.

067 Anna didn't give up studying / despite all the noise <around her>.
Anna는 공부하는 것을 포기하지 않았다 / 모든 소음에도 불구하고 <그녀 주변의>

Anna는 그녀 주변의 모든 소음에도 불구하고 공부하는 것을 포기하지 않았다.

068 I sometimes imagine / being a famous singer / and performing / on the stage.

나는 가끔 상상한다 / 유명한 가수가 되는 것을 / 그리고 공연하는 것을 / 무대에서

나는 가끔 유명한 가수가 되어 무대에서 공연하는 것을 상상한다.

069 I enjoy eating pizza, // but I want to have a salad / for dinner.

나는 피자 먹는 것을 즐긴다, // 하지만 샐러드를 먹고 싶다 / 저녁으로

나는 피자 먹는 것을 즐기지만 저녁으로 샐러드를 먹고 싶다.

070 The company expects / to attract more customers / by making eco-friendly products.

그 회사는 기대한다 / 더 많은 고객을 끌어모으기를 / 친환경 제품들을 만듦으로써

그 회사는 친환경 제품들을 만듦으로써 더 많은 고객을 끌어모으기를 기대한다.

Unit Practice

pp.20~21

STEP 1

1 He held an exhibition / of his photos.

풀이 동사 hold를 과거형 held로 바꿔 쓰고, 목적어로 an exhibition을 쓴 뒤, 목적어를 수식하는 전치사구 of his photos가 뒤에 오도록 배열한다.

2 We have to decide / where to stay.

풀이 동사구 have to decide의 목적어를 「where+to-v」의 순서로 배열한다.

구문 ▶ have to+동사원형: ~해야 한다

▶ where to-v: 어디에서 ~해야 할지

3 We are planning / to go hiking / next weekend.

풀이 '~하는 중이다'는 현재진행형으로 표현한다. 동사 plan은 to부정사를 목적어로 쓰는 동사이므로, 목적어를 to go hiking으로 쓴다.

STEP 2

1 Do you mind opening the window?

당신은 창문 여는 것을 상관하나요? (= 창문을 열어도 될까요?)

풀이 동사 mind의 목적어로 동명사구 opening the window가 쓰였으며, '~하는 것을[하기를]'로 해석한다.

구문 Do you mind v-ing ~?: ~해도 될까요?

2 I don't know what to wear on the first date.

나는 첫 데이트에 무엇을 입어야 할지 모르겠다.

풀이 동사 don't know의 목적어로 「what+to부정사」가 쓰였으며, '무엇을 ~해야 할지'로 해석한다.

3 Carefully, the firefighters rescued the trapped cat.

조심스럽게 소방관들은 갇힌 고양이를 구조했다.

풀이 동사 rescued의 목적어로 과거분사 trapped의 수식을 받는 명사구 the trapped cat이 쓰였으며, '~해진[된]'으로 해석한다.

4 He hurt himself while he was playing soccer with his friends.

그는 그의 친구들과 축구를 하다가 다쳤다.

풀이 주어와 목적어가 동일한 대상이므로, 동사 hurt의 목적어로 재귀대명사 himself가 쓰였다.

5 She has lost the wireless earphones that I gave her for her birthday.

그녀는 내가 그녀의 생일에 준 무선 이어폰을 잃어버렸다.

풀이 동사 has lost의 목적어로 관계대명사절 that ~ birthday의 수식을 받는 명사구 the wireless ~ birthday가 쓰였다.

구문 ▶ have/has+v-ed: ~했다 (현재완료)

▶ that: the wireless earphones를 선행사로 하는 목적격 관계대명사

6 Dorothy and I promised to keep each other's secrets forever.

Dorothy와 나는 서로의 비밀을 영원히 지키기로 약속했다.

풀이 동사 promised의 목적어로 to부정사구 to keep ~ forever가 쓰였으며, '~하는 것을[하기를]'로 해석한다.

STEP 3

1 문장 해석은 아래 해석 참조

Q ③

해석 오늘날의 십 대들은 매일 디지털 기기를 사용한다. 그들은 이른 유년기부터 그것들을 사용해 오고 있다. 그들은 문자 메시지를 보내고 온라인 게임을 함으로써 그들 자신을 즐겁게 한다. 사실 그들은 대부분의 시간을 컴퓨터와 스마트폰 화면 앞에서 보낸다. 이러한 이유로 어떤 사람들은 그들을 'screenager'라고 부른다. 이것은 'screen(화면)'과 'teenager(십 대)'의 조합이다.

구문해설

1행 They **have been using** them *since* early childhood.

▶ have/has been+v-ing: ~해 오고 있다 (현재완료 진행)

▶ since: ~ 이후로[부터]

2행 They amuse themselves **by sending** text messages *and* **playing** online games.

▶ by+v-ing: ~함으로써

▶ and: 전치사 by의 목적어인 두 개의 동명사구 sending text messages와 playing online games를 연결

5행 For this reason, some people **call them "screenagers**."

▶ call+목적어+목적격보어(명사): 목적어를 ~라고 부르다

문제해설

1 주어와 목적어가 동일한 대상일 때 목적어로 재귀대명사(themselves)를 쓰며, '그들 자신을[스스로를]'로 해석한다.

Q 디지털 기기의 화면을 들여다보며 대부분의 시간을 보내는 십 대 청소년들에 관한 글이므로, 글의 제목으로 가장 적절한 것은 ③ '화면을 응시하는 십 대들'이다.

① 더 좋은 화면 만들기

② 십 대들은 왜 그렇게 바쁜가?

2 (1) These days, there are special schools for people who want to become magicians.
(2) For example, students practice dancing, acting, and speaking in public.

해석 요즘에는 마술사가 되기를 원하는 사람들을 위한 특별한 학교들이 있다. 이 학교들에서 장래의 마술사들은 놀라운 마술을 공연하는 방법을 배운다. 그들은 또한 관객들을 즐겁게 하기 위해 필요한 다른 기술들도 개발한다. 예를 들어 학생들은 대중 앞에서 춤추고, 연기하며, 말하는 것을 연습한다.

구문해설

1행 These days, **there are** special schools for people *who* want to become magicians.

▶ there are+복수 명사: ~이 있다

▶ who: 주격 관계대명사로 who 이하는 선행사 people을 수식하는 주격 관계대명사절

2행 They also develop other skills **needed** ***to entertain an audience***.

▶ needed ~ audience: 명사구 other skills를 수식하는 과거분사구

▶ to entertain an audience: 부사 역할의 to부정사구 (목적)

문제해설

2 (1) who가 이끄는 주격 관계대명사절의 동사 want는 to부정사를 목적어로 쓰므로, becoming을 to become으로 고쳐 쓴다.
(2) 동사 practice는 동명사를 목적어로 쓰므로, to dance 이하를 동명사 dancing, acting, and speaking으로 고쳐 쓴다.

Point 03 절 형태 목적어 p.22

075 Janice asked / <how the couple first met>.
Janice는 물었다 / <그 커플이 처음에 어떻게 만났는지>
Janice는 그 커플이 처음에 어떻게 만났는지 물었다.

076 Who can explain to me / <why this room is so messy>?
누가 나에게 설명해줄 수 있니 / <왜 이 방이 너무 지저분한지>
누가 나에게 왜 이 방이 너무 지저분한지 설명해줄 수 있니?

077 I wonder / <whether the plane will take off / tomorrow>.
나는 궁금하다 / <그 비행기가 이륙할지 / 내일>
나는 내일 그 비행기가 이륙할지 궁금하다.

078 People believed / <the earth was flat> / in ancient times.
사람들은 믿었다 / <지구가 평평하다고> / 고대에
고대에 사람들은 지구가 평평하다고 믿었다.

079 I don't know / <if I'll be able to go / to the amusement park / with you>. I'll let you know / later.
나는 모르겠어 / <갈 수 있을지 / 놀이공원에 / 너와 같이>. 너에게 알려 줄게 / 나중에
나는 너와 같이 놀이공원에 갈 수 있을지 모르겠어. 너에게 나중에 알려 줄게.

080 Research has shown / [that there are some jellyfish <that can live forever>].
연구는 보여 주었다 / [일부 해파리가 있다는 것을 <영원히 살 수 있는>]
연구는 영원히 살 수 있는 일부 해파리가 있다는 것을 보여 주었다.

081 John wanted to buy a computer, // and he asked / <what the most recent model was>.
John은 컴퓨터를 사기를 원했다, // 그리고 그는 물어보았다 / <최신 모델이 무엇인지를>
John은 컴퓨터를 사기를 원했고, 최신 모델이 무엇인지를 물어보았다.

Point 04 가목적어 it p.23

085 Some cultures consider / it embarrassing / to ask another person's age.
어떤 문화들은 여긴다 / 난처하다고 / 다른 사람의 나이를 묻는 것이
어떤 문화들은 다른 사람의 나이를 묻는 것이 난처하다고 여긴다.

086 Everyone thought / it strange / <that Betty was silent / on that day>.
모든 사람은 생각했다 / 이상하다고 / <Betty가 조용했던 것이 / 그날>
모든 사람은 Betty가 그날 조용했던 것이 이상하다고 생각했다.

087 Good advice makes / it possible / to achieve better results.

좋은 조언은 만든다 / 가능하게 / 더 나은 결과를 달성하는 것을
좋은 조언은 더 나은 결과를 달성하는 것을 가능하게 만든다.

088 We consider / it important / <that kids play / in a safe environment>.
우리는 생각한다 / 중요하다고 / <아이들이 노는 것이 / 안전한 환경에서>
우리는 아이들이 안전한 환경에서 노는 것이 중요하다고 생각한다.

089 Most people think / it polite / to offer their seat / to an elderly person.
대부분의 사람들은 생각한다 / 예의 바르다고 / 자신의 자리를 권하는 것이 / 어르신께
대부분의 사람들은 어르신께 자신의 자리를 권하는 것이 예의 바르다고 생각한다.

090 He thought / it surprising / <that he could buy those sneakers / at that price>.
그는 생각했다 / 놀랍다고 / <그가 그 운동화를 살 수 있었던 것이 / 그 가격에>
그는 그 가격에 그 운동화를 살 수 있었던 것이 놀랍다고 생각했다.

091 I find it difficult / to have breakfast. However, skipping breakfast makes / it harder / to have a good day.
나는 어렵다고 생각한다 / 아침 식사를 하는 것이. 하지만 아침 식사를 거르는 것은 만든다 / 더 어렵게 / 좋은 하루를 보내는 것을
나는 아침 식사를 하는 것이 어렵다고 생각한다. 하지만 아침 식사를 거르는 것은 좋은 하루를 보내는 것을 더 어렵게 만든다.

Unit Practice pp.24~25

STEP 1

1 People believed / the earth was flat / in ancient times.
풀이 동사 believed의 명사절 목적어를 「주어(the earth)+동사(was)+주격보어(flat)」의 순서로 배열한다. 목적어로 쓰인 명사절을 이끄는 접속사 that은 생략되었다.

2 She found / it pleasant / to talk to Joy.
풀이 진목적어를 뒤로 보내고 그 자리에 가목적어 it이 오도록 배열한다. 빈칸 개수와 직독직해에 맞게 진목적어는 to부정사구인 to talk to Joy로 쓴다.

3 He considered / it brave / that she decided to travel / to Europe / alone.
풀이 진목적어를 뒤로 보내고 그 자리에 가목적어 it이 오도록 배열한다. 빈칸 개수와 직독직해에 맞게 진목적어는 that절인 「접속사(that)+주어(she)+동사(decided)+목적어구(to travel to Europe alone)」의 순서로 배열한다.
구문 decide+to-v: ~하기로 결심하다

STEP 2

1 He described which bicycle he wanted to buy.
그는 그가 어떤 자전거를 사고 싶은지를 말했다.
풀이 동사 described의 목적어로 의문사 which가 이끄는 명사절이 쓰였으며, '어떤[무슨] ~를 …하는지를'로 해석한다.
구문 want+to-v: ~하기를 원하다

2 Sam noticed that someone was following him.
Sam은 누군가가 그를 따라오고 있다는 것을 알아차렸다.
풀이 동사 noticed의 목적어로 접속사 that이 이끄는 명사절이 쓰였으며, '~하다는 것을'로 해석한다.

3 I find it difficult to stay calm in front of an audience.
나는 관중들 앞에서 침착함을 유지하는 것이 어렵다고 생각한다.
풀이 가목적어 it, 진목적어 to부정사구 구문이다. 진목적어인 to부정사구 to stay ~ audience를 가목적어 it 자리에 넣어서 해석한다.
구문 stay+형용사: ~을 유지하다

4 Before we go out, we should check if the theater is open today.
나가기 전에, 우리는 그 영화관이 오늘 문을 여는지 확인해야 한다.
풀이 동사 check의 목적어로 접속사 if가 이끄는 명사절이 쓰였으며, '~인지(를)'로 해석한다.

5 These days, she often forgets what she is supposed to do.
요즘 그녀는 무엇을 할 예정이었는지를 자주 잊어버린다.
풀이 동사 forgets의 목적어로 의문사 what이 이끄는 명사절이 쓰였으며, '무엇을 ~하는지를'로 해석한다.
구문 often: 자주 (빈도부사는 일반동사 앞에 위치)

6 Our teacher made it clear that the assignment should be submitted by next Tuesday.
우리 선생님께서는 그 과제가 다음 주 화요일까지 제출되어야 한다는 것을 확실히 하셨다.
풀이 가목적어 it, 진목적어 that절 구문으로, 진목적어 that ~ Tuesday를 가목적어 it 자리에 넣어서 해석한다.
구문 ▶ make+목적어+목적격보어(형용사): 목적어를 ~하게 만들다
▶ should: ~해야 한다 (의무)
▶ by: ~까지

STEP 3

1 that only others can tickle them
Q ①

해석 여러분은 자기 자신을 간지럼 태울 수 있는지 없는지 아는가? 대부분의 사람들은 오직 다른 사람들만이 그들을 간지럼 태울 수 있다고 말한다. 이것은 우리가 움직일 때 우리가 어떻게 느낄지를 뇌가 예측할 수 있기 때문이다. 우리가 스스로를 간질이기 위해 자신의 몸을 건드릴 때, 뇌는 이런 접촉에 대비하고 어떠한 불편한 느낌도 없애 버린다. 그것이 우리가 스스로를 간지럼 태운다면 그다지 크게 반응하지 않는 이유이다.

구문해설

1행 Do you know **whether** you can tickle *yourself* or not?

▶ whether: 동사 know의 명사절 목적어를 이끄는 접속사

▶ yourself: 여러분 자신을[스스로를] (재귀대명사)

3행 **This is because** the brain can predict *how* we will feel when we move.

▶ This is because ~: 이것은 ~하기 때문이다

▶ how: 동사 predict의 명사절 목적어를 이끄는 의문사

4행 When we touch our own body **to tickle ourselves**, ~.

▶ to tickle ourselves: 부사 역할의 to부정사구 (목적)

문제해설

1 동사 say의 명사절 목적어가 와야 하므로, 「접속사(that)+주어(only others)+동사(can tickle)+목적어(them)」의 순서로 배열한다.

Q 우리 몸의 움직임에 뇌가 미리 대비하기 때문에 스스로를 간지럼 태우는 것이 어렵다는 내용의 글이므로, 글의 주제로는 ① '왜 스스로를 간지럼 태우는 것이 어려운가'가 가장 적절하다.

② 왜 우리는 간지럼을 느낄 때 웃는가

③ 어떻게 뇌는 신체의 반응을 예측하는가

2 (A) You can tell whether[if] someone is lying
(B) we have to choose which gestures look natural

해석 (A)당신은 누군가가 거짓말을 하고 있는지를 그들의 몸짓을 봄으로써 알 수 있다. 우리가 진실을 말할 때는, 우리의 말과 몸짓 언어가 매우 자연스럽다. 그러나 우리가 거짓말을 할 때, 우리의 말에 대해 주의 깊게 생각해야 한다. (B)동시에 우리는 어떤 몸짓이 자연스럽게 보이는지를 선택해야 한다. 이런 모든 생각은 우리의 말과는 맞지 않는 몸짓 언어로 이어질지도 모른다.

구문해설

1행 You can tell whether[if] someone is lying **by watching** their gestures.

▶ by+v-ing: ~함으로써

3행 At the same time, we **have to** choose which gestures *look natural*.

▶ have to: ~해야 한다

▶ look+형용사: ~하게 보이다

4행 All this thinking may lead to body language **that** doesn't match our words.

▶ that: body language를 선행사로 하는 주격 관계대명사

문제해설

2 (A) '~인지를'이라는 뜻의 접속사 whether[if]가 이끄는 절이 동사구 can tell의 목적어가 되어야 한다. 따라서 「접속사(whether[if])+주어(someone)+동사(is lying)」의 순서로 배열한다.

(B) 동사구 have to choose의 명사절 목적어가 와야 하는데, '어떤'이라는 의미의 의문사가 필요하므로, 「의문사(which)+주어(gestures)+동사(look)+주격보어(natural)」의 순서로 배열한다.

Wrap Up

p.26

❶ to부정사 ❷ whether ❸ it ❹ that절

1 Luke didn't remember where he put his key.

2 Dana expects to pass the exam.

3 The new student introduced herself.

4 I don't know what to tell him.

5 She found it necessary to get eight hours of sleep.

6 I don't know whether[if] I'm allergic to peaches.

UNIT 03 보어 찾기

Point 01 주격보어_명사, 형용사, 분사

p.28

097 I felt depressed / <when my best friend moved away>.

나는 우울했다 / <나의 가장 친한 친구가 이사를 갔을 때>

나는 나의 가장 친한 친구가 이사를 갔을 때 우울했다.

098 <After adding some pepper>, / the soup tasted better.

<약간의 후추를 넣은 뒤>, / 그 수프는 더 맛있어졌다.

099 They got excited / <when they heard / about the free concert>.

그들은 신났다 / <그들이 들었을 때 / 무료 콘서트에 대해>

그들이 무료 콘서트에 대해 들었을 때 그들은 신났다.

100 Edwin became / the most successful businessman <in the city>.

Edwin은 되었다 / 가장 성공한 사업가가 <그 도시에서>

Edwin은 그 도시에서 가장 성공한 사업가가 되었다.

101 Having a healthy diet / is a good way <to stay in shape>.

건강한 식습관을 갖는 것은 / 좋은 방법이다 <건강을 유지하는>

건강한 식습관을 갖는 것은 건강을 유지하는 좋은 방법이다.

102 Your idea sounds creative, // but it should be more realistic.

너의 아이디어는 창의적으로 들린다, // 하지만 그것은 좀 더 현실적이어야 한다.

너의 아이디어는 창의적으로 들리지만 그것은 좀 더 현실적이어야 한다.

103 The comedy show was amusing, // so the audience was entertained.

그 코미디 쇼는 재미있었다, / 그래서 관객들이 즐거워했다

그 코미디 쇼는 재미있어서 관객들이 즐거워했다.

Point 02 주격보어_동명사, to부정사, 명사절 p.29

109 The question is / <who will win the Nobel Prize>.

문제는 ~이다 / <누가 노벨상을 탈 것인가>

문제는 누가 노벨상을 탈 것인가이다.

110 The mystery is / <how he survived the accident / without any injuries>.

수수께끼는 ~이다 / <어떻게 그가 그 사고에서 살아남았는가 / 어떤 부상도 없이>

수수께끼는 그가 어떻게 어떤 부상도 없이 그 사고에서 살아남았는가이다.

111 The most important thing <for a team> is / to have the same goal.

가장 중요한 것은 <팀에게> ~이다 / 같은 목표를 갖는 것

팀에게 가장 중요한 것은 같은 목표를 갖는 것이다.

112 One of my good habits is / washing the dishes <right after having a meal>.

나의 좋은 습관 중 하나는 ~이다 / 설거지를 하는 것 <식사를 한 뒤에 바로>

나의 좋은 습관 중 하나는 식사를 한 뒤에 바로 설거지를 하는 것이다.

113 The purpose <of this email> is / to announce a change <in the schedule>.

목적은 <이 이메일의> ~이다 / 변경을 알리는 것 <일정의>

이 이메일의 목적은 일정의 변경을 알리는 것이다.

114 <When people come late>, / a common excuse is / <that there was a traffic jam>.

<사람들이 늦게 올 때>, / 한 가지 흔한 변명은 ~이다 / <교통 체증이 있었다는 것>

사람들이 늦게 올 때 한 가지 흔한 변명은 교통 체증이 있었다는 것이다.

115 The topic <of the debate> was / <whether money brings true happiness / to our lives>.

주제는 <토론의> ~였다 / <돈이 진정한 행복을 가져오는가 / 우리의 삶에>

토론의 주제는 돈이 우리의 삶에 진정한 행복을 가져오는가였다.

Unit Practice pp.30~31

STEP 1

1 After adding some pepper, / the soup tasted better.

풀이 형용사 better가 동사 tasted 뒤에서 주격보어로 쓰이도록 단어를 배열한다.

구문 ▶ adding ~ pepper: 전치사 After의 동명사구 목적어
▶ taste+형용사: ~한 맛이 나다

2 The old house / on the hill / has remained locked / for years.

풀이 과거분사 locked가 동사 has remained 뒤에서 주격보어로 쓰이도록 단어를 배열한다.

구문 ▶ have/has+v-ed: ~해 왔다 (현재완료)
▶ for+기간: ~ 동안

3 The problem is / that we haven't saved / enough money / for the trip.

풀이 that이 이끄는 명사절이 be동사의 주격보어로 쓰였으므로, 「접속사(that)+주어(we)+동사(haven't saved)+목적어(enough money)+수식어구(for the trip)」의 순서로 배열한다.

STEP 2

1 One of my hobbies is taking pictures with my film camera.

내 취미 중 하나는 필름 카메라로 사진 찍는 것이다.

풀이 동명사구 taking ~ camera가 주격보어이며, '주어는 ~하는 것이다'로 해석한다.

2 I had a nightmare last night, and it was really terrifying.

나는 어젯밤에 악몽을 꾸었고 그것은 정말 무서웠다.

풀이 be동사 was 뒤의 현재분사구 really terrifying이 주격보어이며, '주어는 ~였다'로 해석한다.

구문 ▶ and: 앞뒤 절 연결

▶ it: 앞 절의 목적어 a nightmare를 가리키는 대명사

3 The question is <u>why the basketball player suddenly decided to retire</u>.

문제는 그 농구 선수가 왜 갑자기 은퇴하기로 결심했는지이다.

풀이 be동사 is 뒤의 의문사절 why ~ retire가 주격보어이며, '주어는 왜 ~했는지이다'로 해석한다.

구문 decide+to-v: ~하기로 결심하다

4 The best way to comfort someone is <u>to listen to their complaints</u>.

누군가를 위로하는 가장 좋은 방법은 그들의 불만을 듣는 것이다.

풀이 be동사 is 뒤의 to부정사구 to listen ~ complaints가 주격보어이며, '주어는 ~하는 것이다'로 해석한다.

구문 to comfort someone: 명사구 The best way를 수식하는 형용사 역할의 to부정사구

5 When the storm approached, the waves grew <u>more powerful</u>.

폭풍이 가까이 왔을 때 파도는 더 거세졌다.

풀이 동사 grew 뒤에 형용사구 more powerful이 주격보어이며, '주어는 ~해졌다'로 해석한다.

구문 more+형용사: 더 ~한 (비교급)

6 The main question is <u>whether the new technology will improve efficiency</u>.

주요 문제는 새로운 기술이 능률을 향상시킬 것인지이다.

풀이 접속사 whether가 이끄는 명사절 whether the new technology ~ efficiency가 주격보어이며, '주어는 ~인지이다'로 해석한다.

STEP ③

1 (A) living things (B) bigger
문장 해석은 아래 해석 참조
Q ②

해석 (A)<u>돌은 살아 있는 것이 아니다.</u> 그것들은 보통 시간이 흐르면서 더 커지지 않는다. 그러나 루마니아에 있는 'Trovants'라고 불리는 돌들은 자라는 것처럼 보인다. 그곳의 비는 그 안에 광물을 가지고 있다. 돌 안의 모래가 그 광물들과 화학적으로 반응한다. 그 반응 동안, 돌의 (표면) 위에 층이 형성된다. (B)<u>그러면서 그 돌들은 더 커진다!</u>

구문해설

2행 However, stones **called "Trovants"** *in Romania* **look like** they grow.

▶ called "Trovants": 명사 stones를 수식하는 과거분사구

▶ in Romania: 명사구 stones called "Trovants"를 수식하는 전치사구

▶ look like+주어+동사: ~이 …하는 것처럼 보이다 (like는 절을 이끄는 접속사)

4행 The sand **in the stones** *reacts* chemically *with* the minerals.

▶ in the stones: 명사 The sand를 수식하는 전치사구

▶ react with: ~와 반응하다[반응을 보이다]

문제해설

1 (A) be동사 are 뒤의 명사구 living things가 주격보어이며, '주어는 ~이다'로 해석한다.
(B) 동사 become 뒤에 나오는 형용사의 비교급 bigger가 주격보어로 쓰였고, '주어는 ~하게 되다'로 해석한다.

Q 빗물 속의 광물과 돌 안의 모래가 화학 반응을 일으켜 크기가 커지는 루마니아의 특별한 돌에 대한 글이다. 따라서 글의 제목으로는 ② '루마니아의 자라나는 돌들'이 가장 적절하다.
① 빗물 속 해로운 광물들
③ 루마니아: 돌의 나라

2 His only goal was to help others during his own difficult times.

해석 한 남자가 실직했을 때, 그는 특이한 무언가를 하기로 결심했다. 그의 결심은 가난한 낯선 사람에게 매일 10달러를 주는 것이었다. 그는 답례로 아무것도 원하지 않았다. <u>그의 유일한 목표는 자신의 힘든 시기 동안 다른 사람들을 돕는 것이었다.</u> 곧, 많은 사람들이 그의 친절한 행동을 알게 되었다. 그리고 그들 중 일부도 가난한 사람들을 돕기 시작했다.

구문해설

1행 When a man became **unemployed**, he *decided to do* **something unusual**.

▶ unemployed: 주격보어로 쓰인 과거분사

▶ decide+to-v: ~하기로 결심하다

▶ something unusual: -thing으로 끝나는 대명사는 형용사가 뒤에서 수식

His decision was **that** he would give away $10 to a poor stranger every day.

▶ that: 명사절 주격보어를 이끄는 접속사

4행 And some of them **began to help** *the poor* as well.

▶ begin+to-v[v-ing]: ~하기 시작하다

▶ the+형용사: ~한 사람들

문제해설

2 밑줄 친 우리말에 따라, 「주어(그의 유일한 목표는)+동사(이었다)+주격보어(다른 사람들을 돕는 것)+전치사구(자신의 힘든 시기 동안)」 형태로 문장을 쓴다. 보기의 단어 중 to가 있으므로 주격보어로 to부정사구를 쓰고, 시제가 과거이므로 be동사 과거형을 사용해서 문장을 쓴다.

Point 03 목적격보어_명사와 형용사 p.32

120 The writer named / the main character <of his novel> Rick.
그 작가는 이름을 지었다 / 주인공을 <그의 소설의> Rick으로
그 작가는 그의 소설의 주인공 이름을 Rick으로 지었다.

121 We found / the new system fast and efficient.
우리는 생각했다 / 새로운 시스템이 빠르고 효율적이라고
우리는 새로운 시스템이 빠르고 효율적이라고 생각했다.

122 Many people consider / the *Mona Lisa* the greatest painting <of all time>.
많은 사람들은 여긴다 / 모나리자를 가장 위대한 그림이라고 <역대>
많은 사람들은 모나리자를 역대 가장 위대한 그림이라고 여긴다.

123 They found / the festival enjoyable and moving.
그들은 생각했다 / 그 축제가 즐겁고 감동적이라고
그들은 그 축제가 즐겁고 감동적이라고 생각했다.

124 The members <of the club> elected / James the next president.
회원들은 <그 동아리의> 선출했다 / James를 다음 회장으로
그 동아리 회원들은 James를 다음 회장으로 선출했다.

125 Wearing thick boots keeps / you warm / in winter.
두꺼운 부츠를 신는 것은 유지하게 한다 / 너를 따뜻하게 / 겨울에
두꺼운 부츠를 신는 것은 겨울에 너를 따뜻하게 만든다.

126 Colorful lights will make / the show more memorable.
다채로운 조명은 만들 것이다 / 그 공연을 더 기억에 남을 만하게
다채로운 조명은 그 공연을 더 기억에 남을 만하게 만들 것이다.

Point 04 목적격보어_to부정사, 동사원형, 분사 p.33

132 I had / all the unnecessary programs removed.
나는 했다 / 모든 불필요한 프로그램들이 제거되도록
나는 모든 불필요한 프로그램들이 제거되도록 했다.

133 The prince had / his servant find the owner <of the shoe>.
왕자는 시켰다 / 그의 하인이 주인을 찾도록 <그 구두의>
왕자는 그의 하인이 그 구두의 주인을 찾도록 시켰다.

134 <When the sun set>, / I felt / the temperature drop.
<해가 질 때>, / 나는 느꼈다 / 기온이 떨어지는 것을
해가 질 때 나는 기온이 떨어지는 것을 느꼈다.

135 People didn't expect / the explorers to find treasure.
사람들은 기대하지 않았다 / 그 탐험가들이 보물을 찾을 거라고
사람들은 그 탐험가들이 보물을 찾을 거라고 기대하지 않았다.

136 I saw / him riding an electric scooter / on the street.
나는 보았다 / 그가 전동 킥보드를 타고 있는 것을 / 길에서
나는 그가 길에서 전동 킥보드를 타고 있는 것을 보았다.

137 Everyone <in the room> heard / Christmas carols playing / on the radio.
모든 사람들은 <방에 있던> 들었다 / 크리스마스 캐럴이 흘러나오는 것을 / 라디오에서
방에 있던 모든 사람들은 크리스마스 캐럴이 라디오에서 흘러나오는 것을 들었다.

138 Diana found / herself lost / in the shopping mall.
Diana는 깨달았다 / 자신이 길을 잃었다는 것을 / 쇼핑몰에서
Diana는 쇼핑몰에서 자신이 길을 잃었다는 것을 깨달았다.

Unit Practice pp.34~35

STEP 1

1 George considers / his dad a great musician.
풀이 동사 considers의 목적어 his dad의 목적격보어로 명사구 a great musician이 오도록 배열한다.

2 The writer wants / her book to be a bestseller.
풀이 동사 wants는 목적격보어로 to부정사(구)를 쓰므로, 목적어 her book 뒤에 목적격보어 to be a bestseller가 오도록 배열한다.

3 The teacher let / me read the poem / out loud.
풀이 동사 let은 목적격보어로 동사원형을 쓰므로, 목적어 me 뒤에 목적격보어 read the poem out loud가 오도록 배열한다.

STEP 2

1 My younger sister named her new doll Jolly.
나의 여동생은 그녀의 새 인형을 Jolly라고 이름지었다.
풀이 「name+목적어+목적격보어(명사)」는 '목적어를 ~라고 이름짓다'로 해석한다.

2 You should have its battery replaced.
너는 그것의 건전지가 교체되도록 해야 한다.
풀이 「have+목적어+목적격보어(v-ed)」는 '목적어가 ~되도록 하다'로 해석한다.

3 The blueberry juice turned my tongue purple when I drank it.

그 블루베리 주스는 내가 그것을 마셨을 때 내 혀가 보라색으로 변하게 만들었다.

풀이 「turn+목적어+목적격보어(형용사)」는 '목적어가 ~되게 만들다'로 해석한다.

4 Eating spicy foods like tteokbokki makes my stomach hurt.

떡볶이 같은 매운 음식을 먹는 것은 내 배를 아프게 한다.

풀이 「make+목적어+목적격보어(동사원형)」는 '목적어가 ~하게 하다'로 해석한다.

구문 ▶ Eating spicy foods: 동명사구 주어

▶ like: ~ 같은(전치사)

5 The doctor advised her to eat more fruits and vegetables.

그 의사는 그녀에게 더 많은 과일과 채소를 먹으라고 조언했다.

풀이 「advise+목적어+목적격보어(to-v)」는 '목적어에게 ~하라고 조언하다'로 해석한다.

6 I heard the dogs barking loudly from the backyard.

나는 뒷마당에서 개들이 크게 짖고 있는 소리를 들었다.

풀이 「hear+목적어+목적격보어(v-ing)」는 '목적어가 ~하고 있는 것을 듣다'로 해석한다.

STEP ❸

1 (A) feel good (B) to feel more creative
문장 해석은 아래 해석 참조

Q ①

해석 실내 화초는 좋아 보이고 (A) 그것들은 또한 우리를 기분 좋게 한다. 그것은 그것(식물)들이 공기 중 해로운 화학 물질들을 제거하기 때문이다. 사무실에 실내 화초를 가지고 있는 사람들은 일반적으로 더 낮은 혈압을 가진다. 연구에 따르면, 그것들이 우리의 스트레스를 낮춰 주기 때문에 (B) 실내 화초는 우리가 더 창의성을 느끼게 도움을 주기도 한다.

구문해설

3행 People **who** keep houseplants in their office generally have *lower* blood pressure.

▶ who: People을 선행사로 하는 주격 관계대명사로, who keep ~ office가 주격 관계대명사절

▶ 형용사-er: 더 ~한 (비교급)

6행 ~, **as** they lower our stress.

▶ as: ~하기 때문에

문제해설

1 (A) 사역동사 make는 동사원형을 목적격보어로 쓰며, '목적어가 ~하게 하다'로 해석한다.

(B) 동사 help는 to부정사 또는 동사원형을 목적격보어로 쓸 수 있으며, '목적어가 ~하도록 돕다'로 해석한다.

Q 실내 화초는 보기에 좋고, 기분과 건강에도 좋다는 내용이므로, 이 글의 주제로는 ① '실내 화초를 기르는 것의 이점'이 가장 적절하다.

② 실내 화초를 관리하는 것의 어려움

③ 실내 화초를 성공적으로 기르기 위한 조언

2 ② place → placed
④ conveniently → convenient

해석 한 남자가 손을 흔들자 전등이 켜진다. 무엇이 그로 하여금 이것을 할 수 있게 하는가? 그것은 RFID라고 불리는 컴퓨터 칩이다. 그는 그것을 피부 밑에 심어지도록 했고, 그것은 전등에 신호를 보낼 수 있다. RFID에는 많은 용도가 있다. 예를 들어, 어떤 사람들은 칩을 반려동물에 심어지도록 한다. 만약 그들(= 반려동물들)이 길을 잃어버리면, RFID는 그들(= 사람들)이 반려동물들을 찾도록 돕는다. 이 특별한 칩은 우리의 삶을 여러모로 더 편리하게 만들 수 있다!

구문해설

1행 **What** *enables him to do this*?

▶ What: 의문사 주어

▶ enable+목적어+목적격보어(to-v): 목적어가 ~할 수 있게 하다

It is a computer chip **called an RFID**.

▶ called an RFID: 명사구 a computer chip을 수식하는 과거분사구

4행 The RFIDs **help them find their pets** *if* they get lost.

▶ help+목적어+목적격보어(동사원형[to-v]): 목적어가 ~하도록 돕다

▶ if: ~한다면

문제해설

2 ② 동사 had의 목적어 it(= a computer chip)과 목적격보어 place는 수동 관계이므로, 동사원형 place를 과거분사 placed로 고쳐야 한다.

④ 「make+목적어+목적격보어」에서 목적격보어로 부사를 쓸 수 없다. 따라서 부사 conveniently를 형용사 convenient로 고쳐야 한다.

Wrap Up p.36

❶ that절 ❷ whether절 ❸ 목적격 ❹ 분사

1 Spoiled milk smells terrible.
2 Mark saw his dog running toward him.
3 His best quality is that he is honest.
4 Our main goal is helping poor children.
5 Suzy's shocking behavior left me speechless.
6 I'll let my son go camping with his friends.

UNIT 04 시제와 수동태

Point 01 시제와 진행형 p.38

145 Andrew played the drums / in a band / last year.
Andrew는 드럼을 연주했다 / 한 밴드에서 / 작년에
Andrew는 작년에 한 밴드에서 드럼을 연주했다.

146 We were playing basketball / two hours ago.
우리는 농구를 하고 있었다 / 두 시간 전에
우리는 두 시간 전에 농구를 하고 있었다.

147 The workers have not finished / building the gym / yet.
일꾼들은 끝내지 못했다 / 체육관을 짓는 것을 / 아직
일꾼들은 체육관을 짓는 것을 아직 끝내지 못했다.

148 Luke noticed / <that he had lost / his key>.
Luke는 알아차렸다 / <그가 잃어버렸다는 것을 / 그의 열쇠를>
Luke는 자신이 열쇠를 잃어버렸다는 것을 알아차렸다.

149 <Because I have used the program / for 5 years>, / I know it well.
<내가 그 프로그램을 사용해 왔기 때문에 / 5년 동안>, / 나는 그것을 잘 안다
그 프로그램을 5년 동안 사용해 왔기 때문에 나는 그것을 잘 안다.

150 <When I first met Taylor>, / I thought / <(that) I had seen her / before>.
<내가 Taylor를 처음 만났을 때>, / 나는 생각했다 / <내가 그녀를 본 적이 있다고 / 전에>
내가 Taylor를 처음 만났을 때 나는 그녀를 전에 본 적이 있다고 생각했다.

151 I have been learning English / since 2022, // and I'm still taking / English classes.
나는 영어를 배워 오고 있다 / 2022년 이후로, // 그리고 아직도 듣고 있다 / 영어 수업을
나는 2022년 이후로 영어를 배워 오고 있고 아직도 영어 수업을 듣고 있다.

Point 02 주의할 시제 표현 p.39

157 Keep in mind / <that our plane leaves / in an hour>.
명심해라 / <우리 비행기가 떠난다는 것을 / 한 시간 뒤에>
우리 비행기가 한 시간 뒤에 떠난다는 것을 명심해라.

158 She will call you back / <when she gets your message>.
그녀는 너에게 다시 전화할 것이다 / <그녀가 네 메시지를 받으면>
그녀는 네 메시지를 받으면 너에게 다시 전화할 것이다.

159 You will miss the movie / <unless you take a taxi>.
너는 그 영화를 못 볼 것이다 / <네가 택시를 타지 않으면>
택시를 타지 않으면 너는 그 영화를 못 볼 것이다.

160 Daniel is coming back / from China / tonight.
Daniel이 돌아올 것이다 / 중국에서 / 오늘 밤에
Daniel이 오늘 밤에 중국에서 돌아올 것이다.

161 He will go camping / with his family / <after he gets his driver's license>.
그는 캠핑을 갈 것이다 / 그의 가족과 / <그가 그의 운전면허증을 얻은 후>
그는 그의 운전면허증을 딴 후 그의 가족과 캠핑을 갈 것이다.

162 Parker will stay / in the hospital / <until he recovers / completely>.
Parker는 머물 것이다 / 병원에 / <그가 회복할 때까지 / 완전히>
Parker는 완전히 회복할 때까지 병원에 입원해 있을 것이다.

163 The museum opens / at 10:00 a.m. <If we arrive there / at 9:00 a.m.>, / we won't be able to go / inside.
그 박물관은 문을 연다 / 오전 10시에. <만약 우리가 그곳에 도착한다면 / 오전 9시에>, / 우리는 갈 수 없을 것이다 / 안으로
그 박물관은 오전 10시에 문을 연다. 만약 우리가 오전 9시에 그곳에 도착한다면 우리는 들어갈 수 없을 것이다.

Unit Practice pp.40~41

STEP 1

1 Luke noticed / that he had lost / his key.
풀이 Luke가 자신이 열쇠를 잃어버린 것을 알아차린 과거 시점 이전에 열쇠를 잃어버린 것이므로, that절의 동사는 과거완료 had lost로 쓴다.

2 The company is launching / the new product / next year.
풀이 부사구 next year가 예정된 가까운 미래를 나타내므로, 현재진행형 is launching이 쓰였다.

3 We are going to sweep the street / when the snow stops / tomorrow.

풀이 시간 부사절에서는 현재시제로 미래를 표현하므로, when절의 동사는 현재시제 stops로 쓴다.

구문 when: ~할 때

STEP ❷

1 When we visited Paul, he was doing the dishes.

우리가 Paul을 방문했을 때, 그는 설거지를 하고 있었다.

풀이 과거진행형 was doing은 '~하고 있었다'로 해석한다.

2 The science museum exhibition opens in a couple of days.

과학 박물관 전시회가 며칠 내에 열릴 것이다.

풀이 현재시제로 예정된 가까운 미래를 나타낼 수 있다. 부사구 in a couple of days는 예정된 가까운 미래이므로, 현재시제 opens를 미래시제로 해석한다.

3 I'm volunteering at a local charity event next weekend.

나는 다음 주말에 지역 자선 행사에서 자원봉사를 할 것이다.

풀이 현재진행형으로 예정된 가까운 미래를 나타낼 수 있다. 부사구 next weekend는 예정된 가까운 미래이므로, 현재진행형 am volunteering을 미래시제로 해석한다.

4 If the pants I ordered don't arrive tomorrow, I'll just wear this skirt.

만약 내가 주문한 바지가 내일 도착하지 않으면 나는 그냥 이 치마를 입을 것이다.

풀이 접속사 If가 이끄는 조건 부사절에서는 현재시제로 미래를 표현한다.

구문 I ordered: the pants를 선행사로 하는 목적격 관계대명사절 (목적격 관계대명사 that[which] 생략)

5 The pianist has been playing the piano for fifteen years.

그 피아니스트는 15년 동안 피아노를 연주해 오고 있다.

풀이 for fifteen years가 과거부터 지금까지의 시간의 경과를 나타내며, 현재완료 진행형 has been playing은 과거에 일어난 일이 지금도 진행되고 있음을 나타낸다. 현재완료 진행형은 '~해 오고 있다'로 해석한다.

구문 for+기간: ~ 동안

6 This historic site had remained untouched until the explorer discovered it.

그 탐험가가 그것을 발견할 때까지 그 유적지는 계속 훼손되지 않은 상태로 있어 왔다.

풀이 과거의 특정 시점 이전에 일어난 일이 과거의 어느 시점까지 영향을 미치는 과거완료 had remained는 '~해 왔다'로 해석한다.

구문 remain+형용사: 계속 ~이다

STEP ❸

1 (A) visit (B) end
문장 해석은 아래 해석 참조
Q ③

해석 행복한 밸런타인데이 보내세요! 마틴 백화점에서는 여러분을 위해 특별 할인 행사들을 합니다. 저희 백화점을 방문하시면 여러분은 저희의 새로운 수제 초콜릿을 보게 될 것입니다. 초콜릿을 사시면 무료로 예쁜 상자에 포장해 드릴 것입니다. 또한, 은반지를 구입하시면 무료 귀걸이를 받게 될 것입니다. 이러한 행사들은 2월 15일에 끝날 것입니다. 기회를 놓치지 마세요!

구문해설

3행 **If** you *buy* some, we will wrap them in a pretty box for free.

▶ if: ~한다면

▶ buy: 조건 부사절에서 현재시제로 미래를 표현

6행 **Don't miss** your chance!

▶ Don't[Do not]+동사원형: ~하지 마라 (부정명령문)

문제해설

1 (A) 접속사 If가 이끄는 조건 부사절에서는 현재시제 visit로 미래를 표현한다.
(B) 현재시제 end로 예정된 가까운 미래를 나타낼 수 있다. 이때 end는 미래시제로 해석한다.

Q 백화점에서 밸런타인데이를 위한 수제 초콜릿 판매, 초콜릿 무료 포장, 귀걸이 증정 등의 특별한 행사에 대해 홍보하는 내용의 글이므로, 글의 목적으로 가장 적절한 것은 ③이다.

2 ③ has written → wrote
④ had printed → has printed

해석 Alec Greven은 평범한 아이처럼 보인다. 하지만 그는 베스트셀러 책 *How to Talk to Girls*(여자아이들에게 말을 건네는 방법)의 저자이다. 그 책은 전 세계적으로 수만 부가 팔렸다. 3학년 때, Alec은 작문 수업 시간에 그 책을 썼고 학교 축제에서 그것을 팔았다. 곧, 그의 책은 매우 유명해졌다. 지금까지, 출판사는 그의 책을 17개의 언어로 출판했다.

구문해설

1행 Alec Greven **seems like** an ordinary kid.

▶ seem like+명사: ~처럼 보이다

But he is the author of the best-selling book ***How to Talk*** *to Girls*.

▶ how+to-v: ~하는 방법

2행 It **has sold** tens of thousands of copies *around the world*.

▶ have/has+v-ed: ~해 왔다, ~했다 (현재완료)

▶ around the world: 전 세계적으로

문제해설

2 ③ 문장에 In the third grade라는 특정 과거 시점이 나오고 그때 책을 쓴 것이므로, 과거시제 wrote가 적절하다.
④ So far가 과거부터 지금까지의 시간의 경과를 나타내므로, '~해 왔다'의 의미인 현재완료 has printed가 적절하다.

Point 03 수동태의 개념과 형태 p.42

168 These pictures were drawn / by a famous artist.
이 그림들은 그려졌다 / 한 유명한 화가에 의해
이 그림들은 한 유명한 화가에 의해 그려졌다.

169 The main dish will not be served / by the chef.
주요리는 내어지지 않을 것이다 / 주방장에 의해
주요리는 주방장에 의해 내어지지 않을 것이다.

170 The surgery will be performed / by the doctor / tomorrow.
그 수술은 행해질 것이다 / 그 의사에 의해 / 내일
그 수술은 내일 그 의사에 의해 행해질 것이다.

171 This book was not originally written / in Korean.
이 책은 원래 쓰이지 않았다 / 한국어로
이 책은 원래 한국어로 쓰이지 않았다.

172 Several paintings were moved / from his house to the museum.
여러 그림들이 옮겨졌다 / 그의 집에서 박물관으로
여러 그림들이 그의 집에서 박물관으로 옮겨졌다.

173 <After the potatoes are boiled>, / they are cut / into small pieces.
<감자들은 삶아진 뒤에>, / 그것들은 썰린다 / 작은 조각들로
감자들은 삶아진 뒤에 작은 조각들로 썰린다.

174 The price <of the travel package> / includes your hotel bill, // but breakfast is not included.
금액은 <여행 상품의> / 당신의 호텔 숙박료를 포함한다, // 하지만 아침 식사는 포함되지 않는다.
여행 상품의 금액은 당신의 호텔 숙박료를 포함하지만 아침 식사는 포함되지 않는다.

Point 04 4형식·5형식 수동태 p.43

180 New sneakers were promised / to her / by her father.
새 운동화가 약속되었다 / 그녀에게 / 그녀의 아버지에 의해
새 운동화가 그녀의 아버지에 의해 그녀에게 약속되었다.

181 They were seen / singing and dancing <on TV>.
그들이 보여졌다 / 노래하고 춤추는 것이 <TV에서>
TV에서 그들이 노래하고 춤추는 것이 보여졌다.

182 These books were bought / for my son / by his English teacher.
이 책들은 구매되었다 / 나의 아들을 위해 / 그의 영어 선생님에 의해
이 책들은 나의 아들을 위해 그의 영어 선생님에 의해 구매되었다.

183 The old castle <with the red door> / was believed to be haunted.
그 오래된 성은 <빨간 문이 있는> / 귀신이 출몰하는 것으로 믿어졌다
빨간 문이 있는 그 오래된 성은 귀신이 출몰하는 것으로 믿어졌다.

184 Visitors are not allowed / to speak loudly / or drink beverages / here.
방문객들은 허락되지 않는다 / 큰 소리로 말하는 것이 / 또는 음료를 마시는 것이 / 여기서
방문객들은 여기서 큰 소리로 말하거나 음료를 마시는 것이 허락되지 않는다.

185 <Since Joe was made / to clean his room>, / he couldn't go out.
<Joe는 시켜졌기 때문에 / 그의 방을 청소하도록>, / 그는 외출할 수 없었다
Joe는 그의 방을 청소하도록 시켜졌기 때문에 외출할 수 없었다.

186 I was called a "problem-solver." I was asked / to solve difficult tasks.
나는 '문제 해결사'라고 불렸다. 나는 부탁받았다 / 어려운 일들을 해결해 달라고
나는 '문제 해결사'라고 불렸다. 나는 어려운 일들을 해결해 달라고 부탁받았다.

Point 05 동사구 수동태와 수동태 관용 표현 p.44

191 The form was filled out / by Joanna.
그 양식은 작성되었다 / Joanna에 의해
그 양식은 Joanna에 의해 작성되었다.

192 The dumplings were filled / with tofu and vegetables.
그 만두들은 가득 차 있었다 / 두부와 채소들로
그 만두들은 두부와 채소들로 가득 차 있었다.

193 I was surprised / at the way <Joel behaved yesterday>.
나는 놀랐다 / 방식에 <Joel이 어제 행동한>

나는 어제 Joel이 행동한 방식에 놀랐다.

194 Many flyers are handed out / in front of the subway station.
많은 광고지들이 배부된다 / 지하철역 앞에서
지하철역 앞에서 많은 광고지들이 배부된다.

195 Your dream is sometimes laughed at / by others, // but don't get discouraged.
너의 꿈은 때때로 비웃음당한다 / 다른 사람들에 의해, // 하지만 좌절하지 마라
너의 꿈은 때때로 다른 사람들에 의해 비웃음당하지만 좌절하지 마라.

196 My house was broken into / by someone.
우리 집은 침입당했다 / 누군가에 의해
우리 집은 누군가에 의해 침입당했다.

197 New York is known / as the center <of fashion>, // and many stylish people are seen / there.
뉴욕은 알려져 있다 / 중심지로 <패션의>, // 그리고 많은 멋진 사람들이 보인다 / 그곳에는
뉴욕은 패션의 중심지로 알려져 있고 그곳에는 많은 멋진 사람들이 보인다.

Point 06 수동태의 다양한 형태 p.45

203 I still remember being lost / at the square.
나는 길을 잃었던 것을 아직도 기억한다 / 그 광장에서
나는 그 광장에서 길을 잃었던 것을 아직도 기억한다.

204 He wanted to be forgiven / by his father / for his actions.
그는 용서받기를 원했다 / 그의 아버지에게 / 그의 행동에 대해
그는 자기 행동에 대해 그의 아버지에게 용서받기를 원했다.

205 Her car used to be parked / next to my house.
그녀의 차는 주차되어 있곤 했다 / 우리 집 옆에
그녀의 차는 우리 집 옆에 주차되어 있곤 했다.

206 My cell phone is being repaired / now, // so I can't answer any calls.
나의 핸드폰은 수리되고 있다 / 지금, // 그래서 나는 어떤 전화도 받을 수 없다
나의 핸드폰은 지금 수리되고 있어서 나는 어떤 전화도 받을 수 없다.

207 I found out / <that the product had been manufactured / by the company / years ago>.
나는 알게 되었다 / <그 상품이 제조된 것을 / 그 회사에 의해 / 몇 년 전에>
나는 그 상품이 그 회사에 의해 몇 년 전에 제조된 것을 알게 되었다.

208 Something must be done / <before the problem becomes worse>.
무언가가 행해져야 한다 / <문제가 더 나빠지기 전에>
문제가 더 나빠지기 전에 무언가가 행해져야 한다.

209 I didn't know / [that my conversation <with Ryan> / was being recorded].
나는 몰랐다 / [나의 대화가 <Ryan과> / 녹음되고 있다는 것을]
나는 Ryan과 나의 대화가 녹음되고 있다는 것을 몰랐다.

Unit Practice pp.46~47

STEP 1

1 The surgery will be performed / by the doctor / tomorrow.
풀이 미래시제 수동태 문장으로, 「주어(The surgery)+미래시제 수동태(will be performed)+by+행위자(the doctor)+수식어구(tomorrow)」의 순서로 배열한다.

2 My pumpkin pie recipe / is written down / in my diary.
풀이 「동사+전치사」 형태의 동사구 write down이 쓰인 수동태 문장으로, 「주어(My pumpkin pie recipe)+수동태(is written down)+수식어구(in my diary)」의 순서로 배열한다.

3 How to assemble the furniture / is being shown / to us / in the video.
풀이 4형식 진행형 수동태 문장으로, 직접목적어 How to ~ furniture가 주어로 오면 간접목적어 us 앞에 전치사를 쓰므로, 「주어(How to ~ furniture)+진행형 수동태(is being shown)+전치사(to)+목적어(us)+수식어구(in the video)」의 순서로 배열한다.
구문 How+to-v: ~하는 방법, 어떻게 ~하는지

STEP 2

1 The surfer was seen riding the massive waves with ease.
그 서퍼가 거대한 파도를 쉽게 타고 있는 것이 보여졌다.
풀이 지각동사 see가 쓰인 5형식 수동태에서는 be v-ed 뒤에 보어가 남는다. 보어로 남은 현재분사 riding은 '타고 있는 것'으로 해석한다.

2 I'm worried about the interview scheduled for tomorrow.
나는 내일 예정되어 있는 면접이 걱정된다.
풀이 수동태 관용 표현 「be worried about」은 '~에 대해 걱정하다'로 해석한다.
구문 scheduled for tomorrow: 명사 the interview를 수식하는 과거분사구

3 Food waste should be thrown away in plastic bags for food waste.

음식물 쓰레기는 음식물 쓰레기를 위한 비닐봉지에 버려져야 한다.

풀이 조동사 should가 있는 동사구 수동태 should be thrown away는 '~는 버려져야 한다'로 해석한다.

구문 for food waste: 명사구 plastic bags를 수식하는 전치사구

4 He was made to help his younger sister with her math homework by his parents.

그는 그의 부모님에 의해 여동생의 수학 숙제를 도와주도록 시켜졌다.

풀이 5형식 문장 His parents made him help his younger sister with her math homework.를 수동태로 쓰면서 사역동사 make의 수동태 was made의 보어로 to부정사 to help가 쓰였다. was made to help는 '도와주도록 시켜졌다'로 해석한다.

구문 help A with B: A가 B하는 것을 돕다

5 Your password has not been changed for the past three months.

당신의 암호는 지난 3개월 동안 변경되지 않았다.

풀이 현재완료시제 부정형 수동태 문장으로, has not been changed는 '변경되지 않았다'로 해석한다.

구문 for+기간: ~ 동안

6 They were deeply disappointed with the lack of progress in the negotiations.

그들은 협상에 진전이 없어서 깊이 실망했다.

풀이 수동태 관용 표현 「be disappointed with」는 '~에 실망하다'로 해석한다.

구문 ▶ deeply: 동사구 were disappointed with를 수식하는 부사

▶ of progress in the negotiations: 명사 the lack을 수식하는 전치사구

▶ in the negotiations: 명사 progress를 수식하는 전치사구

STEP 3

1 (A) was called (B) was asked (C) made
Q (1) F (2) F

해석 흥미롭게도 돼지 저금통은 우연히 만들어졌다. 18세기에 도공들이 사용했던 점토는 'pygg'라고 불렸다. 한번은 한 영국인 도공이 pygg(로 만들어진) 항아리를 만들어 달라고 부탁받았다. 그는 그 고객이 '돼지' (모양의) 항아리를 원한다고 생각하여, 실수로 그 동물의 모양으로 항아리를 만들었다. 수 년 뒤에 20세기쯤 이 물품은 매우 인기를 끌게 되었다.

구문해설

1행 **Interestingly**, piggy banks *were created* accidentally.

▶ Interestingly: 문장 전체를 수식하는 부사

▶ was/were+v-ed: ~되었다 (과거시제 수동태)

In the 18th century, the clay **that** potters used was called "*pygg*."

▶ that: the clay를 선행사로 하는 목적격 관계대명사

▶ pygg: 수동태 was called의 명사 보어

(← In the 18th century, people called the clay that potters used "pygg.")

3행 Once, an English potter was asked **to create a pygg jar**.

▶ 수동태 was asked의 to부정사구 보어

(← Once, someone asked an English potter to create a pygg jar.)

4행 He thought (**that**) the customer wanted a "pig" jar, ~.

▶ 동사 thought의 명사절 목적어를 이끄는 접속사 that 생략

문제해설

1 (A) 주어 the clay ~ used가 pygg라고 '불리는' 것이므로, 수동태 was called로 써야 한다.

(B) 한 영국인 도공이 고객으로부터 '부탁을 받은' 것이므로, 수동태 was asked로 써야 한다.

(C) 도공이 실수로 동물 모양의 항아리를 '만든' 것이므로, made로 써야 한다.

Q (1) 고객이 부탁했던 것은 pygg로 만들어진 항아리였으나 도공이 착각하여 돼지 모양의 항아리를 만든 것이라고 했으므로, 내용과 일치하지 않는다.

(2) 돼지 저금통은 18세기에 처음 만들어졌고 그것이 인기를 끈 것은 20세기쯤이라고 했으므로, 내용과 일치하지 않는다.

2 (A) this money is called a "tip"
(B) tips are given to waiters / have been served

해석 한 이야기에 따르면 1688년에 Edward Lloyd에 의해 한 커피점이 문을 열었다. 안에는 통이 하나 있었고, 그 위에 '신속함을 보장하기 위해서'라고 쓰여 있었다. 고객들은 들어올 때 그 통 안에 돈을 넣을 수 있었다. 그렇게 하면 그들은 종업원들로부터 빠른 서비스를 받았다. (A)이제 이 돈은 'tip(봉사료)'이라고 불린다. (B)오늘날에는 고객들이 서비스를 제공받은 뒤에 종업원들에게 봉사료가 주어진다.

구문해설

2행 Inside, **there was** a container, and "To Insure Promptness" *was written* on it.

▶ there was+단수 명사: ~이 있었다

▶ was/were+v-ed: ~되었다 (과거시제 수동태)

3행 If they **did**, they got fast service from the waiters.

▶ 앞 문장에 언급된 put money inside it when they entered를 의미

문제해설

2 (A) '이 돈은 'tip'이라고 불린다'라는 의미의 현재시제 수동태 문장으로, 「주어(this money)+수동태 동사(is called)+명사 보어(a "tip")」의 순서로 배열한다.
(B) '봉사료가 종업원들에게 주어진다'라는 의미의 수동태 문장으로, 직접목적어 tips가 주어로 오면 간접목적어 waiters 앞에 전치사를 쓰므로, 「주어(tips)+수동태 동사(are given)+전치사(to)+목적어(waiters)」의 순서로 배열한다. 또한 봉사료가 주어지는 것은 고객들이 서비스를 제공받은 뒤의 일이므로, 접속사 after가 이끄는 절의 동사는 현재완료 수동태 have been served로 쓴다.

Wrap Up

p.48

❶ be동사 ❷ v-ed ❸ be ❹ been

1 I am meeting my friends this weekend.
2 A gift was given to me by him.
3 The car will be washed by my dad.
4 John was satisfied with his grade.
5 The wedding is being held outdoors.
6 I had lived in Tokyo before I moved to Osaka.

UNIT 05 조동사와 가정법

Point 01 조동사의 의미 I

p.50

214 He must be very thirsty / after finishing a race.
그는 매우 목이 마른 것이 틀림없다 / 경주를 끝낸 뒤에
그는 경주를 끝낸 뒤에 매우 목이 마른 것이 틀림없다.

215 You can stay here / <if you promise / to be quiet>.
너는 여기에 머물러도 된다 / <약속한다면 / 조용히 하기로>
조용히 하기로 약속한다면 너는 여기에 머물러도 된다.

216 Clara will take care of my cat / <while I'm on vacation>.
Clara가 내 고양이를 돌볼 것이다 / 〈내가 휴가 간 동안〉
내가 휴가 간 동안 Clara가 내 고양이를 돌볼 것이다.

217 You may look around / the museum, // but you may not take pictures.
너는 둘러보아도 된다 / 박물관을, // 하지만 사진을 찍어서는 안 된다
너는 박물관을 둘러보아도 되지만 사진을 찍어서는 안 된다.

218 My little brothers / are still afraid of heights. They will not ride / this rollercoaster.
나의 남동생들은 / 아직도 높은 곳을 무서워한다. 그들은 타지 않을 것이다 / 이 롤러코스터를
나의 남동생들은 아직도 높은 곳을 무서워한다. 그들은 이 롤러코스터를 타지 않을 것이다.

219 She's avoiding / eye contact, // and her voice is shaking. She might be lying.
그녀는 피하고 있다 / 내 눈을, // 그리고 그녀의 목소리는 떨리고 있다. 그녀는 거짓말을 하고 있는지도 모른다.
그녀는 내 눈을 피하고 있고 그녀의 목소리는 떨리고 있다. 그녀는 거짓말을 하고 있는지도 모른다.

220 Those people claim / <that they have seen a dragon / in the sky>, // but it cannot be true.
저 사람들은 주장한다 / <그들이 용을 봤다는 것을 / 하늘에서>, // 하지만 그것은 사실일 리가 없다
저 사람들은 하늘에서 용을 봤다고 주장하지만, 그것은 사실일 리가 없다.

Point 02 조동사의 의미 II

p.51

225 You will have to come / to my office / before nine o'clock.
너는 와야 할 것이다 / 내 사무실에 / 9시 전에
너는 9시 전에 내 사무실에 와야 할 것이다.

226 People must not park / their cars / in this area.
사람들은 주차해서는 안 된다 / 그들의 차를 / 이 구역에
사람들은 이 구역에 그들의 차를 주차해서는 안 된다.

227 You had better go to bed early / on the night <before the exam>.
너는 일찍 잠자리에 드는 것이 좋겠다 / 밤에 <시험 전날>
너는 시험 전날 밤에 일찍 잠자리에 드는 것이 좋겠다.

228 You should not bully / or make fun of others.
너는 괴롭혀서는 안 된다 / 다른 사람들을 놀리거나
너는 다른 사람들을 괴롭히거나 놀려서는 안 된다.

229 <As he always breaks / his promises>, / you had better not trust him.
<그는 항상 어기기 때문에 / 그의 약속을>, / 너는 그를 믿지 않는 것이 좋겠다
그는 항상 약속을 어기기 때문에 너는 그를 믿지 않는 것이 좋겠다.

230 <Before you go abroad>, / you must visit City Hall / and get a passport.

<해외에 가기 전에>, / 너는 시청을 방문해야 한다 / 그리고 여권을 받아야 한다
해외에 가기 전에 너는 시청을 방문해서 여권을 받아야 한다.

231 You don't have to pay / the entrance fee / <if you have / a membership card>.
너는 낼 필요가 없다 / 입장료를 / <네가 가지고 있으면 / 회원 카드를>
회원 카드를 가지고 있으면 너는 입장료를 낼 필요가 없다.

Point 03 조동사+have v-ed p.52

236 Joey cannot have heard / our conversation.
Joey가 들었을 리가 없다 / 우리의 대화를
Joey가 우리의 대화를 들었을 리가 없다.

237 You should not have driven / so fast / on the highway.
너는 달리지 않았어야 했다 / 그렇게 빨리 / 고속도로에서
너는 고속도로에서 그렇게 빨리 달리지 않았어야 했다.

238 The tennis player / must have trained hard / for the match.
그 테니스 선수는 / 열심히 훈련했음이 틀림없다 / 그 경기를 위해
그 테니스 선수는 그 경기를 위해 열심히 훈련했음이 틀림없다.

239 They cannot have cleaned / their rooms. They're still a mess.
그들은 청소를 했을 리가 없다 / 그들의 방을. 그것들은 여전히 지저분한 상태이다.
그들은 그들의 방을 청소했을 리가 없다. 그것들은 여전히 지저분한 상태이다.

240 Felix should have apologized / to her / <when he had the chance>.
Felix는 사과했어야 했다 / 그녀에게 / <그가 기회를 가지고 있었을 때>
Felix는 기회가 있었을 때 그녀에게 사과했어야 했다.

241 He thought / <that he might have given his friends / the wrong information>.
그는 생각했다 / <자신이 친구들에게 주었을지도 모른다고 / 잘못된 정보를>
그는 자신이 친구들에게 잘못된 정보를 주었을지도 모른다고 생각했다.

242 You may have been tired, // but you should have gone / to work. Your colleagues must have been angry.
너는 피곤했을지도 모른다, // 하지만 너는 갔어야 했다 / 일하러. 너의 동료들은 화가 났음이 틀림없다.
너는 피곤했을지도 모르겠지만 일하러 갔어야 했다. 너의 동료들은 화가 났음이 틀림없다.

Point 04 다양한 조동사 표현 p.53

247 Alberto and I / would go skiing / every winter.
Alberto와 나는 / 스키를 타러 가곤 했다 / 겨울마다
Alberto와 나는 겨울마다 스키를 타러 가곤 했다.

248 I would like to talk / about my worries.
나는 이야기하고 싶다 / 나의 고민에 대해
나는 나의 고민에 대해 이야기하고 싶다.

249 I would rather drive / than go by train.
나는 차라리 운전을 하겠다 / 기차로 가느니
나는 기차로 가느니 차라리 운전을 하겠다.

250 Jimmy used to eat / a lot of junk food / on weekends.
Jimmy는 먹곤 했다 / 많은 정크푸드를 / 주말에
Jimmy는 주말에 많은 정크푸드를 먹곤 했다.

251 I would rather have / one true friend / than a million fake ones.
나는 차라리 가지겠다 / 한 명의 진정한 친구를 / 수많은 거짓된 친구들보다
나는 수많은 거짓된 친구들보다 차라리 한 명의 진정한 친구를 가지겠다.

252 I would like to ask someone / to help me / <because I cannot do it / by myself>.
나는 누군가에게 부탁하고 싶다 / 나를 도와줄 것을 / <왜냐하면 나는 그것을 할 수 없기 때문에 / 혼자>
나는 그것을 혼자 할 수 없기 때문에 누군가에게 나를 도와달라고 부탁하고 싶다.

253 Sophia used to have / long hair, // but she cut it short / yesterday.
Sophia는 갖고 있었다 / 긴 머리를, // 하지만 그녀는 머리를 짧게 잘랐다 / 어제
Sophia는 긴 머리를 갖고 있었지만 어제 머리를 짧게 잘랐다.

Unit Practice pp.54~55

STEP 1

1 He must be / very thirsty / after finishing a race.
풀이 '~임이 틀림없다'는 강한 확신을 나타내는 조동사 must를 써서 「주어(He)+조동사(must)+동사원형(be)+주격보어(very thirsty) ~」의 순서로 배열한다.
구문 ▶ after: ~한 뒤에
▶ finishing a race: 전치사 after의 동명사구 목적어

2 I cannot hold my breath / underwater / for 30 seconds.

풀이 '~할 수 없다'는 능력을 나타내는 조동사 can의 부정형 cannot[can't]을 써서 「주어(I)+조동사(cannot)+동사원형(hold)+목적어(my breath) ~」의 순서로 배열한다.

3 You should have checked / your answers / before submitting the answer sheet.

풀이 '~했어야 했다'는 과거의 일에 대한 후회를 나타내는 「should have v-ed」를 써서 「주어(You)+동사(should have checked)+목적어(your answers) ~」의 순서로 배열한다.

구문 ▶ before: ~하기 전에

▶ submitting the answer sheet: 전치사 before의 동명사구 목적어

STEP 2

1 I would like to order a large pizza with extra cheese.

나는 치즈를 추가한 큰 사이즈의 피자를 주문하고 싶다.

풀이 would like to는 '~하고 싶다'로 해석한다.

구문 with extra cheese: 명사구 a large pizza를 수식하는 전치사구

2 You had better turn down the music or the neighbors will complain.

너는 음악 소리를 낮추는 것이 좋겠다. 그렇지 않으면 이웃들이 항의할 것이다.

풀이 충고를 나타내는 had better는 '~하는 것이 좋겠다'로 해석한다.

구문 or: 그렇지 않으면

3 Victor used to have a fear of water, but he has overcome it.

Victor는 물 공포증이 있었지만 그는 그것을 극복했다.

풀이 과거의 상태를 나타내는 used to는 '~이었다'로 해석한다.

구문 ▶ of water: 명사 a fear를 수식하는 전치사구

▶ have/has+v-ed: ~했다 (현재완료)

▶ it: a fear of water를 가리키는 대명사

4 The package might have been delivered to the wrong address.

그 소포는 잘못된 주소로 배달되었을지도 모른다.

풀이 과거의 일에 대한 추측을 나타내는 「might have v-ed」는 '~했을지도 모른다'로 해석한다.

구문 have/has been+v-ed: ~되었다 (현재완료 수동태)

5 She would always read a bedtime story to her children when they were young.

그녀는 그녀의 아이들이 어렸을 때 그들에게 잠들기 전 동화를 항상 읽어주곤 했다.

풀이 과거의 습관을 나타내는 would는 '~하곤 했다'로 해석한다.

6 We cannot have missed the bus because we were there earlier than the planned schedule.

우리는 버스를 놓쳤을 리가 없다. 왜냐하면 우리는 예정된 시간보다 더 일찍 그곳에 있었기 때문이다.

풀이 과거의 일에 대한 추측을 나타내는 「cannot have v-ed」는 '~했을 리가 없다'로 해석한다.

구문 ▶ 형용사-er than: ~보다 더 …한 (비교급)

▶ planned: 명사 schedule을 수식하는 과거분사

STEP 3

1 (A) will (B) might not

Q ①

해석 우울하게 느낄 때, 당신은 밖에 나가 다른 사람들을 만나는 것이 좋다. 집에 머무르면 당신은 결국 기분이 더 나빠질지도 모른다. 운동도 도움이 된다. 신체적으로 활동적이라면 기분이 더 나아질 (A) 것이다. 이런 활동들이 당신의 우울함을 완전히 쫓아내지는 (B) 않을지 모르지만 그것들은 도움이 될 것이다.

구문해설

1행 When you feel depressed, you **should** get out and meet other people.

▶ should: ~하는 것이 좋겠다[낫다] (충고)

2행 If you stay home, you **might** *end up* ***feeling*** **worse**.

▶ might: ~일지도 모른다 (추측)

▶ end up+v-ing: 결국 ~하게 되다

▶ feel+형용사: ~하게 느끼다

문제해설

1 (A) 문맥상 '신체적으로 활동적이라면 기분이 더 나아질 것이다'라는 의미가 자연스러우므로, 예정을 나타내는 will이 알맞다.

(B) 문맥상 '완전히 쫓아내지는 않을지 모르지만'이라는 의미가 자연스러우므로, 추측을 나타내는 might not이 알맞다.

Q 우울할 때는 밖에 나가 사람들을 만나거나 운동을 하는 등 활동적으로 행동하는 것이 도움이 된다는 내용의 글이므로, 글의 요지로 가장 적절한 것은 ①이다.

2 they would rather lose 1,000 dollars than gain nine kilograms

해석 한 설문 조사에 따르면 사람들은 자신의 체중에 신경을 많이 쓴다. 절반 이상의 사람들은 그들이 9킬로그램을 찌우느니 차라리 1,000 달러를 잃겠다고 응답했다. 이 놀라운 결과는 과체중인 사람들에 대한 사회의 의견과 관련되어 있을지도 모른다. 그들은 종종 게으르고 덜 매력적이라고 여겨진다.

구문해설

2행 This surprising result **might** be related to society's opinion of overweight individuals.

▶ might: ~일지도 모른다 (추측)

3행 They are often considered **to be lazy *and* less attractive**.

▶ 수동태 are considered의 to부정사구 보어

▶ and: 형용사 lazy와 less attractive 연결

문제해설

2 '…하느니 차라리 ~하겠다'는 「would rather ~ than ...」으로 나타낸다. 조동사 would rather 뒤에 동사원형 lose를 쓰고, 접속사 than 뒤에 동사 lose의 비교 대상이 되는 동사 gain을 동사원형으로 쓴다.

Point 05 가정법 과거/과거완료, 혼합 가정법 p.56

258 <If he had worn / a helmet>, / he might not have injured / his head.
<그가 썼더라면 / 헬멧을>, / 그는 다치지 않았을지도 모를 텐데 / 그의 머리를
그가 헬멧을 썼더라면 머리를 다치지 않았을지도 모를 텐데.

259 <If we took / a different route>, / we might avoid / the traffic jam.
<우리가 간다면 / 다른 길로>, / 우리는 피할지도 모를 텐데 / 교통 체증을
우리가 다른 길로 간다면 교통 체증을 피할지도 모를 텐데.

260 <If he had not sat / on the chair>, / it would not be broken / now.
<그가 앉지 않았더라면 / 그 의자에>, / 그것은 부서져 있지 않을 텐데 / 지금
그가 그 의자에 앉지 않았더라면 그것은 지금 부서져 있지 않을 텐데.

261 <If she had gotten / the award>, / she would have been proud / of herself.
<그녀가 받았더라면 / 그 상을>, / 그녀는 자랑스러웠을 텐데 / 그녀 스스로가
그녀가 그 상을 받았더라면 스스로가 자랑스러웠을 텐데.

262 [If I had known / <that he was / in the hospital>], / I would have visited / him.
[내가 알았더라면 / <그가 있는 것을 / 병원에>], / 나는 방문했을 텐데 / 그를
그가 병원에 있는 것을 내가 알았더라면 나는 그를 방문했을 텐데.

263 <If we had not played computer games / all night>, / we would not feel sleepy / now.
<우리가 컴퓨터 게임을 하지 않았더라면 / 밤새도록>, / 우리는 졸리지 않을 텐데 / 지금
우리가 밤새도록 컴퓨터 게임을 하지 않았더라면 지금 졸리지 않을 텐데.

264 <If I had lived in Paris / in the 1920s>, / I could have met / many famous artists.
<내가 파리에 살았더라면 / 1920년대에>, / 나는 만날 수 있었을 텐데 / 많은 유명한 예술가들을
내가 1920년대에 파리에 살았더라면 많은 유명한 예술가들을 만날 수 있었을 텐데.

Point 06 I wish/as if 가정법 p.57

269 I wish / <Bob had come to London / with me>.
좋았을 텐데 / <Bob이 런던에 왔더라면 / 나와 함께>
Bob이 나와 함께 런던에 왔더라면 좋았을 텐데.

270 Daniel acted / <as if we had not had / a fight>.
Daniel은 행동했다 / <마치 우리가 하지 않았던 것처럼 / 싸움을>
Daniel은 마치 우리가 싸움을 하지 않았던 것처럼 행동했다.

271 The car looks / <as if it had been / in an accident>.
그 차는 보인다 / <마치 났던 것처럼 / 사고가>
그 차는 마치 사고가 났던 것처럼 보인다.

272 I wish / <today were Saturday // so I could take a nap>.
좋을 텐데 / <오늘이 토요일이어서 // 내가 낮잠을 잘 수 있다면>
오늘이 토요일이어서 내가 낮잠을 잘 수 있다면 좋을 텐데.

273 She treats me / <as if I were / her private secretary>.
그녀는 나를 대한다 / <마치 내가 ~인 것처럼 / 그녀의 개인 비서>
그녀는 마치 내가 그녀의 개인 비서인 것처럼 나를 대한다.

274 I wish / [I had said goodbye / to all of my friends / <before I left>].
좋았을 텐데 / [내가 작별 인사를 했더라면 / 내 친구들 모두에게 / <내가 떠나기 전에>]
내가 떠나기 전에 내 친구들 모두에게 작별 인사를 했더라면 좋았을 텐데.

275 Kamila always talks / to me / <as if she were older / than me>.
Kamila는 항상 말한다 / 내게 / <마치 그녀가 나이가 더 많은 것처럼 / 나보다>
Kamila는 항상 마치 그녀가 나보다 나이가 더 많은 것처럼 내게 말한다.

Unit Practice

pp.58~59

STEP 1

1 If he had not sat / on the chair, / it would not be broken / now.

풀이 과거 사실과 반대되는 가정이 현재 상황에 영향을 미치는 혼합 가정법을 사용하여 「If+주어+had v-ed ~, 주어+조동사 과거형+동사원형 ….」으로 쓴다.

구문 be동사+v-ed: ~되다 (수동태)

2 I wish / I had a cute pet / at home.

풀이 '~하면 좋을 텐데'는 「I wish+가정법 과거」로 나타내므로, 「I wish+주어+동사의 과거형 ~.」으로 쓴다.

3 He ate the chicken / as if he had not eaten anything / in days.

풀이 '마치 ~였던 것처럼'은 「as if+가정법 과거완료」로 나타내므로, 「as if+주어+had v-ed ~」로 쓴다.

STEP 2

1 I wish he had let me know that he needed some help.

그가 약간의 도움이 필요했다는 것을 내게 알려 줬더라면 좋았을 텐데.

풀이 「I wish+가정법 과거완료」는 과거 사실과 반대되는 일을 나타내며 '~했더라면 좋았을 텐데'로 해석한다.

구문 ▶ let+목적어+목적격보어(동사원형): 목적어가 ~하게 하다
▶ that: 동사 know의 명사절 목적어를 이끄는 접속사

2 Jason and Ellen talked as if they had known each other for years.

Jason과 Ellen은 마치 서로를 몇 년간 알았던 것처럼 이야기했다.

풀이 「as if+가정법 과거완료」는 과거 사실과 반대되는 일을 나타내며 '마치 ~였던 것처럼'으로 해석한다.

3 If you had listened to the instructions, you wouldn't be in trouble now.

네가 그 설명을 들었더라면 넌 지금 난처하지 않을 텐데.

풀이 「If+주어+had v-ed ~, 주어+조동사 과거형+동사원형 ….」은 과거 사실과 반대되는 가정이 현재 상황에 영향을 미칠 때 쓰는 혼합 가정법 구문으로, '(만약) ~했더라면 …할 텐데'로 해석한다.

4 If the sun did not exist, we would not be here today.

태양이 존재하지 않는다면 우리는 오늘날 여기에 없을 텐데.

풀이 「If+주어+동사의 과거형 ~, 주어+조동사 과거형+동사원형 ….」은 현재 사실과 반대되는 일을 가정할 때 쓰는 가정법 과거 구문으로, '(만약) ~하면 …할 텐데'로 해석한다.

5 If we had read the reviews, we could have avoided going to the restaurant.

우리가 그 비평을 읽었더라면 우리는 그 식당에 가는 것을 피할 수 있었을 텐데.

풀이 「If+주어+had v-ed ~, 주어+조동사 과거형(could)+have v-ed ….」는 과거 사실과 반대되는 일을 가정할 때 쓰는 가정법 과거완료 구문으로, '만일 ~했더라면 …할 수 있었을 텐데'로 해석한다.

구문 avoid+v-ing: ~하는 것을 피하다

6 When Lily is in the water, she swims as if she were a mermaid.

Lily가 물속에 있을 때, 그녀는 마치 인어인 것처럼 수영한다.

풀이 「as if+가정법 과거」는 현재 사실과 반대되는 일을 나타내며 '마치 ~인 것처럼'으로 해석한다.

STEP 3

1 traveled, 문장 해석은 아래 해석 참조
Q ①

해석 여러분이 달에 간다면 여러분은 산맥과 분화구라고 불리는 그릇 모양의 구덩이를 보게 될 것이다. 그것들(산맥과 분화구)은 우주에서 온 바위들이 달과 충돌했을 때 형성되었다. 그 바위들은 달 표면의 일부분을 밀어 올렸고 일부분에는 구덩이를 만들었다. <u>여러분이 달에 간다면 여러분은 거대한 평원들도 보게 될 것이다.</u> 이런 평원들의 대다수가 용암이 분화구 안에서 식고 굳어진 뒤에 그것(용암)에 의해 만들어졌다.

구문해설

1행 **If** you **went** to the moon, you **would see** mountain ranges and bowl-shaped holes *called craters.*
▶ 가정법 과거로, 현재 일어날 가능성이 거의 없는 일을 가정
▶ called craters: 명사구 bowl-shaped holes를 수식하는 과거분사구

2행 They **were formed** when rocks *from space* crashed into the moon.
▶ was/were+v-ed: ~되었다 (과거시제 수동태)
▶ from space: 명사 rocks를 수식하는 전치사구

5행 **If** you **traveled** to the moon, you **would** also see huge plains.
▶ 가정법 과거로, 현재 일어날 가능성이 거의 없는 일을 가정

6행 Many of these plains **were made by** lava after it cooled and hardened in craters.
▶ was/were+v-ed+by: ~에 의해…되었다 (과거시제 수동태)

문제해설

1 현재 일어날 가능성이 거의 없는 일을 가정하는 가정법 과거 구문 「If+주어+동사의 과거형 ~, 주어+조동사 과거형+동사원형 ….」으로 if절의 동사는 과거형 traveled가 알맞다. '(만약) ~하면 …할 텐데'로 해석한다.

Q 달에 산맥, 분화구, 거대 평원과 같은 지형이 형성된 과정을 설명하는 글이므로, 글의 주제로 가장 적절한 것은 ①이다.

2 (A) I didn't have these ugly legs
(B) my life would be happier

해석 어느 날, 한 어린 순록이 호수에 비친 자신을 보았다. 그는 말했다. "내 뿔은 아름다워. (A) 하지만 내가 이 못생긴 다리들을 가지고 있지 않다면 좋을 텐데. (B) 내가 아름다운 다리들을 가지고 태어났다면 내 인생은 더 행복할 텐데!" 바로 그때, 그는 사냥꾼의 총소리를 들었다. 그가 도망가려고 할 때 그의 뿔이 나뭇가지에 걸렸다. 하지만 그의 다리가 그가 빠져나가도록 도왔다. "휴우!" 그는 말했다. "내가 이 튼튼한 다리를 가지고 있지 않다면 나는 지금 죽어 있을 거야!"

구문해설

1행 One day, a young reindeer saw **himself** in a lake.
▶ himself: 그[자기] 자신 (재귀대명사)

3행 **As** he *tried to run* away, his horns **became caught** in some branches.
▶ as: ~할 때
▶ try+to-v: ~하려고 하다[애쓰다]
▶ become+v-ed: (~인 상태가) 되다

4행 But his legs **helped him escape**.
▶ help+목적어+목적격보어(동사원형): 목적어가 ~하도록 돕다

문제해설

2 (A) 현재 이루기 힘든 소망이나 아쉬움은 「I wish+가정법 과거」로 표현하므로, 「I wish+주어+동사의 과거형 ~」으로 쓴다.
(B) 과거 사실과 반대되는 가정이 현재 상황에 영향을 미치고 있으므로 혼합 가정법을 사용하여 「If+주어+had v-ed ~, 주어+조동사 과거형+동사원형 ….」으로 쓴다.

Wrap Up p.60

❶ 의무·충고·금지 ❷ 추측·후회 ❸ 동사원형 ❹ 과거
❺ 과거완료

1 You must[should] not throw trash on the street.
2 She screamed as if she had seen a ghost.
3 We can see a full moon on Chuseok.
4 She would[used to] drink coffee every morning.
5 If I had a lot of money, I could buy a fancy car.
6 He may[might] have left his cell phone in the classroom.

UNIT 06 수식어구의 쓰임

Point 01 형용사적 수식어구_형용사와 전치사구 p.62

281 The government introduced / a law <against spitting / on the street>.
정부는 도입했다 / 법을 <침 뱉는 것을 금지하는 / 길에서>
정부는 길에서 침 뱉는 것을 금지하는 법을 도입했다.

282 Have you ever been / to a country <colder than Russia>?
너는 가 본 적이 있니 / 나라에 <러시아보다 더 추운>
너는 러시아보다 더 추운 나라에 가 본 적이 있니?

283 This book gives you / tips <for growing houseplants>.
이 책은 너에게 제공한다 / 조언을 <실내 화초를 키우는 것에 관한>
이 책은 너에게 실내 화초를 키우는 것에 관한 조언을 제공한다.

284 The artist is famous / for her <unique> style <of painting>.
그 예술가는 유명하다 / 그녀의 <독특한> 방식으로 <그림 그리기의>
그 예술가는 그녀의 독특한 화풍으로 유명하다.

285 If you want Indian food, / visit the <new> restaurant <opposite the theater>.
네가 인도 음식을 원한다면, / <새로운> 음식점을 방문하라 <극장 맞은편의>
네가 인도 음식을 원한다면 극장 맞은편의 새로운 음식점을 방문하라.

286 Could you bring me / the wallet <on the table>?
제게 가져다주실 수 있나요 / 지갑을 <탁자 위에 있는>
탁자 위에 있는 지갑을 제게 가져다주실 수 있나요?

287 Remember / not to keep anything valuable / inside your locker.
기억해라 / 귀중한 어떤 것도 보관하지 않을 것을 / 너의 사물함 안에
너의 사물함 안에 귀중한 어떤 것도 보관하지 않을 것을 기억해라.

Point 02 형용사적 수식어구_분사와 to부정사 p.63

293 The police officer found / the <stolen> car / last night.

경찰관은 발견했다 / <도난당한> 차를 / 지난밤에
지난밤에 경찰관은 도난당한 차를 발견했다.

294 When I was young, / I had / nothing <to worry about>.
내가 어렸을 때, / 나는 없었다 / 아무것도 <걱정할>
내가 어렸을 때 나는 걱정할 것이 아무것도 없었다.

295 I ate / the waffle <covered with strawberries and syrup>.
나는 먹었다 / 와플을 <딸기와 시럽으로 덮여 있는>
나는 딸기와 시럽으로 덮여 있는 와플을 먹었다.

296 A boy <singing on the stage> / waved his hand / at me.
남자아이가 <무대에서 노래를 부르고 있던> / 손을 흔들었다 / 나에게
무대에서 노래를 부르고 있던 남자아이가 나에게 손을 흔들었다.

297 Tara heard / the people <riding on the roller coaster> / scream.
Tara는 들었다 / 사람들이 <롤러코스터를 타고 있는> / 비명을 지르는 것을
Tara는 롤러코스터를 타고 있는 사람들이 비명을 지르는 것을 들었다.

298 [Because the doctor had / many patients <to take care of>], / she couldn't rest.
[그 의사는 있었기 때문에 / 많은 환자가 <돌볼>], / 그녀는 쉴 수 없었다
그 의사는 돌볼 환자가 많았기 때문에 쉴 수 없었다.

299 The shopping mall sets up / a Christmas tree <decorated with lights and ribbons> / every December.
그 쇼핑몰은 설치한다 / 크리스마스트리를 <전등과 리본으로 장식된> / 매년 12월에
그 쇼핑몰은 매년 12월에 전등과 리본으로 장식된 크리스마스 트리를 설치한다.

Unit Practice pp.64~65

STEP 1

1 The price of an airline ticket / is fairly high / these days.
풀이 전치사구 of an airline ticket이 명사 The price를 뒤에서 수식하도록 배열한다.

2 Tara heard / the people / riding on the roller coaster / scream[screaming].
풀이 현재분사구 riding on the roller coaster가 명사 the people을 뒤에서 수식하도록 배열한다.
구문 hear+목적어+목적격보어(동사원형[현재분사]): 목적어가 ~하는[하고 있는] 것을 듣다

3 He was looking / in the refrigerator / for milk / to put on his cereal.
풀이 to부정사구 to put ~ cereal이 명사 milk를 뒤에서 수식하도록 배열한다.
구문 was/were+v-ing: ~하고 있었다 (과거진행)

STEP 2

1 I love looking up at the sky full of stars on a clear night.
나는 맑게 갠 밤에 별들로 가득한 하늘을 올려다보는 것을 아주 좋아한다.
풀이 형용사구 full of stars가 명사 the sky를 수식하고, 형용사 clear가 명사 a night를 수식한다.
구문 love+v-ing[to-v]: ~하는 것을 대단히 좋아하다

2 The fallen leaves covered the ground like a soft blanket.
떨어진 나뭇잎들은 부드러운 담요처럼 땅을 덮었다.
풀이 과거분사 fallen이 명사 The leaves를 수식하고 형용사 soft가 명사 a blanket을 수식한다. 명사를 수식하는 과거분사는 '~된'으로 해석한다.
구문 like: ~처럼

3 Having friends to rely on makes life more pleasant.
의지할 친구들을 갖는 것은 인생을 더 즐겁게 만든다.
풀이 to부정사구 to rely on이 명사 friends를 수식한다. 명사를 수식하는 to부정사는 '~하는[할]'로 해석한다.
구문 ▶ Having friends ~ on: 동명사구 주어
▶ make+목적어+목적격보어(형용사): 목적어를 ~하게 만들다
▶ more+형용사: 더 ~한 (비교급)

4 My mom often tries to change clothes of no use into unique items.
우리 엄마는 종종 쓸모없는 옷들을 독특한 물품으로 바꾸려고 애쓰신다.
풀이 전치사구 of no use가 명사 clothes를 수식하고, 형용사 unique가 명사 items를 수식한다.
구문 ▶ often: 종종, 자주 (빈도부사)
▶ try+to-v: ~하기 위해 애쓰다
▶ change A into B: A를 B로 바꾸다

5 Ivan doesn't like math because it's the most challenging subject for him.
Ivan에게 수학은 가장 도전적인 과목이기 때문에 그는 수학을 좋아하지 않는다.

풀이 형용사구 the most challenging이 명사 subject를 수식한다.

구문 it: math를 가리키는 대명사

6 I saw someone strange leave a note on my desk.

나는 낯선 누군가가 내 책상 위에 쪽지를 두고 가는 것을 보았다.

풀이 -one으로 끝나는 대명사 someone을 형용사 strange가 뒤에서 수식한다.

구문 see+목적어+목적격보어(동사원형): 목적어가 ~하는 것을 보다

STEP ❸

1 (A) written (B) describing
Q ②

해석 *Dancing Lessons for the Advanced in Age*는 체코 작가 Bohumil Hrabal에 의해 쓰여진 소설이다. 그 이야기에는, 자신의 삶을 서술하는 한 나이 지긋한 남성이 있다. 다른 책들과는 달리, Hrabal의 책은 단 하나의 문장만을 가지고 있다! 그러나 그 책은 128페이지이다. Hrabal의 글쓰기 방식은 관심을 끌기에 매우 좋은, 독특한 형식이다.

구문해설

2행 In the story, **there is** an elderly man describing his life.

▶ there is+단수 명사: ~이 있다

4행 Hrabal's writing method is a unique style **great for *grabbing attention.***

▶ great for grabbing attention: 명사 a style을 수식하는 형용사구

▶ grabbing attention: 전치사 for의 동명사구 목적어

문제해설

1 (A) Bohumil Hrabal에 의해 '쓰여진' 소설이므로, 수동의 의미를 나타내는 과거분사 written이 어법상 맞다.

(B) 한 노인이 자신의 삶을 '서술하는' 것이므로, 능동의 의미를 나타내는 현재분사 describing이 어법상 맞다.

Q Hrabal의 소설은 128개의 문장으로 이루어진 것이 아니라 한 문장으로 되어 있고, 총 128페이지에 달한다고 하였으므로, 글의 내용과 일치하지 않는 것은 ②이다.

2 people living in the South eat Hoppin' John / made with peas

해석 미국에서는 새해 첫날 먹는 음식들이 각 지역마다 다르다. 예를 들어 남부에 사는 사람들은 완두콩으로 만들어진 걸쭉한 수프인 Hoppin' John을 먹는다. 그들은 또한 양배추 같은 녹색 채소도 먹는다. 이 채소들은 돈을 상징한다. 사람들은 그것들을 먹음으로써 많은 돈을 벌기를 바란다.

구문해설

1행 In the United States, the foods **eaten on New Year's Day** are different in each area.

▶ 명사 the foods를 수식하는 과거분사구

2행 For example, people ~ eat **Hoppin' John, a thick soup made with peas**.

▶ Hoppin' John과 a thick soup made with peas는 같은 음식을 지칭 (동격을 나타내는 콤마)

4행 People **hope to earn** a lot of money *by eating* **them**.

▶ hope+to-v: ~하기를 바라다

▶ by+v-ing: ~함으로써

▶ them: green vegetables를 가리키는 대명사

문제해설

2 현재분사구 living in the South가 명사 people을 뒤에서 수식하고, 과거분사구 made with peas가 명사구 a thick soup를 뒤에서 수식하도록 배열한다.

Point 03 부사적 수식어구_부사와 전치사구 p.66

305 <For a long time>, / shells were used / as money.

<오랫동안>, / 조개껍데기는 사용되었다 / 돈으로

오랫동안 조개껍데기는 돈으로 사용되었다.

306 The musical instruments / in this store / are <quite> expensive.

악기들은 / 이 매장의 / <꽤> 비싸다

이 매장의 악기들은 꽤 비싸다.

307 She is worried / <about her upcoming job interview>.

그녀는 걱정한다 / <그녀의 곧 있을 취업 면접에 대해>

그녀는 곧 있을 취업 면접에 대해 걱정한다.

308 Since we have met / <fairly> often, / we know each other / <well>.

우리는 만나 왔기 때문에 / <꽤> 자주, / 서로를 안다 / <잘>

우리는 꽤 자주 만나 왔기 때문에 서로를 잘 안다.

309 <Unfortunately>, / the game was canceled / due to bad weather.

<유감스럽게도>, / 그 경기는 취소되었다 / 안 좋은 날씨 때문에

유감스럽게도 안 좋은 날씨 때문에 그 경기는 취소되었다.

310 She carefully read the instructions / before starting the experiment.

그녀는 설명서를 신중하게 읽었다 / 실험을 시작하기 전에

그녀는 실험을 시작하기 전에 설명서를 신중하게 읽었다.

311 Nancy was terrible at cooking, // but now she is pretty good / at it.
Nancy는 요리에 서툴렀다, // 하지만 지금 그녀는 꽤 잘한다 / 그것을
Nancy는 요리에 서툴렀지만 지금 그녀는 요리를 꽤 잘한다.

Point 04 부사적 수식어구_to부정사 p.67

317 Everyone was shocked / to hear the price <of the tickets>. 감정의 원인
모두가 충격을 받았다 / 가격을 듣고서 <표의>
모두가 표의 가격을 듣고서 충격을 받았다.

318 My great-grandfather lived / to be ninety-five. 결과
나의 증조할아버지는 사셨다 / 95세가 되도록
나의 증조할아버지는 95세가 되셨다.

319 She joined the school choir / to develop her singing skills. 목적
그녀는 학교 합창단에 들어갔다 / 그녀의 노래 실력을 향상시키기 위해
그녀는 노래 실력을 향상시키기 위해 학교 합창단에 들어갔다.

320 My mother was disappointed / to hear / <that I failed the test>. 감정의 원인
어머니는 실망하셨다 / 듣고서 / <내가 시험에서 떨어졌다는 것을>
어머니는 내가 시험에서 떨어졌다는 것을 듣고서 실망하셨다.

321 <After it snows>, / the slope freezes / and becomes dangerous / to walk on. 형용사 수식
<눈이 온 뒤에>, / 경사지는 언다 / 그리고 위험해진다 / 걷기에
눈이 온 뒤에 경사지는 얼어서 걷기에 위험해진다.

322 He went to the store / to buy groceries, // but it was already closed.
그는 가게에 갔다 / 식료품을 사기 위해, // 하지만 가게는 이미 닫혀 있었다
그는 식료품을 사기 위해 가게에 갔지만 가게는 이미 닫혀 있었다.

323 Many paintings <in the museum> are hard / to understand.
많은 그림들은 <박물관에 있는> 어렵다 / 이해하기에
박물관에 있는 많은 그림들은 이해하기 어렵다.

Unit Practice pp.68~69

STEP 1

1 She is worried / about her upcoming job interview.
풀이 전치사구 about her ~ interview가 형용사 worried를 뒤에서 수식하도록 배열한다.
구문 be worried about: ~에 대해 걱정하다

2 Eric searched on the internet / to find the lyrics / of the song.
풀이 '목적'을 나타내는 부사 역할의 to부정사구 to find ~ song이 동사구 searched on the internet을 뒤에서 수식하도록 배열한다.
구문 of the song: 명사 the lyrics를 수식하는 전치사구

3 I always feel too sleepy / on Monday mornings.
풀이 빈도부사 always가 동사구 feel too ~ mornings를 앞에서 수식한다. 부사 too가 형용사 sleepy를 앞에서 수식하도록 배열하고, 전치사구 on Monday mornings는 동사구 feel too sleepy를 뒤에서 수식하도록 배열한다.
구문 always: 항상 (빈도부사는 일반동사 앞에 위치)

STEP 2

1 My rival runs really fast, so I must practice running as best as I can.
내 경쟁 상대는 아주 빨리 달려서 나는 내가 할 수 있는 한 최선을 다해 달리기를 연습해야 한다.
풀이 부사 really가 부사 fast를 앞에서 수식한다.
구문 ▶ practice+v-ing: ~하는 것을 연습하다
▶ as+부사+as+주어+can: ~가 할 수 있는 한 …하게 (원급 비교)

2 It seemed that she was embarrassed to forget her lines during the school play.
그녀는 학교 연극 중에 그녀의 대사를 잊어버려서 당황한 것처럼 보였다.
풀이 to forget ~ play는 embarrassed라는 '감정의 원인'을 나타내는 부사 역할의 to부정사구로 '~해서[하게 되어서]'로 해석한다.
구문 ▶ it 가주어, that절 진주어
▶ during+기간: ~ 동안, ~ 중에

3 A nice hotel room is expensive to book during the holiday season.
휴가철 동안 좋은 호텔 객실은 예약하기에 비싸다.
풀이 to book ~ season은 형용사 expensive를 수식하는 부사 역할의 to부정사구로 '~하기에'로 해석한다.

4 In the morning, Matthew woke up to find himself late for school.

아침에 Matthew는 일어나 보니 그가 학교에 지각한 것을 알게 되었다.

풀이 to find himself late for school은 woke up의 '결과'를 나타내는 부사 역할의 to부정사구로 '~해서 결국 …하다'로 해석한다.

5 With his creativity and talent, Steve Jobs absolutely deserved to win the Nobel Prize.

그의 창의력과 재능으로 스티브 잡스는 틀림없이 노벨상을 받을 만했다.

풀이 부사 absolutely는 동사 deserved를 수식한다.

구문 deserve+to-v: ~을 받을 만하다

6 The movie must be amazing to have been seen by so many people.

그렇게 많은 사람들에게 보여진 것을 보면 그 영화는 굉장한 것임이 틀림없다.

풀이 to have ~ people은 must be amazing이라는 '판단의 근거'를 나타내는 부사 역할의 to부정사구로 '~하는 것을 보면[하다니]'로 해석한다.

구문 ▶ must: ~임이 틀림없다 (강한 확신)

▶ have/has been v-ed: ~되어 왔다 (현재완료 수동태)

STEP 3

1 문장 해석은 아래 해석 참조
Q ②

해석 타이거피시는 아프리카에서 발견된다. 그들의 이름에서 추측할 수 있듯이, 그들은 큰 이빨을 가졌다. 타이거피시는 자라서 1.5미터 길이가 될 수 있고, 무게가 70킬로그램이 넘을 수 있다. 몇몇 배고픈 타이거피시들은 물 밖으로 튀어나와 날고 있는 새들을 잡아챈다! 이것은 심지어 카메라의 필름에도 잡혔다. 사람들은 타이거피시가 먹이를 잡기 위해 뛰어오르는 것을 보고서 종종 놀란다.

구문해설

1행 Tigerfish **are found** in Africa.

▶ am/are/is+v-ed: ~되다 (수동태)

2행 Tigerfish can grow **to be 1.5 meters long**, and they can weigh over 70 kilograms.

▶ 부사 역할의 to부정사구 (결과)

4행 Some hungry tigerfish grab **flying** birds *out of the air*!

▶ flying: 날고 있는 (현재분사)

▶ out of the air: 동사 grab을 수식하는 전치사구

5행 People are **often** surprised to *see them jump* to catch their prey.

▶ often: 자주 (빈도부사)

▶ see+목적어+목적격보어(동사원형): 목적어가 ~하는 것을 보다

문제해설

1 to see ~ prey는 surprised의 원인 즉, '감정의 원인'을 나타내는 부사 역할의 to부정사구로 '~해서[하게 되어서]'로 해석한다. 또한 to catch their prey는 앞의 동사 jump의 '목적'을 나타내는 부사 역할의 to부정사구로 '~하기 위해'로 해석한다.

Q 타이거피시라는 이름에서 연상할 수 있듯이 큰 이빨을 가지고 있다고는 했지만 호랑이의 이빨보다 크다고 하지는 않았으므로, 글의 내용과 일치하지 않는 것은 ②이다.

2 ② causing → to cause
③ careful → carefully

해석 사람들은 스트레스를 풀기 위해 종종 음식을 먹는다. 문제는 사람들이 일반적으로 정크푸드를 선택한다는 것이다. 시간이 흐르면서, 이러한 행동은 체중 증가와 높은 콜레스테롤 수치를 야기할 수 있다. 따라서 스트레스를 받을 때 신중하게 생각하라. 긴장을 풀 필요가 있을 때는, 프렌치프라이를 먹는 대신에 산책을 하는 것이 어떨까?

구문해설

1행 People often eat **to relieve stress**.

▶ 부사 역할의 to부정사구 (목적)

The problem is **that** they generally choose junk food.

▶ that: 명사절 주격보어를 이끄는 접속사

3행 When you **need to relax**, *why not go* for a walk **instead of** *eating french fries*?

▶ need+to-v: ~할 필요가 있다

▶ why not+동사원형 ~?: ~하는 게 어때?

▶ instead of: ~ 대신에

▶ eating french fries: 전치사 instead of의 동명사구 목적어

문제해설

2 ② 「be동사+likely+to부정사」에서 형용사 likely를 수식하는 부사 역할의 to부정사이므로, causing을 to cause로 고쳐야 한다.
③ 동사 think를 수식하려면 형용사가 아닌 부사가 와야 한다. 따라서 careful을 carefully로 고쳐야 한다.

Wrap Up

p.70

❶ 형용사 ❷ 과거분사 ❸ 부사 ❹ to부정사(구)

1 We're[We are] glad to see you graduate.
2 Jimmy grew up to become a professor.
3 She probably likes your present.
4 In a hurry, we ran across the road.
5 The elementary school near my home will be closed.
6 The girl smiling brightly must be Luna.

UNIT 07 관계사절

Point 01 관계대명사와 관계부사 p.72

328 *The man* <who saved the child / from drowning> / is a hero.
그 남자는 <어린이를 구했던 / 물에 빠진> / 영웅이다
물에 빠진 어린이를 구했던 그 남자는 영웅이다.

329 Do you know / *the reason* <why they changed their minds>?
너는 아니 / 이유를 <그들이 마음을 바꾼>
너는 그들이 마음을 바꾼 이유를 아니?

330 Last Saturday was / *the day* <when my best friend got married>.
지난 토요일은 ~이었다 / 날 <나의 가장 친한 친구가 결혼한>
지난 토요일은 나의 가장 친한 친구가 결혼한 날이었다.

331 I need / *a big bag* <into which I can put / all my books>.
나는 필요하다 / 큰 가방이 <안에 넣을 수 있는 / 나의 모든 책들을>
나는 내 모든 책들을 넣을 수 있는 큰 가방이 필요하다.

332 Be careful / [when you drive / on *a road* <where traffic is heavy>].
조심해라 / [운전할 때 / 도로에서 <교통이 혼잡한>]
교통이 혼잡한 도로에서 운전할 때 조심해라.

333 Can you tell me / *the way* <you manage your time>?
내게 말해줄 수 있니 / 방법을 <네가 시간을 관리하는>
내게 네가 시간을 관리하는 방법을 말해줄 수 있니?

334 *The principles* <on which his theory is based> / are out of date.
원리들은 <그의 이론의 근거가 되는> / 구식이다
그의 이론의 근거가 되는 원리들은 구식이다.

Point 02 관계사의 계속적 용법과 생략 p.73

339 James is going out / with *Clara*, / <who is his classmate>.
James는 사귀고 있는데 / Clara와, / <그녀는 그의 학급 친구이다>
James는 Clara와 사귀고 있는데, 그녀는 그의 학급 친구이다.

340 Rudolph was / *a reindeer* <(which[that]) others laughed at>.
루돌프는 ~이었다 / 순록 <다른 이들이 비웃던>
루돌프는 다른 이들이 비웃던 순록이었다.

341 Ally met *a man*, / <who was a firefighter>, / on the train.
Ally는 한 남자를 만났는데, / <그는 소방관이었다>, / 기차에서
Ally는 기차에서 한 남자를 만났는데, 그는 소방관이었다.

342 Who is / *the person* <(whom[who/that]) you traveled / to Vietnam with>?
누가 ~이니 / 사람 <네가 여행 갔던 / 베트남으로 같이>
누가 네가 베트남으로 같이 여행 갔던 사람이니?

343 Benjamin said / *<he lived in Toronto>*, / <which turned out / to be false>.
Benjamin은 말했다 / <그가 토론토에 산다고>, / <그것은 드러났다 / 거짓으로>
Benjamin은 그가 토론토에 산다고 말했는데, 그것은 거짓으로 드러났다.

344 Louis spent the summer / with *his aunt*, / <who taught him / to speak English>.
Louis는 여름을 보냈다 / 그의 이모와, / <그녀는 그에게 가르쳐 주었다 / 영어로 말하는 것을>
Louis는 그의 이모와 여름을 보냈는데, 그녀는 그에게 영어로 말하는 것을 가르쳐 주었다.

345 Mechanical problems were found / with *the cars*, / <which led to lower sales>.
기계상의 문제가 발견되었다 / 그 차들에서, / <그것은 더 낮은 판매량으로 이어졌다>
그 차들에서 기계상의 문제가 발견되었는데, 그것은 더 낮은 판매량으로 이어졌다.

Unit Practice pp.74~75

STEP 1

1 He bought *a sofa* / that four people can sit on.
풀이 선행사 a sofa 뒤에 관계대명사절 that four ~ on이 오도록 배열한다. 선행사가 전치사의 목적어일 때 관계대명사 앞으로 전치사를 이동할 수 있으나 관계대명사가 that일 때는 전치사를 이동할 수 없으므로, 전치사 on을 문장 맨 끝에 쓴다.

2 My closest friend is *Katlin*, / who is honest and diligent.
풀이 주격보어로 쓰인 명사 Katlin 뒤에, Katlin을 선행사로 하는 계속적 용법의 주격 관계대명사절 who ~ diligent가 오도록 배열한다.
구문 형용사-est: 가장 ~한 (최상급)

3 Do you know *the reason* / why they changed their minds?

풀이 선행사 the reason 뒤에 관계부사절 why they ~ minds 가 오도록 배열한다.

STEP ❷

1 *The fireworks exploded*, which made the sky look colorful.

폭죽이 터졌는데, 그것은 하늘을 형형색색으로 보이게 만들었다.

풀이 which ~ colorful은 선행사인 앞 절 전체에 부가적인 설명을 더하는 계속적 용법의 주격 관계대명사절이다.

구문 ▶ make+목적어+목적격보어(동사원형): 목적어를 ~하게 만들다

▶ look+형용사: ~하게 보이다

2 The high school gives a scholarship to *students* whose grades are excellent.

그 고등학교는 성적이 탁월한 학생들에게 장학금을 준다.

풀이 whose grades are excellent는 선행사 students를 수식하는 소유격 관계대명사절이다.

구문 give A to B: B에게 A를 주다

3 Fabian does volunteer work at *the hospital* where he was born.

Fabian는 그가 태어난 병원에서 자원봉사를 한다.

풀이 where he was born은 장소를 나타내는 선행사 the hospital을 수식하는 관계부사절이다.

4 He was excited to interview *the woman* he had read about in a magazine article.

그는 잡지 기사에서 읽었던 그 여성을 인터뷰하게 되어 신이 났다.

풀이 (whom[who/that]) he had ~ article은 선행사 the woman을 수식하는 목적격 관계대명사절이다. 목적격 관계대명사 whom[who/that]은 생략되었다.

구문 ▶ to interview ~ article: 부사 역할의 to부정사구 (감정의 원인)

▶ had v-ed: ~했었다 (과거완료, 과거보다 앞선 시제)

5 I saw *a bird building a nest*, which was common in my area.

나는 새가 둥지를 짓는 것을 보았는데, 그것은 우리 지역에서 흔했다.

풀이 which ~ area는 선행사 a bird building a nest에 부가적인 설명을 더하는 계속적 용법의 주격 관계대명사절이다.

구문 see+목적어+목적격보어(현재분사): 목적어가 ~하고 있는 것을 보다

6 She returned the product to *the clerk* from whom she had made the purchase.

그녀는 그녀가 구매했던 직원에게 그 상품을 반납했다.

풀이 from whom ~ purchase는 선행사 the clerk를 수식하는 목적격 관계대명사절이다. 선행사 the clerk가 관계대명사절에서 전치사 from의 목적어로 쓰였고, 관계대명사 whom 앞으로 전치사 from이 이동했다.

STEP ❸

1 (A) which / in which they grow
(B) which / which injured plants need
Q ③

해석 식물들은 배려심이 있다. (A)그들은 자신들이 자라는 생태계를 돌본다. 예를 들어 식물들은 그들 주변의 토양이 필요로 하는 것에 관심을 갖는다. 만일 토양에 어떤 영양소가 부족하면, 그들은 그 특정 영양소를 만들기 시작한다. 게다가 건강한 식물들은 가까운 곳에 있는 다친 식물들을 돕기도 한다. (B)그들은 다친 식물들이 필요로 하는 영양소를 그들의 뿌리 망을 통해 보낸다.

구문해설

2행 For example, plants pay attention to the needs **of the soil *around them.***

▶ of the soil around them: 명사 the needs를 수식하는 전치사구

▶ around them: 명사 the soil을 수식하는 전치사구

3행 **If** the soil lacks a nutrient, *they* **start to produce** that particular nutrient.

▶ If: ~한다면

▶ they: plants를 가리키는 대명사

▶ start+to-v[v-ing]: ~하기 시작하다

6행 They send *nutrients* **which injured plants need** *through their root networks*.

▶ which injured plants need: 선행사 nutrients를 수식하는 목적격 관계대명사절

▶ through their root networks: 동사 send를 수식하는 전치사구

문제해설

1 (A) 선행사 the ecosystems가 관계대명사절에서 전치사 in의 목적어이고, 전치사 in이 관계대명사 which 앞으로 이동했다. 이때 관계대명사 that이 쓰이면 전치사가 관계대명사절 앞으로 이동할 수 없다.

(B) 선행사 nutrients가 사물이므로 목적격 관계대명사 which가 적절하며, 이때 which는 생략할 수 있다.

Q 식물들이 주변의 토양이나 다른 식물들이 필요로 하는 영양소를 공급하면서 생태계를 돌본다는 내용이므로, 글의 주제로는 ③ '어떻게 식물들이 자신들의 공동체를 돕는가'가 가장 적절하다.

① 왜 식물들에게 건강한 토양이 필요한가

② 식물들과 의사소통하는 방법

2 (A) which leave the water to lay eggs
(B) which[that] they were born on / on which they were born

해석 과학자들은 암컷 바다거북에 관심을 갖고 있는데, (A)그들은 알을 낳기 위해 물에서 나온다. 그들은 이 거북들이 (B)그들이 태어났던 같은 해변으로 돌아온다는 것을 알게 되었다. 그들은 모래에 구덩이를 파고 알을 낳는다. 그러고 나서 그들은 그것들(알)을 먹는 동물들로부터 그것들(알)을 숨기기 위해 땅 속에 알을 묻는다. 마침내 그들은 바다로 돌아간다.

구문해설

1행 Scientists **are interested in** female sea turtles, which leave the water *to lay eggs*.
- ▶ be interested in: ~에 관심이 있다
- ▶ to lay eggs: 부사 역할의 to부정사구 (목적)

2행 They **have found** *that* these turtles return to the same beach **on which** they were born.
- ▶ have/has v-ed: ~했다 (현재완료)
- ▶ that: 동사 have found의 명사절 목적어를 이끄는 접속사
- ▶ on which: 선행사 the same beach가 관계대명사절에서 전치사 on의 목적어이므로, 전치사는 관계대명사 which 앞으로 이동 가능

3행 Then they bury the eggs **to hide them from animals *that* eat them**.
- ▶ to hide ~ them: 부사 역할의 to부정사구 (목적)
- ▶ that: animals를 선행사로 하는 주격 관계대명사

문제해설

2 (A) 빈칸 앞에 콤마(,)가 있는 것으로 보아 계속적 용법의 관계대명사절이고, 명사구 female sea turtles가 선행사이므로 which를 사용한다. 또한, 목적을 나타내는 to부정사구 to lay eggs를 써서 문장을 완성한다.
(B) the same beach를 선행사로 하는 관계대명사절을 쓴다. 선행사가 관계대명사절에서 전치사 on의 목적어 역할을 하므로, 전치사가 관계대명사절 뒤에 있는 「관계대명사(which[that])+주어(they)+동사(were born)+전치사(on)」로 쓰거나, 관계대명사 앞으로 전치사가 이동한 「전치사(on)+관계대명사(which)+주어(they)+동사(were born)」로 쓴다. 관계대명사가 that일 때는 전치사를 앞으로 이동할 수 없음에 유의한다.

Point 03 관계대명사 what p.76

350 People couldn't believe / <what they were seeing>.
사람들은 믿을 수 없었다 / <그들이 보고 있는 것을>
사람들은 자신들이 보고 있는 것을 믿을 수 없었다.

351 Students should bring / <what they need for class>.
학생들은 가져와야 한다 / <그들이 수업에 필요한 것을>
학생들은 수업에 필요한 것을 가져와야 한다.

352 <What you experienced / at the camp> / sounds very interesting.
<네가 경험한 것은 / 캠프에서> / 매우 흥미롭게 들린다
네가 캠프에서 경험한 것은 매우 흥미롭게 들린다.

353 <What happened to Eric> / can happen / to anyone.
<Eric에게 일어난 것은> / 일어날 수 있다 / 누구에게나
Eric에게 일어난 것은 누구에게나 일어날 수 있다.

354 I went shopping, // but I couldn't find / <what I wanted to buy>.
나는 쇼핑하러 갔다, // 하지만 찾을 수 없었다 / <내가 사고 싶었던 것을>
나는 쇼핑하러 갔지만 내가 사고 싶었던 것을 찾을 수 없었다.

355 <What you did for us / today> / was very brave, // and I'm proud of you.
<네가 우리를 위해 한 일은 / 오늘> / 매우 용감했다, // 그리고 나는 네가 자랑스럽다
네가 오늘 우리를 위해 한 일은 매우 용감했고 나는 네가 자랑스럽다.

356 Volunteering <at an orphanage> is / <what she has done / for over ten years>.
자원봉사를 하는 것은 <보육원에서> ~이다 / <그녀가 해 온 것 / 10년이 넘는 동안>
보육원에서 자원봉사를 하는 것은 그녀가 10년 넘게 해 온 것이다.

Point 04 복합관계사 p.77

362 <Wherever I go>, / I always bring my smartphone.
<어디에 가더라도>, / 나는 항상 스마트폰을 가지고 다닌다.

363 <Whenever I feel sad>, / my little puppy comforts me.
<내가 슬플 때마다>, / 내 작은 강아지가 나를 위로해 준다.

364 He doesn't wear a scarf / <however cold it is / outside>.
그는 목도리를 하지 않는다 / <아무리 추워도 / 밖이>
그는 밖이 아무리 추워도 목도리를 하지 않는다.

365 <Whatever you do / to persuade me>, / I won't change my mind.

<네가 무엇을 하더라도 / 나를 설득하기 위해>, / 나는 내 마음을 바꾸지 않을 것이다

네가 나를 설득하기 위해 무엇을 하더라도 나는 내 마음을 바꾸지 않을 것이다.

366 <Whoever leaves the classroom / last> / should turn off the lights.

<교실을 나가는 사람은 누구든지 / 마지막으로> / 불을 꺼야 한다

마지막으로 교실을 나가는 사람은 누구든지 불을 꺼야 한다.

367 <However busy you are>, / you should help with the group project.

<네가 아무리 바쁘더라도>, / 너는 그룹 과제를 도와야 한다.

368 <If you feel hungry>, / you can have / <whatever is in the refrigerator>.

<배가 고프면>, / 너는 먹어도 된다 / <냉장고에 있는 것은 무엇이든>

배가 고프면 너는 냉장고에 있는 것은 무엇이든 먹어도 된다.

Unit Practice pp.78~79

STEP 1

1 This is what I prepared / for my father's birthday.

풀이 관계대명사 what이 이끄는 명사절이 주격보어로 쓰였으며 「관계대명사(what)+주어(I)+동사(prepared)+수식어구(for my father's birthday)」의 순서로 배열한다.

2 What I need / these days / is some peace and quiet.

풀이 관계대명사 what이 이끄는 명사절이 주어로 쓰였으며 「관계대명사(what)+주어(I)+동사(need)+수식어구(these days)」의 순서로 배열한다.

3 However busy you are, / you should help with the group project.

풀이 however가 이끄는 양보 부사절로, 「복합관계부사(however)+형용사(busy)+주어(you)+동사(are)」의 순서로 배열한다.

STEP 2

1 Honestly, I don't understand what you're trying to say.

솔직히 나는 네가 무슨 말을 하려고 하는 것인지 이해가 안 된다.

풀이 관계대명사 what이 이끄는 명사절 what ~ say가 동사 don't understand의 목적어로 쓰였으며, '~하는 것'으로 해석한다.

구문 ▶ Honestly: 문장 전체를 수식하는 부사

▶ try+to-v: ~하려고 노력하다[애쓰다]

2 Whichever route you take during rush hour, there will be a traffic jam.

혼잡 시간대에는 네가 어느 길을 가든지 교통 체증이 있을 것이다.

풀이 복합관계대명사 whichever가 부사절 Whichever ~ rush hour를 이끌고 있고, whichever는 '~하는 것은 어느 것이나'로 해석한다.

3 Whenever Charlotte eats delicious food, she likes to take pictures of it.

Charlotte은 맛있는 음식을 먹을 때마다 그것의 사진을 찍는 것을 좋아한다.

풀이 복합관계부사 whenever가 부사절 Whenever ~ food를 이끌고 있고, whenever는 '~할 때마다'로 해석한다.

구문 ▶ like+to-v[v-ing]: ~하는 것을 좋아하다

▶ of it: 명사 pictures를 수식하는 전치사구

4 What you've learned in today's class will be tested in our quiz next week.

너희가 오늘 수업 시간에 배웠던 것은 다음 주 퀴즈에서 평가될 것이다.

풀이 관계대명사 what이 이끄는 명사절 What ~ class가 문장의 주어로 쓰였으며, '~하는 것'으로 해석한다.

구문 ▶ have/has+v-ed: ~했다 (현재완료)

▶ will be v-ed: ~될 것이다 (미래시제 수동태)

5 Wherever we looked, there were singing birds and blossoming flowers.

우리가 어디를 보더라도 노래하는 새들과 피어나는 꽃들이 있었다.

풀이 복합관계부사 Wherever가 부사절 Wherever we looked를 이끌고 있고, wherever는 '어디를 ~하더라도'로 해석한다.

구문 ▶ there were+복수 명사: ~이 있었다

▶ singing: 명사 birds를 수식하는 현재분사

▶ blossoming: 명사 flowers를 수식하는 현재분사

6 Whoever wants to join the club needs to fill out this application.

동아리에 가입하고 싶은 사람은 누구든지 이 지원서를 작성할 필요가 있다.

풀이 복합관계대명사 whoever가 명사절 주어인 Whoever ~ club을 이끌고 있고, whoever는 '~하는 사람은 누구든지'로 해석한다.

구문 ▶ want+to-v: ~하기를 원하다

▶ need+to-v: ~할 필요가 있다

STEP 3

1 (A) whatever you want

(B) wherever you move the pen

해석은 아래 해석 참조

Q (1) T (2) F

해석 그림을 그리는 것은 멋지다! 하지만 보통의 펜으로 그려진 그림들은 2차원일 뿐이다. 그것이 바로 여러분이 3D 펜이 필요한 이유이다! 여러분은 (A) 여러분이 원하는 것은 무엇이든지 3차원으로 그릴 수 있다. 약간의 플라스틱을 펜 안에 넣고 펜에 전원을 연결하기만 하면 된다. 가열된 플라스틱은 (B) 여러분이 펜을 움직이는 곳은 어디든지, 심지어 공중에도, 나올 것이다. 그 플라스틱은 재빨리 식어 단단해진다. 얼마나 재미있는가!

구문해설

1행 **Drawing** is great!

▶ 동명사 주어

But drawings **made with a normal pen** are only two-dimensional.

▶ 명사 drawings를 수식하는 과거분사구

2행 **That's why** you need a 3D pen!

▶ That's why: 그것이 (바로) ~한 이유이다

7행 **How fun!**

▶ How+형용사!: 얼마나 ~한가! (감탄문)

문제해설

1 (A) 동사 draw의 목적어로 쓰인 복합관계대명사절로, 「복합관계대명사(whatever)+주어(you)+동사(want)」의 순서로 배열한다. whatever는 '무엇을 하더라도'로 해석한다.
(B) wherever가 이끄는 복합관계부사절로, 「복합관계부사(wherever)+주어(you)+동사(move)+목적어(the pen)」의 순서로 배열한다. wherever는 '어디에 ~하더라도'로 해석한다.

Q (1) 약간의 플라스틱을 3D 펜 안에 넣고 펜에 전원을 연결하기만 하면 된다고 했으므로, 펜 안에 플라스틱을 넣어서 3차원 조형물을 만들 수 있음을 알 수 있다.
(2) 펜에서 나온 가열된 플라스틱은 재빨리 식어 단단해진다고 했으므로, 굳는 데 시간이 오래 걸리는 것이 아님을 알 수 있다.

2 ③ that → which
④ However → Whoever

해석 연주회에서 여러분은 음악이 끝날 때마다 박수를 친다. 하지만 클래식 음악 연주회에서는 언제 박수를 칠지 아는 것이 어렵다. 클래식 곡들은 자신만의 끝을 가진 여러 부분을 갖고 있다. 따라서 여러분이 박수를 쳐야 하는 끝부분을 아는 것은 어렵다. 만약 확신이 서지 않으면 다른 사람들이 박수를 칠 때까지 그냥 기다려라. 먼저 (박수를) 시작하는 사람이 누구든 아마도 가장 잘 알고 있을 것이다.

구문해설

1행 At concerts, you clap **whenever the music stops**.

▶ whenever+주어+동사: 시간 부사절로 쓰인 복합관계부사절

But **it** is tough **to know *when to clap* at a classical music concert.**

▶ it은 가주어, to know 이하가 진주어

▶ when+to-v: 「의문사+to-v」로 동사 know의 목적어 (언제 ~할지를)

2행 Classical songs have many parts **that** have their own endings.

▶ many parts를 선행사로 하는 주격 관계대명사

3행 Thus, **it** is hard **to recognize the ending** ~.

▶ it은 가주어, to recognize 이하가 진주어

4행 **Whoever starts first** probably knows best.

▶ Whoever+동사 ~: 문장의 주어로 쓰인 복합관계대명사절

문제해설

2 ③ 선행사 the ending이 관계대명사절에서 전치사 for의 목적어이고 관계대명사 앞에 전치사 for가 있으므로, 관계대명사 that을 which로 고쳐 쓴다. 관계대명사가 that일 때는 전치사를 앞으로 이동할 수 없다.
④ However는 양보 부사절을 이끄는 복합관계부사이므로, 문장의 주어 역할을 하는 명사절을 이끌면서 사람을 가리키는 복합관계대명사 Whoever로 고쳐 쓴다.

Wrap Up p.80

❶ 선행사 ❷ 목적격 ❸ what ❹ ever

1 Whoever violates the law will be punished.
2 This is the game (which[that]) we used to play.
3 Whenever he visits me, he brings cookies.
4 Brooks is my friend with who(m) I exercise.
(= Brooks is my friend who(m)[that] I exercise with.)
5 I showed him what I bought.
6 He won the lottery, which surprised everyone.

UNIT 08 부사절과 분사구문

Point 01 시간·이유 부사절 p.82

373 You can rest / on the sofa / <until your clients arrive>.
너는 쉬어도 된다 / 소파에서 / <너의 고객들이 도착할 때까지>
너는 너의 고객들이 도착할 때까지 소파에서 쉬어도 된다.

374 Sam didn't bring / his laptop / <because it was not working>.
Sam은 가져오지 않았다 / 그의 노트북을 / <왜냐하면 그것이 작동하지 않아서>
Sam은 그의 노트북이 작동하지 않아서 그것을 가져오지 않았다.

375 Five years have passed / <since Monica went abroad / to study>.
5년이 흘렀다 / <Monica가 해외에 간 이후로 / 공부하기 위해>
Monica가 공부하기 위해 해외에 간 이후로 5년이 흘렀다.

376 <As she was allergic / to seafood>, / she couldn't eat / the shrimp dish.
<그녀는 알레르기가 있었기 때문에 / 해산물에>, / 그녀는 먹을 수 없었다 / 새우 요리를
그녀는 해산물에 알레르기가 있었기 때문에 새우 요리를 먹을 수 없었다.

377 <As soon as my younger sister looked / at my picture>, / she laughed aloud.
<내 여동생은 보자마자 / 내 사진을>, / 그녀는 크게 웃었다
내 여동생은 내 사진을 보자마자 크게 웃었다.

378 You should not answer / your phone / <while you're / inside the theater>.
너는 받아서는 안 된다 / 네 전화를 / <네가 있는 동안 / 극장 안에>
너는 극장 안에 있는 동안 전화를 받아서는 안 된다.

379 <As he is busy / these days>, / he won't be able to come / to the wedding.
<그는 바빠서 / 요즘>, / 그는 올 수 없을 것이다 / 그 결혼식에
그는 요즘 바빠서 그 결혼식에 올 수 없을 것이다.

Point 02 조건·양보 부사절 p.83

384 I won't see him / again / <unless he says sorry / to me>.
나는 그를 보지 않을 것이다 / 다시는 / <그가 미안하다고 말하지 않으면 / 나에게>
그가 나에게 미안하다고 말하지 않으면 나는 다시는 그를 보지 않을 것이다.

385 <If you want to make / good friends>, / be kind to others / first.
<네가 만들기를 원한다면 / 좋은 친구를>, / 다른 사람들에게 친절하게 대해라 / 먼저
네가 좋은 친구를 만들고 싶다면 다른 사람들에게 먼저 친절하게 대해라.

386 <Even though Finn took / some medicine>, / his symptoms didn't get better.
<Finn은 먹었지만 / 약을>, / 그의 증상은 호전되지 않았다
Finn은 약을 먹었지만 그의 증상은 호전되지 않았다.

387 <Although she was holding back / her tears>, / everyone knew / <that she felt sad>.
<비록 그녀는 참고 있었지만 / 눈물을>, / 모두가 알았다 / <그녀가 슬프다는 것을>
그녀는 눈물을 참고 있었지만 그녀가 슬프다는 것을 모두가 알았다.

388 <Even if I work hard>, / it may be difficult / to earn enough money / to buy a house.
<내가 열심히 일해도>, / 어려울지도 모른다 / 충분한 돈을 버는 것은 / 집을 살 만큼
내가 열심히 일해도 집을 살 만큼 충분한 돈을 버는 것은 어려울지도 모른다.

389 The dog won't attack you / <unless you move suddenly / or scare him>.
그 개는 너를 공격하지 않을 것이다 / <네가 갑자기 움직이지 않거나 / 그를 겁주지 않으면>
네가 갑자기 움직이거나 그를 겁주지 않으면 그 개는 너를 공격하지 않을 것이다.

390 <As long as you follow / the rules>, / you can use / the school library.
<네가 따르는 한 / 규칙을>, / 너는 사용할 수 있다 / 학교 도서관을
네가 규칙을 따르는 한 너는 학교 도서관을 사용할 수 있다.

Unit Practice pp.84~85

STEP 1

1 Even though it was quite expensive, / it was a nice dinner.
풀이 접속사 even though가 이끄는 양보 부사절은 「접속사(Even though)+주어(it)+동사(was)+주격보어(quite expensive)」의 순서로 배열한다.

2 While the teacher wrote / on the blackboard, / the students took notes.
풀이 접속사 while이 이끄는 시간 부사절은 「접속사(While)+주어(the teacher)+동사(wrote)+수식어구(on the blackboard)」의 순서로 배열한다.

3 If you want to make / good friends, / be kind to others / first.
풀이 접속사 if가 이끄는 조건 부사절은 「접속사(If)+주어(you)+동사(want)+목적어(to make good friends)」의 순서로 배열한다.

구문 ▶ want+to-v: ~하기를 원하다
▶ 동사원형 ~: ~해라 (긍정 명령문)

STEP 2

1 I didn't see the sign because I was too busy looking at my cell phone.
나는 내 휴대 전화를 보느라 너무 바빴기 때문에 그 표지판을 보지 못했다.
풀이 접속사 because가 이끄는 이유 부사절로, because는 '~ 때문에'로 해석한다.
구문 busy+v-ing: ~하느라 바쁜

2 It is bad for your health to go to sleep as soon as you finish your meal.
식사를 마치자마자 잠을 자는 것은 당신의 건강에 해롭다.
풀이 접속사 as soon as가 이끄는 시간 부사절로, as soon as는 '~하자마자'로 해석한다.
구문 ▶ It은 가주어, to go ~ meal이 진주어
▶ bad for: ~에 해로운[나쁜]

3 When he tasted the soup, he realized that he had put too much salt in it.
그는 그 수프를 맛보았을 때 그가 그 안에 너무 많은 소금을 넣었다는 것을 깨달았다.
풀이 접속사 When이 이끄는 시간 부사절로, When은 '~했을 때'로 해석한다.
구문 ▶ that: 동사 realized의 명사절 목적어를 이끄는 접속사
▶ had v-ed: ~했었다 (과거완료)

4 My parents allow me to stay out late as long as I let them know where I am.
나의 부모님은 내가 어디에 있는지를 그들에게 알려드리는 한 늦게까지 밖에 있는 것을 허락하신다.
풀이 접속사 as long as가 이끄는 조건 부사절로, as long as는 '~하는 한'으로 해석한다.
구문 ▶ allow+목적어+목적격보어(to-v): 목적어가 ~하는 것을 허락하다
▶ let+목적어+목적격보어(동사원형): 목적어가 ~하게 하다
▶ where(의문사)+주어+동사: 동사 know의 목적어로 쓰인 의문사절

5 After we baked some cookies, we shared them with our neighbors.
약간의 과자를 굽고 난 뒤에 우리는 그것을 이웃과 나누었다.
풀이 접속사 after가 이끄는 시간 부사절로, after는 '~한 뒤에'로 해석한다.
구문 ▶ them: some cookies를 가리키는 대명사
▶ share A with B: A를 B와 나누다[나누어 갖다]

6 Unless you hurry, you won't be able to buy the concert tickets.
서두르지 않으면 너는 그 콘서트 표를 살 수 없을 것이다.
풀이 접속사 unless가 이끄는 조건 부사절로, unless는 '만약 ~하지 않으면'으로 해석한다.
구문 Unless you hurry: 현재시제로 미래를 나타내는 조건 부사절

STEP 3

1 ②
Q ②

해석 당신이 무언가를 빨리 요리할 필요가 있을 (A) 때, 전자레인지는 매우 유용하다. 그런데 그것은 어떻게 작동하는 걸까? 당신이 시작 버튼을 (B) 누르면, 전자레인지는 음식 속으로 마이크로파를 보낸다. 마이크로파 안의 에너지는 음식 속 물 분자에 영향을 미친다. 물 분자들은 빠르게 앞뒤로 움직이기 시작한다. 이러한 움직임이 열을 만들어 내기 (C) 때문에, 전자레인지는 음식을 조리할 수 있다.

구문해설

3행 The energy **in the microwaves** affects the water molecules *in the food.*
▶ in the microwaves: 명사 The energy를 수식하는 전치사구
▶ in the food: 명사구 the water molecules를 수식하는 전치사구

4행 They **begin to move** quickly back and forth.
▶ begin+to-v[v-ing]: ~하기 시작하다

문제해설

1 (A) 문맥상 '빨리 요리할 필요가 있을 때'가 적절하므로, 시간을 나타내는 접속사 when이 알맞다.
(B) 문맥상 '시작 버튼을 누르면'이 적절하므로, 조건을 나타내는 접속사 if가 알맞다.
(C) 문맥상 '열을 만들어 내기 때문에'가 적절하므로, 이유를 나타내는 접속사 since가 알맞다.

Q 전자레인지가 어떠한 원리로 작동하여 열을 발생시키고 음식을 조리할 수 있는지에 대해 설명하는 글이므로, 글의 제목으로는 ② '전자레인지로 음식을 가열하는 것의 원리'가 가장 적절하다.
① 전자레인지로 조리하는 빠르고 쉬운 레시피
③ 우리의 일상 생활 속 전자레인지의 다양한 쓰임

2 because[since/as] beans taste good with many other foods

해석 콩은 많은 건강상의 이점을 가지고 있다. 예를 들어 그것들은 심장 질환과 암을 예방하도록 돕는다. 그리고 그것들은 비록 열량이 높지만, 섬유질의 함량 또한 높다. 섬유질은 당신이 빨리 배부르게 느끼도록 하므로, 당신은 과식하는 것을 피할 수 있다. 게다가 콩은 많은 다른 음식들과 같이 먹어도 맛이 좋으므로, 당신의 식단에 콩을 추가하는 것은 쉽다.

구문해설

1행 For example, they **help prevent** heart disease and cancer.

▶ help+동사원형[to-v]: ~하도록 돕다

2행 And **although** they are high in calories, they are also high in fiber.

▶ although: 비록 ~하지만

3행 Fiber **makes you feel** full quickly, so you can *avoid eating* too much.

▶ make(사역동사)+목적어+목적격보어(동사원형): 목적어가 ~하게 하다

▶ avoid+v-ing: ~하는 것을 피하다

문제해설

2 주절이 콩을 식단에 추가하기가 쉽다는 내용이므로, 종속절로 쓰인 부사절에는 그 이유가 제시되는 것이 자연스럽다. 따라서 이유 접속사를 추가하여 「접속사(because[since, as])+주어(beans)+동사(taste)+주격보어(good)+수식어구(with many other foods)」의 순서로 배열한다.

Point 03 분사구문의 의미 p.86

395 <Turning right>, / you will find a bank.
= <If you turn right>
<오른쪽으로 돌면>, / 너는 은행을 찾게 될 것이다.

396 <Having no money>, / Issac couldn't pay for dinner.
= <Because he had no money>
<돈이 없어서>, / Issac은 저녁 식사 비용을 지불할 수 없었다.

397 <Looking out the window>, / I saw / a stranger wandering.
= <When I looked out the window>
<창밖을 내다봤을 때>, / 나는 보았다 / 낯선 사람이 돌아다니고 있는 것을
창밖을 내다봤을 때 나는 낯선 사람이 돌아다니고 있는 것을 보았다.

398 <Taking a shower>, / he sang a song <from his favorite movie>.
= <As he took a shower>
<샤워를 하면서>, / 그는 노래를 불렀다 <그가 가장 좋아하는 영화에서 나온>
샤워를 하면서 그는 그가 가장 좋아하는 영화에서 나온 노래를 불렀다.

399 <Driving down the road / in heavy rain>, / David witnessed an accident.
= <While he drove down the road / in heavy rain>
<길을 운전하는 동안 / 폭우 속에서>, / David는 사고를 목격했다.
폭우 속에서 길을 운전하는 동안 David는 사고를 목격했다.

400 <Listening to loud music / through earphones>, / you'll damage / your hearing.
= <If you listen to loud music / through earphones>
<시끄러운 음악을 들으면 / 이어폰으로>, / 손상을 줄 것이다 / 너의 청각에
이어폰으로 시끄러운 음악을 들으면 너의 청각에 손상을 줄 것이다.

Point 04 분사구문의 다양한 형태 p.87

404 <When buying something / online>, / you should compare prices.
<무언가를 살 때 / 온라인으로>, / 너는 가격을 비교해야 한다
온라인으로 무언가를 살 때 너는 가격을 비교해야 한다.

405 <The test being difficult>, / many of the students / failed.
<그 시험이 어려워서>, / 많은 학생들이 / 낙제했다.

406 <Considering it's his first job>, / he is doing pretty well.
<이것이 그의 첫 직업임을 고려하면>, / 그는 꽤 잘하고 있다.

407 <Frankly speaking>, / I don't think / <that our plan is a good idea>.
<솔직히 말하면>, / 나는 생각하지 않는다 / <우리의 계획이 좋은 방안이라고>
솔직히 말하면 나는 우리의 계획이 좋은 방안이라고 생각하지 않는다.

408 <Surrounded by the police>, / the criminal came / out of the house.
<경찰에 둘러 싸여>, / 범인이 나왔다 / 집 밖으로
경찰에 둘러 싸여 범인이 집 밖으로 나왔다.

409 <Hidden by a big tree>, / this "no smoking" sign / is easy to miss.
<큰 나무에 가려져 있어서>, / 이 '금연' 표지판은 / 놓치기 쉽다.

410 <Having already read the book / several times>, / she knew the whole story.
<그 책을 이미 읽었기 때문에 / 여러 번>, / 그녀는 모든 이야기를 알고 있었다
그 책을 이미 여러 번 읽었기 때문에 그녀는 모든 이야기를 알고 있었다.

Unit Practice pp.88~89

STEP 1

1 The test being difficult, / many of the students / failed.

풀이 부사절의 주어와 주절의 주어가 다르면, 부사절을 분사구문으로 바꿀 때 부사절의 주어를 생략하지 않는다. 부사절의 주어인 The test가 '어려운' 것이므로(능동), 현재분사 being을 쓴다.

구문 The test being difficult
= Because[Since / As] the test was difficult

2 Cleaning her house, / Emma found some old photos.

풀이 주절의 주어인 Emma가 그녀의 집을 '청소한' 것이므로(능동), 현재분사 Cleaning을 쓴다.

구문 Cleaning her house = As she cleaned her house

3 Being cheered / by the crowd, / the athlete felt encouraged.

풀이 '응원을 받은'이라는 수동의 의미이므로 수동 분사구문을 쓴다. 「Being+과거분사(cheered)+수식어구(by the crowd)」의 순서로 배열한다.

구문 ▶ Being cheered by the crowd = Because[Since / As] he[she] was cheered by the crowd
▶ feel+형용사: ~하게 느끼다

STEP 2

1 Taking a taxi, we will be able to save time and avoid walking in the rain.

택시를 타면 우리는 시간을 절약하고 빗속에서 걷는 것을 피할 수 있을 것이다.

풀이 문맥상 우리가 시간을 절약하고 빗속을 걷는 것을 피할 수 있는 조건을 제시하는 분사구문이므로, '(만약) ~라면'으로 해석한다.

구문 ▶ Taking a taxi = If we take a taxi (조건 부사절에서는 현재시제로 미래를 표현)
▶ and: 동사 save와 avoid를 연결
▶ avoid+v-ing: ~하는 것을 피하다

2 While talking on the phone, I looked at the calendar to check my schedule.

통화를 하는 동안 나는 내 일정을 확인하기 위해 달력을 보았다.

풀이 분사구문의 의미를 분명히 하기 위해 접속사를 남긴 형태로, 접속사 while은 '~하는 동안'으로 해석한다.

구문 ▶ While talking on the phone
= While I talked on the phone
▶ to check my schedule: 부사 역할의 to부정사구 (목적)

3 Generally speaking, taking breaks from studying improves your concentration.

일반적으로 말하면 공부를 하다가 휴식을 취하는 것은 너의 집중력을 향상시킨다.

풀이 Generally speaking은 분사구문 관용 표현으로, '일반적으로 말하면'으로 해석한다.

구문 taking breaks from studying: 동명사구 주어

4 Not remembering the password, Samuel couldn't log into his account.

비밀번호를 기억하지 못했기 때문에 Samuel은 그의 계정에 접속할 수 없었다.

풀이 문맥상 Samuel이 그의 계정에 접속할 수 없었던 이유를 설명하는 분사구문의 부정형이므로, '~하지 못했기 때문에'로 해석한다.

구문 Not remembering the password = Because [Since / As] he didn't remember the password

5 Warned about the storm, they decided to cancel their outdoor activities.

폭풍에 대한 경고를 받았기 때문에 그들은 야외 활동을 취소하기로 결정했다.

풀이 문맥상 그들이 야외 활동을 취소하게 된 이유를 설명하는 수동형 분사구문이므로, '~되었기 때문에'로 해석한다. 분사구문의 시제가 주절의 시제를 앞서는 완료형 분사구문으로 분사구문 앞에 Having been이 생략되었다.

구문 ▶ Warned about the storm = Because[Since / As] they had been warned about the storm
▶ decide+to-v: ~하기로 결정하다

6 Having seen the accident, he called an ambulance at once.

사고를 본 뒤 그는 즉시 구급차를 불렀다.

풀이 구급차를 부르기 전에 사고를 먼저 본 것이므로 완료형 분사구문이 쓰였고, '~한 뒤[후]'로 해석한다.

구문 ▶ Having seen the accident
= After he had seen the accident
▶ at once: 즉시

STEP 3

1 문장 해석은 아래 해석 참조
Q ②

해석 우리는 미소를 흉내 내는 것으로써 미소가 진짜인지 판단할 수 있다. 한 연구에서 사람들은 그들의 입에 연필을 물고 있는 동안 미소가 진짜인지를 추측했다. 이것(입에 연필을 물고 있는 행동)은 그들이 미소 짓지 못하게 했다. 그들이 연필을 입에 물고 있을 때, 그들은 결정하는 데 어려움을 겪었다. 그러나 그들은 연필 없이는 그것을 더 쉽게 알아냈다. 이것은 그들이 같은 식으로 미소를 지을 수 있고 미소 짓는 사람의 감정을 이해할 수 있었기 때문이다.

구문해설

1행 We can judge **if** a smile is real *by imitating* **it**.

▶ if: 동사 judge의 명사절 목적어를 이끄는 접속사 (~인지)

▶ by+v-ing: ~함으로써

▶ it: a smile을 가리키는 대명사

In a study, people guessed **whether** a smile was real *while holding a pencil in their mouth*.

▶ whether: 동사 guessed의 명사절 목적어를 이끄는 접속사 (~인지)

▶ while holding a pencil in their mouth: 접속사를 남긴 분사구문 (= while people held a pencil ~)

3행 This **stopped them from smiling**.

▶ stop+목적어+from+v-ing: 목적어가 ~하는 것을 막다

5행 they **had a hard time deciding**

▶ have a hard time+v-ing: ~하는 데 어려움을 겪다, ~하느라 고생하다

6행 **This is because** they could smile the same way ~.

▶ this is because: 이것은 ~이기 때문이다

문제해설

1 분사구문의 의미를 분명히 하기 위해 접속사 while을 남긴 형태로, 접속사의 의미를 살려 '~하는 동안'으로 해석한다.

Q 연필을 물고 있지 않을 때는 미소 짓는 사람처럼 미소를 지어볼 수 있어서 그 미소가 진짜인지 아닌지를 판단하기가 더 쉽다고 하였으므로, 빈칸에는 ② '흉내 내는 것'이 가장 적절하다.

① 숨김 ③ 상상함

2 The weather being terrible, living in Oymyakon is very difficult.

해석 Oymyakon(오이먀콘)은 약 5백 명의 인구를 가진 러시아의 마을이다. 지구 상에서 가장 추운 거주지로 여겨져서, 그곳은 '추위의 극'이라는 별명이 붙었다. 날씨가 끔찍하기 때문에, Oymyakon에서 사는 것은 매우 어렵다. 배터리는 빨리 방전되고 금속은 피부에 달라붙는다. 일부 주민들은 심지어 차 엔진이 어는 것을 방지하기 위해 가을부터 봄까지 차 엔진을 계속 작동시킨다.

구문해설

2행 ~, it **is nicknamed** *the "Pole of Cold."*

▶ am/are/is+v-ed: ~되다 (수동태)

▶ the "Pole of Cold": 5형식 수동태에서 목적격보어인 명사구가 수동태 뒤에 남은 형태

3행 **The weather being terrible**, living in Oymyakon is very difficult.

▶ The weather being terrible
= Because[Since/As] the weather is terrible

4행 Some residents even **keep their car engine running** from fall till spring *to **prevent it from freezing***.

▶ keep+목적어+v-ing: 목적어가 계속해서 ~하게 하다

▶ to prevent ~ freezing: 부사 역할의 to부정사구 (목적)

▶ prevent+목적어+from+v-ing: 목적어가 ~하는 것을 방지하다[막다]

문제해설

2 부사절을 분사구문으로 바꿀 때, 부사절의 주어와 주절의 주어가 다르면 부사절의 주어를 생략하지 않고 분사 앞에 남긴다. 또한 주절의 주어가 '~에서 사는 것은'이므로 동명사구나 to부정사구를 써야 하는데, 빈칸 개수로 보아 동명사구를 쓴다.

Wrap Up p.90

❶ 접속사 ❷ since ❸ 조건 ❹ 분사구문

1 Although he was tired, he went to the library.
2 Since this shirt is big for me, I'll get it tailored.
3 Having quit his job, he started a new business.
4 Walking out of the room, Amy turned off the light.
5 The weather being good, we went to the beach.
6 Cooking dinner, she burned her hand.

UNIT 09 특수구문

Point 01 짝을 이루는 접속사 p.92

415 You may send it / either by email or by fax.
너는 그것을 보내면 된다 / 이메일 또는 팩스 둘 중 하나로
너는 그것을 이메일 또는 팩스 둘 중 하나로 보내면 된다.

416 I like / both watching sports and playing them.
나는 좋아한다 / 스포츠를 보는 것과 그것들을 하는 것 둘 다
나는 스포츠를 보는 것과 그것들을 하는 것 둘 다를 좋아한다.

417 Lily will go to Japan / not for travel, / but for work.
Lily는 일본에 갈 것이다 / 여행을 위해서가 아니라 / 일을 위해서
Lily는 여행이 아니라 일로 일본에 갈 것이다.

418 <When I speak / in front of a lot of people>, / I feel / both excited and nervous.

<나는 말할 때 / 많은 사람들 앞에서>, / 나는 느낀다 / 흥분과 긴장 둘 다
많은 사람들 앞에서 말할 때 나는 흥분과 긴장 둘 다를 느낀다.

419 Ken donates money / to charity / <not <because he is rich>, / <but <because he wants to help others>>.
Ken은 돈을 기부한다 / 자선 단체에 / <그가 부자이기 때문이 아니라>, / <그는 다른 사람들을 돕고 싶기 때문에>
Ken은 부자여서가 아니라 다른 사람들을 돕고 싶어서 자선 단체에 돈을 기부한다.

420 Yoga helps you / relieve stress / as well as strengthen your body.
요가는 너에게 도움이 된다 / 스트레스를 완화하는 데에도 / 너의 신체를 더 튼튼하게 하는 것뿐만 아니라
요가는 너의 신체를 더 튼튼하게 하는 것뿐만 아니라 스트레스를 완화하는 데에도 도움이 된다.

421 I go to work by bike / not only to help the environment / but also to stay healthy.
나는 자전거로 출근한다 / 환경을 돕기 위해서 뿐만 아니라 / 건강을 유지하기 위해서
나는 환경을 돕기 위해서 뿐만 아니라 건강을 유지하기 위해서 자전거로 출근한다.

Point 02 강조와 생략 p.93

426 Kali's son is as old / as Owen's (son).
Kali의 아들은 나이가 있다 / Owen의 아들만큼
Kali의 아들은 Owen의 아들만큼 나이가 있다.
(Kali의 아들은 Owen의 아들과 동갑이다.)

427 <Although (we were) tired>, / we waited / <until the game was over>.
<(우리는) 피곤했지만>, / 우리는 기다렸다 / <경기가 끝날 때까지>
우리는 피곤했지만 경기가 끝날 때까지 기다렸다.

428 My family was worried / about my injury more / than I was (worried about my injury).
우리 가족은 걱정했다 / 내 부상에 대해 더 / 내가 한 것보다 (내가 내 부상에 대해 걱정하는 것보다)
우리 가족은 내 부상에 대해 나보다 더 걱정했다.

429 It was in Paris / <that he got his first job / as a model>.
바로 파리였다 / <그가 첫 일자리를 구한 곳은 / 모델로서>
그가 모델로서 첫 일자리를 구한 곳은 바로 파리였다.

430 It was at the mall / [that I found the perfect birthday gift <for my friend>].
바로 그 쇼핑몰이었다 / [내가 멋진 생일 선물을 찾은 곳은 <내 친구를 위한>]
내가 내 친구를 위한 멋진 생일 선물을 찾은 곳은 바로 그 쇼핑몰이었다.

431 <When (he was) asked / about the accident>, / Patrick didn't say anything.
<질문을 받았을 때 / 그 사고에 대해>, / Patrick은 아무 말도 하지 않았다
그 사고에 대해 질문을 받았을 때 Patrick은 아무 말도 하지 않았다.

432 I do believe / [it was Kelly / <that sent me the invitation>].
나는 정말로 믿는다 / [바로 Kelly였다는 것을 / <나에게 초대장을 보낸 사람이>]
나에게 초대장을 보낸 사람이 바로 Kelly였다는 것을 나는 정말로 믿는다.

Unit Practice pp.94~95

STEP ❶

1 It was my homeroom teacher / that[who(m)] I met / on the street.
풀이 '…한 것은 (바로) ~이었다'라는 의미의 「it was ~ that …」 강조구문으로, It was와 that[who(m)] 사이에 강조할 어구 my homeroom teacher를 썼다.
구문 that[who(m)]: 강조하는 어구가 사람이고 목적격이므로, that 대신 who(m)를 쓸 수 있음

2 You can either buy the book / online / or borrow it / from the library.
풀이 'A 또는 B'는 「either A or B」를 써서 나타낸다. 동사 buy와 borrow가 「either A or B」로 연결되었다.
구문 ▶ it: the book을 가리키는 대명사
▶ from the library: 동사 borrow를 수식하는 전치사구

3 My family enjoys going skiing / not only in winter / but also in summer.
풀이 'A뿐만 아니라 B도'는 「not only A but (also) B」를 써서 나타낸다. 전치사구 in winter와 in summer가 「not only A but (also) B」로 연결되었다.
구문 enjoy+v-ing: ~하는 것을 즐기다

STEP ❷

1 While (we were) walking in the forest, we saw some ducks swimming in a pond.
숲을 걷는 동안 우리는 오리들이 연못에서 헤엄치고 있는 것을 보았다.

풀이 부사절의 주어와 주절의 주어가 같을 때, 부사절의 「주어+be동사」는 생략 가능하다. While we were walking in the forest에서 we were가 생략되었다.

구문 saw+목적어+목적격보어(v-ing): 목적어가 ~하고 있는 것을 보았다

2 Though some people may not remember, I did win an award for painting in school.

몇몇 사람들은 기억하지 못할지도 모르지만 나는 정말 학교에서 그림으로 상을 받았다.

풀이 동사 win을 강조하기 위해 조동사 do의 과거형 did를 썼고, '정말 ~했다'로 해석한다.

구문 for painting: 명사 an award를 수식하는 전치사구

3 Blake was asked to try bungee jumping, but he didn't want to (try bungee jumping).

Blake는 번지 점프를 시도할 것을 요청받았지만, 그는 (번지 점프를 시도하는 것을) 원하지 않았다.

풀이 앞 절에서 언급한 try bungee jumping을 반복하지 않기 위해 didn't want to 뒤의 try bungee jumping이 생략되었다.

구문 ▶ to try bungee jumping: 5형식 문장을 수동태로 바꾸면서 목적격보어인 to부정사구 to try bungee jumping이 수동태 was asked 뒤에 남음

▶ want+to-v: ~하기를 원하다

4 It was the book that I couldn't put down until the end.

끝까지 손에서 내려놓을 수 없었던 것은 바로 그 책이었다.

풀이 「It was ~ that ...」 강조구문으로, 목적어인 the book이 강조되었다. '…한 것은 바로 ~이었다'로 해석한다.

5 Suffering from colds, neither Carter nor Sofia could go on the field trip.

감기를 앓고 있어서 Carter도 Sofia도 현장 학습에 갈 수 없었다.

풀이 명사 Carter와 Sofia가 「neither A nor B」로 연결되었고 「neither A nor B」는 'A도 B도 아닌'으로 해석한다.

구문 Suffering from colds: 이유를 나타내는 분사구문 (= Because[Since/As] they were suffering from colds)

6 The concert hall has standing areas that are close to the stage as well as seating options.

그 콘서트홀은 좌석 선택지뿐만 아니라 무대와 가까운 스탠딩 구역도 갖고 있다.

풀이 명사구 standing areas ~ stage와 seating options가 「B as well as A」로 연결되었고 「B as well as A」는 'A뿐만 아니라 B도'로 해석한다.

구문 ▶ that: 명사구 standing areas를 선행사로 하는 주격 관계대명사

▶ close to: ~에 가까운

STEP 3

1 leather and paper as well as clay and wood
문장 해석은 아래 해석 참조

Q ③

해석 과거에는 장난감들이 주로 점토나 나무로 만들어졌다. 사람들이 처음으로 다른 재료들로 장난감을 만들기 시작한 것은 바로 1700년대였다. 그들은 점토와 나무뿐만 아니라 가죽과 종이도 사용할 수 있다는 것을 깨달았다. 그리고 나중에 기계가 발명되고 난 뒤, 금속이 사용되었다. 물론 오늘날에는 대부분의 장난감들이 플라스틱으로 만들어진다.

구문해설

1행 **It was** in the 1700s **that** people first *began to make* toys with other materials.

▶ 「it was ~ that …」 강조구문으로, in the 1700s를 강조

▶ begin+to-v[v-ing]: ~하기 시작하다

2행 They realized (**that**) they could use ~.

▶ 동사 realized의 명사절 목적어를 이끄는 접속사 that이 생략됨

4행 ~, most toys **are made of** plastic.

▶ be made of: ~로 만들어지다

문제해설

1 ( ) 앞 문장의 내용과 제시된 단어들로 보아 예전부터 사용되었던 점토와 나무뿐만 아니라 가죽과 종이도 사용될 수 있다는 내용이 와야 한다. 제시된 「as well as」를 활용하되, 「not only A but also B」와 달리 「B as well as A」임에 유의해서 배열한다.

Q 장난감은 사람들이 가죽과 종이, 금속을 사용해서 만들기 (A)시작할 때까지는 점토나 나무로 만들어졌지만, 지금은 플라스틱이 대부분 장난감의 (B)주요 재료이다.

과거부터 현재까지 장난감을 만드는 재료가 어떻게 달라져 왔는지에 대해 설명하는 내용의 글이므로, (A)started, (B)primary 순서로 들어가는 것이 적절하다.

2 (A) Texting while walking
(B) prevents you from focusing on your surroundings

해석 당신은 걷고 있는 동안에 문자 메시지를 보내는가? 그렇다면 그만두어야 한다. 한 연구는 그것이 운전을 하면서 문자 메시지를 보내는 것보다 더 위험하다는 것을 보여 주었다. 당신은 걷는 것이 간단하다고 생각할지도 모르지만, 연구자들은 그렇지 않다고 말한다. 안전하게 걷기 위해서는, 당신은 주변 환경에 집중해야 한다. 그러나 문자 메시지를 보낼 때, 당신은 주로 (휴대 전화의) 화면에 집중한다. 이것은 위험한 사고를 유발할 수도 있다.

구문해설

1행 Do you text while (**you are**) walking?

▶ 부사절 while you are walking에서 「주어+be동사」인 you are가 생략됨

Then you should stop (**texting while walking**).

▶ 동사 stop의 목적어 texting while walking이 생략됨 (앞 문장에 반복된 어구가 있을 때, 없어도 내용 파악이 가능하면 생략 가능)

One study has shown <**that** it is *more dangerous than* texting while driving>.

▶ that: 동사 has shown의 명사절 목적어를 이끄는 접속사

▶ more+형용사+than: ~보다 더 …한 (비교급)

2행 You might think (**that**) *walking* is simple, but researchers say (**that**) it isn't (**simple**).

▶ (that): 동사 think와 say의 각 명사절 목적어를 이끄는 접속사가 생략됨

▶ walking: 동사 think의 목적어로 쓰인 명사절의 동명사 주어

▶ 앞 절에 언급된 simple이 반복을 피하기 위해 생략됨

3행 **To walk safely**, you must focus on your surroundings.

▶ 부사 역할의 to부정사구 (목적)

4행 However, when (**you are**) texting, you mostly focus on the screen.

▶ 부사절 when you are texting에서 「주어+be동사」인 you are가 생략됨

문제해설

2 | 문자 메시지를 보내는 것은 (B)당신이 당신 주변 환경에 집중하는 것을 막기 때문에 (A)걷는 동안 문자 메시지를 보내는 것은 매우 위험하다. |

(A) 걷는 동안 문자 메시지를 보내는 것이 매우 위험하다고 했다.
(B) 걷는 동안 문자 메시지를 보내는 것이 왜 위험한지에 대한 이유를 설명하고 있다. 걸을 때는 주변에 집중해야 하는데, 문자 메시지를 보내는 것은 휴대 전화의 화면에 집중하게 해서 당신이 주변에 집중하는 것을 막기 때문이다.

Point 03 부정 표현 p.96

437 Ariana seldom expresses / her thoughts.
Ariana는 좀처럼 표현하지 않는다 / 자기 생각을
Ariana는 좀처럼 자기 생각을 표현하지 않는다.

438 Nobody knows / <how lonely I am / now>.
아무도 알지 못한다 / <내가 얼마나 외로운지를 / 지금>
내가 지금 얼마나 외로운지 아무도 알지 못한다.

439 Asking forgiveness / is not always easy, // but it is important.
용서를 구하는 것이 / 항상 쉽지는 않다, // 하지만 그것은 중요하다
용서를 구하는 것이 항상 쉽지는 않지만 그것은 중요하다.

440 Neither of us had the patience / to wait in a long line / at a restaurant.
우리 둘 중 누구도 인내심이 없었다 / 긴 줄을 기다릴 / 식당에서
우리 둘 다 식당에서 긴 줄을 기다릴 인내심이 없었다.

441 <Even though Jason rarely exercises>, / he has never been overweight.
<Jason은 비록 좀처럼 운동을 하지 않지만>, / 그는 결코 비만이었던 적이 없다.

442 That doesn't necessarily mean / <you have to pay the charge / at once>.
그것은 반드시 의미하지는 않는다 / <네가 요금을 지불해야 한다는 것을 / 당장>
그것은 반드시 네가 요금을 당장 지불해야 한다는 것을 의미하지는 않는다.

443 Not all people achieve / their dreams, // but no one succeeds / without dreaming.
모든 사람들이 이루는 것은 아니다 / 자신의 꿈을, // 하지만 아무도 성공하지 못한다 / 꿈을 꾸는 것 없이
모든 사람들이 자신의 꿈을 이루는 것은 아니지만 꿈을 꾸지 않고는 아무도 성공하지 못한다.

Point 04 도치 p.97

448 Not only is he intelligent, // but he is also kind.
그는 똑똑할 뿐만 아니라, // 친절하기도 하다.

449 Out of the trash can / came a terrible smell.
쓰레기통에서 / 지독한 냄새가 났다.

450 In New York Harbor / stands the Statue of Liberty.
뉴욕항에 / 자유의 여신상이 서 있다.

451 Hardly can we imagine / a world <without the Internet>.
우리는 거의 상상할 수가 없다 / 세상을 <인터넷이 없는>
우리는 인터넷이 없는 세상을 거의 상상할 수가 없다.

452 My friend does not like broccoli, // and neither do I.
내 친구는 브로콜리를 좋아하지 않는다, // 그리고 나도 그렇다
내 친구는 브로콜리를 좋아하지 않고, 나도 그렇다.

453 Little did I imagine / <that our team would actually win / the match>.
나는 거의 상상하지 못했다 / <우리 팀이 실제로 이길 것이라고 / 그 경기를>
나는 우리 팀이 그 경기를 실제로 이길 것이라고 거의 상상하지 못했다.

454 These sculptures were created / by the ancient Greeks, // and so were these paintings.

이 조각상들은 만들어졌다 / 고대 그리스인들에 의해, // 그리고 이 그림들도 마찬가지이다

이 조각상들은 고대 그리스인들에 의해 만들어졌고, 이 그림들도 마찬가지이다.

Unit Practice

pp.98~99

STEP 1

1 Nobody knows / how lonely I am / now.

풀이 '아무도 ~않다'라는 전체부정은 nobody를 써서 나타낸다.

구문 how+형용사+주어+동사: 동사 knows의 목적어로 쓰인 의문사절

2 Never did Becky think / that she would win the lottery.

풀이 부정어 Never가 문장의 맨 앞에 나오면 주어와 동사가 도치되므로, 「부정어(Never)+조동사(did)+주어(Becky)+동사(think) ~」의 순서로 배열한다. 부정어가 문장의 맨 앞에 올 때 일반동사는 반드시 조동사 do를 써서 시제를 나타낸다.

구문 that: 동사 think의 명사절 목적어를 이끄는 접속사

3 There flows a river / through the heart / of the city.

풀이 장소를 나타내는 부사 There가 문장의 맨 앞에 나오면 주어와 동사가 도치되므로, 「부사(There)+동사(flows)+주어(a river) ~」의 순서로 배열한다.

구문 ▶ through: ~을 통해[관통하여]

▶ of the city: 명사 the heart를 수식하는 전치사구

STEP 2

1 In the night sky shines the bright full moon.

밤하늘에 밝은 보름달이 빛난다.

풀이 전치사구 In the night sky가 문장 맨 앞으로 나와서 주어 the bright full moon과 동사 shines가 도치되었다. 전치사구가 강조된 것이므로 전치사구를 먼저 해석하는 것이 자연스럽다.

2 You can't drop things in space because there is no gravity.

우주에는 중력이 없기 때문에 물건을 떨어뜨릴 수 없다.

풀이 no는 전체부정 표현으로, '(결코) ~않다[없다]'로 해석한다.

3 Nathan doesn't believe in any superstitions, and nor do I.

Nathan은 어떠한 미신도 믿지 않고 나도 마찬가지이다.

풀이 nor 다음에 주어 I와 동사 do가 도치되었고, '~도 그렇다[마찬가지이다]'로 해석한다.

4 After a long day, little was she expecting the surprise party waiting at home.

긴 하루 뒤, 그녀는 집에서 기다리고 있는 깜짝 파티를 거의 예상하지 못하고 있었다.

풀이 부정어 little 다음에 주어 she와 동사 was가 도치된 문장으로 '거의 ~않다'로 해석한다. 동사가 be동사이므로 조동사를 사용하지 않는다.

구문 waiting at home: 명사구 the surprise party를 수식하는 현재분사구

5 Not every city has a convenient public transportation system like Seoul.

모든 도시가 서울과 같은 편리한 대중 교통 시스템을 가지고 있는 것은 아니다.

풀이 「not+every」는 부분부정 표현으로, '모두가 ~한 것은 아니다'로 해석한다.

구문 like: ~과 같은

6 Even though it is winter, it rarely snows these days due to the warm weather.

겨울이지만 따뜻한 날씨 때문에 요즘에는 좀처럼 눈이 오지 않는다.

풀이 rarely는 부정의 의미를 가진 부사로, '좀처럼[거의] ~않다'로 해석한다.

구문 ▶ it: 계절을 나타내는 비인칭 주어

▶ due to: ~ 때문에

STEP 3

1 not all of them remain

문장 해석은 아래 해석 참조

Q ③

해석 Meteora는 그리스에 있는 가장 큰 수도원 집단들 중 하나이다. 그것은 사암 봉우리들의 꼭대기에 위치해 있다. 누구도 그것들을 쉽게 올라갈 수 없지만, 11세기 초반에 수도승들이 그 봉우리들 위에 수도원들을 용케 지었다. 원래는 24개의 건물들이 있었으나, 그것들 모두가 남아 있는 것은 아니다. 오늘날에는 단 6개만이 남아 있다.

구문해설

1행 Meteora is **one of the largest groups** of monasteries in Greece.

▶ one of the+최상급+복수명사: 가장 ~한 …들 중 하나

2행 It **is located** on top of sandstone peaks.

▶ am/are/is+v-ed: ~되다 (수동태)

3행 **Nobody** can easily climb *them*, but monks **managed to build** monasteries on them in the early 11th century.

▶ nobody: 아무도 ~않다 (전체부정)

▶ them: sandstone peaks를 가리키는 대명사

▶ manage+to-v: 간신히[용케] ~ 해내다

문제해설

1 마지막 문장에서 오늘날에는 단 6개의 Meteora만 남아 있다는 것으로 보아 24개가 있었으나 모두가 다 남아 있는 것은 아니라는 의미가 되어야 한다. 따라서 '모두가 ~한 것은 아니다'라는 부분부정 표현「not+all」을 써서 나타낸다.

Q 24개의 건물 중 현재 6개만 남아 있다고 하였으므로, ③은 글의 내용과 일치하지 않는다.

2 ② Along another wave comes
→ Along comes another wave
③ so we will → so will we

해석 한 작은 바다 파도가 그의 앞에 있는 파도들이 해변에 부딪치는 것을 본다. "나는 끝장이야!" 그는 소리친다. 또 다른 파도가 따라와서 묻는다. "무슨 일이야?" "봐!" 작은 파도는 울부짖는다. "저 파도들은 부딪쳐서 영원히 사라질 것이고, 우리도 그럴 거야! 나는 사라지는 게 두려워!" 두 번째 파도가 말한다. "무서워하지 마. 부딪히는 것이 결코 사라지는 것을 의미하는 것은 아니야. 우리는 그저 파도가 아니라 바다의 일부분이거든."

구문해설

1행 A small ocean wave **sees the waves *in front of him* crashing** into the seashore.

▶ see+목적어+목적격보어(v-ing): 목적어가 ~하고 있는 것을 보다

▶ in front of him: 명사 the waves를 수식하는 전치사구

4행 I'm afraid of **disappearing**!

▶ 전치사 of의 동명사 목적어

5행 ~, "**Don't be** frightened. Crashing *never* means disappearing."

▶ Don't+동사원형: ~하지 마라 (부정 명령문)

▶ never: 결코 ~않다 (전체부정을 나타내는 부정어)

We are **not** just waves **but** part of the ocean.

▶ not A but B: A가 아니라 B

문제해설

2 ② 방향을 나타내는 부사 along이 문장의 맨 앞에 나올 때 주어와 동사가 도치되므로, 동사 comes 뒤에 주어 another wave가 오도록 고쳐쓴다.

③ 앞 문장의 내용을 받은 so가 문장의 맨 앞에 나올 때 주어와 동사가 도치되므로, 조동사 will 뒤에 주어 we가 오도록 고쳐쓴다. 「so+(조)동사+주어」는 '~도 그렇다[마찬가지이다]'로 해석한다.

Wrap Up

p.100

❶ neither ❷ not only ❸ do ❹ 동사

1. I worked hard and so did Jack.
2. It is Bob that[who] works at the post office.
3. You can choose to either walk or take the bus.
4. Luckily, none of the passengers were[was] hurt.
5. Not every girl likes flowers.
6. While (I was) in the hospital, I kept a diary.

MEMO

MEMO

MEMO

MEMO

MEMO

중학

천문장

LEVEL 3

「구문이 독해로 연결되는 해석 공식」